THE DOG LOVER'S

Elizabeth Meriwether Schuler

by the same author
RAISING PUPPIES FOR PLEASURE AND PROFIT

ANSWER BOOK

SIMON AND SCHUSTER
NEW YORK

*With special thanks for the help given me by
Eric Archer, D.V.M., Old Saybrook, Connecticut
and
O. L. Burr, D.V.M., Chester, Connecticut*

Copyright © 1975 by Elizabeth Meriwether Schuler
All rights reserved
including the right of reproduction
in whole or in part in any form
Published by Simon and Schuster
A Gulf+Western Company
Rockefeller Center, 630 Fifth Avenue
New York, New York 10020
Designed by Edith Fowler
Manufactured in the United States of America
2 3 4 5 6 7 8 9 10

Library of Congress Cataloging in Publication Data

Schuler, Elizabeth Meriwether.
   The dog lover's answer book.

   Includes index.
   1. Dogs—Miscellanea.   2. Dog breeds.   I. Title.
SF426.S36   636.7   75-23492
ISBN 0-671-22089-6

Contents

Introduction	9
SECTION ONE: QUESTIONS AND ANSWERS	13
1. Just About Dogs	15
2. Buying a Dog	41
3. General Care and Handling of Dogs	60
4. Housing	74
5. Feeding	80
6. Grooming	90
7. Training	100
8. Obedience Trials	120
9. Medical Care	126
10. Breeding and Whelping	158
11. Raising Puppies	174
12. Legal Problems	201
13. Dog Shows	208
14. Guard Dogs, Hunting Dogs, Seeing Eye Dogs	219
15. The Old Dog	228
SECTION TWO: BREEDS	235
Credits	403
Index	409

Introduction

I was startled the other day to be asked how I became so interested in dogs. There never was a time in my memory when I wasn't. Dogs have always been my treasured companions.

The first was Hector, the old collie at my grandparents' home in Pewee Valley, Kentucky, who romped with and watched over all the grandchildren. Hector was not the rapier-headed, long-nosed collie you see nowadays; he had a broad head packed with solid intelligence and affection. Just as he was the first to teach me the joy of a dog, he also brought me my first shattering sorrow when three of us found his stiffened, cold body. But the legacy he left me has been continued by a long line of pets.

First, there was a small weepy-eyed poodle who spent most of her puppyhood in my doll carriage. When she died and was buried under the catalpa tree by the tennis court, a wispy fox terrier quickly succeeded her and just as quickly and sadly ended up under the catalpa tree—a victim of distemper. Then there was Pat, a sturdy female wirehaired fox terrier. Pat did not waste much time on people. She had been kennel-raised too long; regardless of entreaties, when she had had her dinner, she stalked upstairs to her bed in the upper hall. But she was ours and we loved her and trained her, and one incredible day Mother told us she had found a fine male wirehaired and we would soon have puppies. Our joy was boundless and, just as promised, we found four tiny puppies in the pen one spring morning. I was a good bit curious about their arrival but also just happy they were there. Those infants taught me something about puppy raising; and what joy it was to be told I could keep a male while my cousin Emily was allowed to have a female. Those two pups were trained to a fine point, bathed and petted, shown in small dog shows, photographed endlessly, and adored; then mourned as all pets must one day be.

They were followed by a charming, dour scottie who spent his infancy lying on my bed for long weeks as I recovered from a serious illness. It would have been wiser to have kept him there, for one black rainy night he was killed by a heedless driver. Time and again when we had such heartbreak my father would vow, "Never again. No more dogs. We can't stand any more of this; it hurts too much." But my wonderful optimistic mother brought home new hope—"Just this last time, Edmund." This time it was a dear pair of silky, cuddly cocker spaniels; one soft fawn and one deep ruby-red, with gentle brown eyes and wavy ears, and each as round and soft as an infant's toy. The soft fawn one left us within a week; that charming roundness was a fine case of roundworms, but we rejoiced that we still had one puppy to love. And love him we did, though it took all the patience we had for he was a ridiculous high-strung idiot. He chased the sunbeams across the polished floors in panting, yipping circles, went berserk when the telephone pealed, and when riding in the car chased each passing vehicle, leaping across seat backs, passengers and driver without cessation. This time we had the unusual pleasure of giving him up and for once rejoiced at a loss and a quiet, still house.

At this point I married and moved to San Francisco. When my husband and I found a first-floor apartment with a tiny yard, my discerning mother-in-law found me a puppy. Mom knew I was often lonely and when she spied a small boy with a basket of minute black pups she flew out of her car and asked the boy what he planned to do with them. He sobbingly told her he had been ordered to sell the lot and would "two dollars and a half be too much?"

Mom was a bit anxious about her sudden purchase for she

knew I had always had purebred dogs, but if this black scrap had won the Westminster Dog Show I could not have been more thrilled. Part scottie and part Skye (as far as we could ascertain), he was all dog. No large investment ever brought such a return as he brought us all. We named him Dan'l Boone, and when we moved to Connecticut he slept by the baby carriage and watched over our daughters as they grew; he loved us all. But one day, much older and grayer and a bit less gay, Dan'l Boone trotted off through the front gate and we never saw him again. He knew his time had come and with Scotch stubbornness he wanted to meet it alone. A year or so later, one of his successors brought home his collar.

That week of hunting, waiting and hoping for Dan'l Boone to return was a nightmare and I did not help matters any by breaking my kneecap. The fact that it was also my birthday brought no cheer whatsoever. A birthday call from my Aunt Cary in Hartford brought the overwhelming news that she wanted to give us a male golden retriever she had just seen in a kennel when she was choosing two pups for her boys. I was not merely overwhelmed; I was stunned. Could I manage a big dog in my fractured state? And what was a golden retriever? I had to know. With the help of a friend, cast and crutches, I went off to the bookstore to find out. Within moments of seeing that first picture, I knew I had come full circle. Goldens reminded me strongly of old Hector.

Since that incredible day twenty-five years ago when Aunt Cary came in with that beautiful Jason, I have never been without a golden and I trust I never shall be. I have trained them. Doctored them. Worried with non-eaters and over-eaters. Scoured the countryside when they strayed. Bred them. Raised so many litters that I've lost count. And when the time came when their lives held nothing but pain, I have held their paws as the merciful drug was injected.

Yes, I am interested in dogs. I love them.

I wrote my first book on raising puppies when I found that so many of my females were being bred by people who knew nothing about how to care for puppies, raise them wisely and sell them carefully.

This book was written for all the many families who wonder if they should have a dog and for all those who do. I care very much how dogs are purchased, trained, cared for and loved. They should be a joy to you and your friends (or at least not an annoyance to them), companions for your children, and in every way a happy, and even useful, addition to your home. I hope this book will help you to attain that goal.

SECTION
ONE

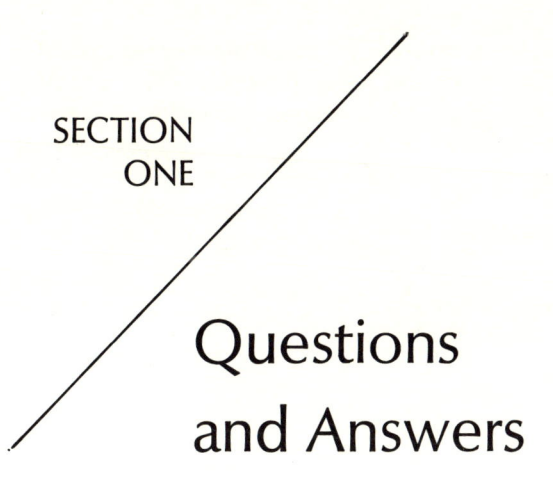

Questions and Answers

1 Just About Dogs

What was the first dog?
The dog family, which includes many other animals besides dogs, dates back roughly 20,000,000 years. The antecedent of the true dog was the wolf. In 3000 B.C. several types of dogs were in existence throughout the world.

How many dogs are there in the United States?
About 25 to 30 million. No one knows for sure. It is estimated that about 5,000,000 dogs are born annually.

How well can a dog see?
He can see as well as man and in some ways better. For instance, he can see much better at night; is extraordinarily sensitive to movement; and has a much larger field of vision. But, like most animals, he has no color vision. His binocular vision—the area he sees with both eyes at once—is narrower than ours.

Isn't a dog's sense of hearing overrated? I've had several dogs who were definitely not deaf, but who didn't move a muscle when a strange sound was made outside the house.
Most likely your dogs simply were not alarmists.
No, a dog's hearing is superior to ours in several ways: The human ear can hear sounds which are only in the frequencies between 20 and 20,000 cycles, and perhaps slightly higher;

dogs can hear sounds at a much higher frequency. Dogs can also hear fainter sounds, which is why they may set up a racket long before you know anyone is outside your door or window. And they are much better at pinpointing the sources of sounds.

Canine hearing is inferior to human hearing in only two respects. Dogs can't estimate how far a sound has traveled, and they can't differentiate as well between pitches.

Do dogs see TV?
I am certain they are attracted to the sound and see something of the picture, though it may be just a flickering of light and dark shapes. I have never had any luck in getting them to notice dogs on TV. Perhaps it is the absence of scent or smell.

It is interesting to me that the younger the pup, the more addicted he may be. Our five-year-old male thinks TV a deadly bore, and if he thinks we're watching too long, he will sit right in front of the set, totally obliterating the screen and yawn again and again in very exaggerated fashion.

Have tests been made of the dog's sense of smell?
Many. And they prove what man has long known from simple observation; the dog's sense is amazing. For instance, if you put just one drop of sulphuric acid in 10,000,000 drops of water, a dog would know that something is wrong.

Isn't it true that a dog's sense of taste is better than a man's? If so, doesn't that mean that dogs would appreciate the change of diet the TV advertisers suggest?
Some authorities believe that a dog's sense of taste is keener than a man's, but they haven't proved the point. But whether it's true or not, there's no reason for catering to a dog's taste buds when you feed him. He is just as happy eating the same food day in and day out as he is in having meat today, fish tomorrow and vegetables on Thursday.

Why do some dogs howl when you strike a certain musical note?
Evidently the note just titillates some sense and makes them

sing. Some dogs are affected by one note; others by another; and still others by none at all.

> *Are dogs changing? When I was growing up I used to hear three or four of them howling together at night as if in a concert. But I haven't heard them do this in 30 or 40 years.*

I feel rather certain that a lot of the natural dog is being bred out of dogs. But I think the main reason neither you nor I have heard a canine concert in recent years is that dogs today are being kept indoors a lot more and they're not allowed to roam as much. So they just don't have as many occasions to get their barbershop quartets together under a full moon.

Another explanation may be that you are not exposed to the same breeds you knew years ago. "Singing" dogs are primarily northern breeds.

> *Isn't it odd for a dog to "purr" when he's being scratched?*

Of the many dogs I've had, my current big fellow had been the only one that did this. But just the other day I noticed my four-year-old doing it, too.

The sound isn't really like a cat's purr. It seems to come from deep in the chest and nose and it's a little rough and sporadic. But when Joshua makes it, he's the most contented-sounding dog I can imagine.

> *I was amazed to hear my mother dog make a sort of humming noise when she was caring for her pups the other day. Isn't that unusual?*

It's not common but it's not unusual either. It's just one of the noises some females make. Usually they make it when the litter is making a racket.

> *Do all dogs shed? Why?*

All dogs shed their coat once a year. Why they do is not really known, but warm temperatures and long hours of daylight obviously have much to do with it because most shedding is done in summer.

> *Why do some dogs shed more or less the year 'round while others get it over within a few months?*

Dogs that live indoors shed almost constantly. Outdoor dogs shed in a much shorter period. This is pretty good evidence that warm temperatures influence shedding.

> *My dog seems to sleep most of the time. Is that natural?*

When a dog has something to do, he will stay awake and active for hours. Sled dogs, for instance, have amazing endurance. Foxhounds have even been known to follow a trail for 48 hours.

But as a rule, dogs are somnolent creatures. It's my guess—and only a guess—that the average dog sleeps about 18 out of 24 hours.

When a dog wants to sleep, he really doesn't care what position he is in.

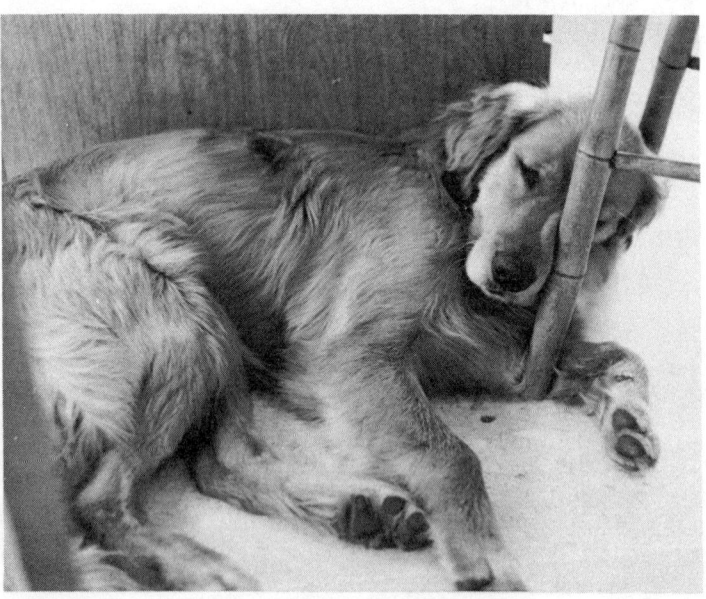

Is it true that dogs lose heat only by panting?
Almost. A dog does have sweat glands on his nose and feet and thus loses some heat—but only a little—by sweating.

How fast can dogs run?
The greyhound, the fastest dog, has been clocked at 36 miles per hour. This is almost as fast as a racehorse, and nearly twice as fast as a man.

At what age can a dog swim?
I've seen large breeds swimming at eight weeks. I shouldn't be surprised if they can swim even earlier. They do it instinctively.

I have a spaniel who absolutely refuses to go into the water. Is there anything I can do about it? All my other spaniels are in and out of the water all day.
There is little you can do to make your spaniel enjoy the water if he does not like it. Toss a few sticks if you wish, encourage him, let him watch the other dogs, but do not insist, and above all do not push or throw him in.

Why do some dogs swim with all four legs while others use mainly their front legs?
It's just one of the differences between individual animals. My younger female golden retriever has mild hip dysplasia and she tucks her hind legs under her body and swims entirely with her forelegs. On the other hand, my older female is free of hip dysplasia, yet she doesn't use her hind legs to any greater extent.

By contrast, two of my daughters have golden retrievers and both dogs are powerful swimmers using all four legs. One is a female without hip dysplasia, the other a male with very bad dysplasia.

And just to compound the enigma, my big male with perfect hips doesn't go near the water except to wade around at ankle-depth.

Is it harmful for my dog to swim in the family pool?
There is little risk to your pet but you would be wise to dis-

courage the idea at the start. It may be amusing to you and fun for the dog, but it will not be so amusing when he returns from a dip in a muddy swamp and decides to clean off in the pool. In addition, accumulations of dog hair will not be helpful to your swimming pool filter system.

One other problem with a dog that is a powerful swimmer with a love of water is that he may jump happily into a pool to join his human companions and accidentally scratch them badly.

How intelligent are dogs?

On the basis of experiments they are rated the most intelligent domestic animal, but rank below some chimpanzees, orangutans and other apes.

How does a dog learn?

By trial and error. For example, I have always been amused when my dogs put a front paw into an empty dog dish in order to hold it steady while they give it a final lick. They learned the trick as youngsters when they accidentally stepped into a dish and found it wouldn't move.

Similarly, a dog sometimes learns to open doors controlled by thumb latches because he stood up against the door one day, begging to get in, and accidentally tripped the latch.

How good is a dog's memory?

It's excellent. For example, one of my aunts gave me a dog some years ago; and although he rarely saw her, he instantly rushed to her and jumped all over her with joy whenever she came to visit.

Similarly, whenever my daughters' dogs come to visit us, the first thing they do is race around the house to the swimming pool, where family and dogs spend so much time in the summer.

I don't pretend to be a deep student of dogs. But my observation over many years leads me to the conclusion that dogs—like people—tend to remember things that make them very happy or very angry. The in-between things they forget.

Does a mother dog remember her offspring?
If she does, she certainly does a magnificent job of concealing her sentiments. In other words, no.

Do dogs understand words or just words accompanied by gestures?
Dogs develop a good understanding of many spoken words in addition to such commands as No, Heel, Stay. When I find a dripping wet dog at the front door I say, "You are wet; go to the kitchen," and she will be there waiting for me within seconds.

Or, I will say, "I'm cleaning, go upstairs," and after a sad look, they go.

I think it amusing and helpful, too, to talk to your dogs; accustom them to words. Use the same phrases, speak in a definite tone and before long you will find they understand very well.

How do dogs communicate with humans?
They make their wishes very clearly known in a variety of ways in addition to barking. Our first dog always gave a great happy shake all over when I went to the door to let her out. All dogs we have had since then learned the habit but use it a bit differently. If I see one looking restless and ask, "Do you want to go out?" my answer is a great happy shake in clear response to the question.

At cocktail time, if I give each dog a couple of dog biscuits, they never think that two are sufficient and stare steadily at the box, then at my face, and then back at the box—all very clearly saying please, just one more.

Other ways that dogs communicate are by bumping against you, tossing their heads in the direction they want to go, pacing back and forth to call attention to themselves, pointing like a hunting dog (but not necessarily at game).

The longer a dog lives with you, the easier his signals are to understand. But don't be surprised if he sometimes comes up with a new signal. And of course you shouldn't expect one dog to "talk" like another unless they live together.

Why do dogs often sneeze when they greet their owners?

I believe it is one of their ways of showing emotion.

Why does a dog turn around in circles before he lies down?

This behavior is a throwback to the early dogs. One theory holds that the dog is trampling down the grass or snow in which he used to live to make a comfortable bed. Another theory is that he's driving away snakes. A third is that the female is pushing her pups into a pile so she won't lie on them.

Whatever the truth—which we'll never know—please note that dogs are perfectly able to flop directly down on the ground and go to sleep without turning in circles beforehand.

Why does a male dog go all around his owner's yard urinating a little here and a little there?

He's staking out the boundaries of his territory.

If a dog is allowed to run loose, why does he choose your neighbor's yard to defecate in?

I guess it's because of his native instinct, evident even in puppies, not to befoul his own nest.

Why do two strange male dogs always sniff each other's hindquarters when they first meet?

It's just standard operating procedure.

Why does a dog roll in carrion or manure?

This unpleasant habit dates back to the primitive dog that killed for his food, slaughtered an attacker and then rolled exultantly in the residue of the kill. Most dogs never indulge themselves, but others are overjoyed at the discovery of a very dead rabbit or squirrel. You cannot win against such a primordial urge. Just keep an aerosol can of dry shampoo on hand and an old towel. You can scold all you like, but your words will soon be forgotten at the sight of the next rabbit.

Why dogs roll in manure I do not know. It's interesting to note, however, that those with an affinity for carrion are the principal culprits.

Will our year-old puppy resent our first new baby when I bring her home?

Probably not if you make no change in the puppy's habits, play with him, love him, spend as much time with him as possible and do not just shut him away while you enjoy and care for the baby. Treat the puppy exactly as if he were an older child, because he needs your attention and affection just as much. A young puppy will soon learn to enjoy the baby as part of his adored family and may wind up sleeping protectively by the carriage.

An older dog, however, may need more watchful care. Some breeds don't trust children of any age no matter what you do to please them. And one-man dogs must be treated with great caution. If they appear bad-tempered and stay that way, you may have to get rid of them.

Can I expect a dog and cat to get along happily?

They may not be happy, but after a few fierce encounters they will begin to accept each other; and eventually they may actually play together and become friends. It takes time. Your real concern will be to prevent the cat from injuring the dog's eyes. The cat is more adept at avoiding injury.

Not all dogs are black, white or brown. What unusual colors do they come in and what are they called?

Apricot. A sort of pinkish-brown. It's usually a poodle color.

Belton. A fine scattering or mottling of white and blue-gray, white and orange, white and brown. It is common in setters.

Brindle. An even mixture of black and gray or brown.

Dappled. A splattering of various colors, none predominating.

Fawn. Ranging from a deep cream to rich gold.

Grizzle. Bluish-gray.

Harlequin. Large patches of color on a base color—usually black on white.

Liver. A deep red-brown.
Merle. A gray so deep and flecked with black that it appears blue. Most people use the redundant term "blue merle."
Parti-color. A coat of several colors.
Roan. A mixture of colored and white hairs.
Sable. A light-toned coat with a lacing of black hairs.
Sedge. The color of dead grass.
Tricolor. White, black and tan.
Wheaten. Pale yellow.

What's the difference between a dog's mantle and mask?
The mantle is the darker area on the shoulders, back and sides, while the mask is the darker tone of the face and muzzle.

What are the various distinct spots of color on a dog called?
You can call these just "spots" if you like. But fanciers use more special words: "blaze" for a clearly marked stripe in the center of the face; "kiss marks" for the spots on the cheeks or above the eyes; "beauty spot" for a colored spot surrounded by white on the top of the head.

What is feathering?
The longer hair on legs, tails and ears. Spaniels, among others, have feathering. The heavy long hair on the back of the thighs is also called a culotte.

The terms apron, mane and ruff seem to refer to pretty much the same thing. Do they?
Not quite. The apron is the full hair on the chest. Collies have gorgeous aprons. The mane is the long hair on the sides and top of the mask. The ruff is the long hair that surrounds the neck.

Do some dogs have double coats of fur?
Many hardy outdoor breeds, especially water dogs, have a clearly visible double coat. The outer one is firm and resistant

to underbrush, the inner is a softer underliner for protection from cold and damp.

Do all dogs have brown eyes?
The great majority. But some, such as Chesapeake retrievers, have almost yellow eyes. And some have what is known as a china eye, meaning they are a crystal-clear blue.

Retrievers are always described as having a "kindly expression." What is really meant?
Expression in a dog is his whole look. Each breed has a typical expression. For example, a Welsh corgi has a foxy expression; a Shetland sheepdog, an alert, questioning expression.

When someone refers to a dog's muzzle, is he speaking of the whole head?
No, the muzzle is just the foreface, the jaw area; everything below the eyes.

What is meant by a dog's "stop"?
It's the change in depth between the muzzle and the skull.

What is the bump or knob on top of some dogs' heads?
The occiput. It is the very back point of the skull. But in some breeds, especially in setters and golden retrievers, it is a definite knob.

What are chops? Flews?
Chops are the heavy hanging folds on the jaw. Flews are the loose hanging folds of the upper lips.

What terms are used to describe the different parts of a dog's forelegs and hindlegs?
On the forelegs, the pastern is the section between the foot and the first joint, which is called the carpus. The forearm is the section between the carpus and upper joint, or elbow. Above the elbow is the upper arm, then the shoulder. The withers are the top of the shoulder right behind the neck.

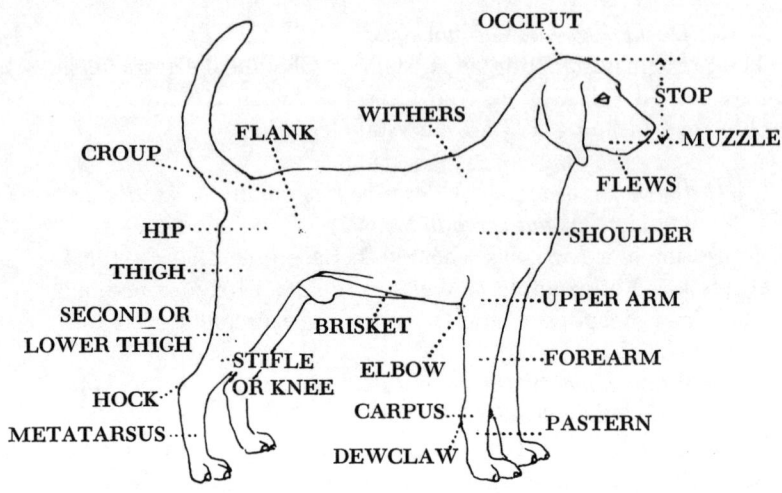

On the hindlegs, the metatarsus corresponds with the pastern; the hock with the carpus. Above the hock is the second, or lower, thigh; then the joint called the stifle. The thigh proper is above the stifle and is connected to the hips.

How is a dog's height measured?
Always from his front shoulder (withers) to the ground.

What is a dewclaw?
This is the extra, useless claw found on the inside of the leg above the foot. They are usually removed when a pup is a few days old; but consult the standard for your breed.

Dewclaws have been bred out of some breeds.

What are some of the worst faults to look for in a dog's legs and gait?
If he's cowhocked, the hocks turn toward each other instead of being straight.

If he has splay feet, the toes are spread apart.

If he knuckles over, the ankles of the front legs are doubled over in an almost deformed way. A Basset that knuckles over is disqualified from the show ring.

Paddling is bad because the dog walks with his legs spread far apart. A weaving, or rolling, gait, in which the feet cross each other, is also undesirable.

What is a dog's brisket?
The brisket is the chest area that lies between the forelegs.

Where is a dog's flank?
This is the area behind the ribs, before the hip section.

Where is a dog's croup?
It's the area before the tail or rump. It's also referred to as a "goose-rump" if too abrupt or sloped.

What is meant by a dog's "brush"?
His very heavily furred tail. If it has a soft, pendulous fringe, that is called a plume. The round ball of fur on the tip of a poodle's tail is a pompon.

How many breeds of dogs are there?
One hundred and sixty-six recognized breeds with more than one or two specimens are to be found in the United States today. There are probably additional breeds with only one or two specimens.

Outside the U.S. there are still more breeds, many in large numbers.

Just what is the American Kennel Club?
Because the AKC is the largest organized group of dog lovers in the world, everything connected with dogs in the United States tends to be dominated by it. This is rather unfair to similar associations which, though much smaller, also do a great deal for dogs and dog owners. On the other hand, it cannot be denied that, despite some arrogant and monopolistic practices and policies, the AKC has done much to improve

28 / THE DOG LOVER'S ANSWER BOOK

dogs and bring order to what might otherwise be a very disorderly business.

The AKC is a non-profit association with membership composed of over 300 breed clubs. Its basic purpose is to promote and safeguard purebred dogs. Among other things, it puts out a monthly *Stud Book Register;* publishes *Purebred Dogs —the American Kennel Club Gazette,* a monthly magazine with general information and details about events in the dog world; has a library of 9,000 books which is open to the public; sets up regulations for dog shows, obedience trials and field trials; and maintains an information service which anyone can call. The address is: American Kennel Club, 51 Madison Avenue, New York, New York 10010.

What other organizations in the U.S. register dogs?

American Coonhound Association, Box 501, Lexington, Tennessee 38531

American Field Stud Book, 222 W. Adams Street, Chicago, Illinois 60606

American International Border Collie Registry, Runnells, Iowa 50237

Full Cry Kennel Club (Coonhounds), Box 190, Sedalia, Missouri 65301

International Fox Hunters' Stud Book, 152 Walnut Street, Lexington, Kentucky 40503

National Coursing Association, 300 North Cedar Street, Abilene, Kansas 67410

National Stock Dog Registry, Rt. 1, Butler, Indiana 46721

North American Sheepdog Society, 210 E. Main Street, McLeansboro, Illinois 62859

Standard Foxhound Stud Book, Sand Springs, Oklahoma 74063

Stodghill ARF Registry, Quinlan, Texas 75474

United Kennel Club, 321 W. Cedar Street, Kalamazoo, Michigan 49007

In addition, many of the clubs representing the breeds listed in Section II maintain stud books.

What is a blooded dog?
A purebred, pedigreed dog. The American Kennel Club defines a purebred as "a dog whose sire and dam belong to the same breed, and are themselves of unmixed descent since recognition of the breed."

What's the difference between a mongrel and a crossbreed?
Since neither are purebreds, they are actually the same thing—a mutt. But if you want to split hairs, a mongrel is a dog descended from so many breeds that he's a total mixture. A crossbreed, on the other hand, is the offspring of two purebred dogs of different breeds. He may have a definite resemblance to one or the other parent.

What breeds are recognized and pedigreed by the American Kennel Club?
The 121 breeds recognized and pedigreed by the AKC are described alphabetically (along with other breeds not recognized by the AKC) in the second section of this book. For show purposes, they are divided into six groups as follows:

GROUP 1—SPORTING DOGS
American water spaniel
Brittany spaniel
Chesapeake Bay retriever
Clumber spaniel
Cocker spaniel
Curly-coated retriever
English cocker spaniel
English setter
English springer spaniel
Field spaniel
Flat-coated retriever
German short-haired pointer
German wirehaired pointer
Golden retriever
Gordon setter
Irish setter
Irish water spaniel
Labrador retriever
Pointer
Sussex spaniel
Vizsla
Weimaraner
Welsh springer spaniel
Wirehaired pointing griffon

Group 2—Hounds

- Afghan hound
- American foxhound
- Basenji
- Basset hound
- Beagle
- Black-and-tan coonhound
- Bloodhound
- Borzoi
- Dachshund
- English foxhound
- Greyhound
- Harrier
- Irish wolfhound
- Norwegian elkhound
- Otter hound
- Rhodesian ridgeback
- Saluki
- Scottish deerhound
- Whippet

Group 3—Working Dogs

- Akita
- Alaskan malamute
- Belgian Malinois
- Belgian sheepdog
- Belgian Tervuren
- Bernese mountain dog
- Bouvier des Flandres
- Boxer
- Briard
- Bull mastiff
- Cardian Welsh corgi
- Collie
- Doberman pinscher
- German shepherd
- Giant schnauzer
- Great Dane
- Great Pyrenees
- Komondor
- Kuvasz
- Mastiff
- Newfoundland
- Old English sheepdog
- Pembroke Welsh corgi
- Puli
- Rottweiler
- Saint Bernard
- Samoyed
- Shetland sheepdog
- Siberian husky
- Standard schnauzer

Group 4—Terriers

- Airedale terrier
- American Staffordshire terrier
- Australian terrier
- Bedlington terrier
- Border terrier
- Bullterrier
- Cairn terrier
- Dandie Dinmont terrier
- Fox terrier
- Irish terrier
- Kerry blue terrier
- Lakeland terrier
- Manchester terrier
- Miniature schnauzer
- Norwich terrier
- Scottish terrier

GROUP 4—TERRIERS
Sealyham terrier
Skye terrier
Soft-coated wheaten terrier
Staffordshire bullterrier
Welsh terrier
West Highland white terrier

GROUP 5—TOYS
Affenpinscher
Brussels griffon
Chihuahua
English toy spaniel
Italian greyhound
Japanese spaniel
Maltese
Miniature pinscher
Papillon
Pekingese
Pomeranian
Pug
Shih Tzu
Silky terrier
Yorkshire terrier

GROUP 6—NON-SPORTING DOGS
Bichon frise
Boston terrier
Bulldog
Chow chow
Dalmatian
French bulldog
Keeshond
Lhasa Apsos
Poodle
Schipperke
Tibetan terrier

The AKC also recognizes but does not accept for registration the following breeds. These are grouped in a Miscellaneous Class.

Australian cattle dog
Australian kelpie
Bearded collie
Cavalier King Charles spaniel
Ibizan hound
Miniature bullterrier
Spinone Italiano

What breeds are recognized and registered by the United Kennel Club?

Airedale terrier
Alaskan malamute
American Eskimo
American (pit) bullterrier
  (American Staffordshire
  terrier)

American water spaniel
Arctic husky (Siberian husky)
Basset hound
Black-and-tan coonhound
Bloodhound
Bluetick coonhound
Chihuahua
Dachshund
English coonhound
English shepherd
German shepherd
Irish setter
Maltese
Miniature pinscher
Pekingese
Plott hound
Pomeranian
Poodle
Redbone coonhound
Saint Bernard
Shetland sheepdog
Toy fox terrier
Treeing Walker coonhound
Weimaraner

What other breeds are there in the United States?
This is a miscellaneous collection of well-known sporting breeds and rare breeds which are not yet accepted by the AKC or UKC because there are not enough of them in the U.S. or for other reasons.

Anatolian shepherd
Australian shepherd
Border collie
Boykin spaniel
Canaan dog
Catahoula leopard dog
Chinese crested dog
Chinese fighting dog
Chinese imperial ch'in
Chinese temple dog
Coton de Tulear
Finnish spitz
Glen of Imaal terrier
Greater Swiss mountain dog
Iceland dog
Jack Russell terrier
Little lion dog
Mexican hairless
Neapolitan mastiff
Pharaoh hound
Picardie shepherd
Portuguese water dog
Redtick coonhound
Telomian
Tennessee treeing brindle
Tibetan mastiff
Tibetan spaniel
Trigg hound
Xoloxcuintle

What are the most popular breeds of dogs in the U.S. today?

Here are the top 25 breeds registered by the AKC in 1974. Comparable statistics are not available from other registries.

Rating	Breed	Number Registered
1	Poodles	171,550
2	German shepherds	86,014
3	Irish setters	61,549
4	Beagles	51,777
5	Dachshunds	47,581
6	Doberman pinschers	45,110
7	Miniature schnauzers	41,392
8	Labrador retrievers	36,689
9	Cocker spaniels	35,492
10	Saint Bernards	31,361
11	Collies	28,068
12	Pekingeses	23,631
13	Shetland sheepdogs	22,944
14	Golden retrievers	20,933
15	Chihuahuas	20,639
16	Great Danes	20,319
17	Brittany spaniels	19,368
18	Yorkshire terriers	19,223
19	Siberian huskies	18,473
20	Lhasa Apsos	17,692
21	Basset hounds	17,251
22	Pomeranians	16,433
23	Old English sheepdogs	16,050
24	German short-haired pointers	15,284
25	English springer spaniels	14,389

Why do breeds rise and fall in popularity?

There are various reasons, some with a sound basis and others simply faddish. For example, cockers became popular in the '30s when a dog named Flush appeared on Broadway in *The Barretts of Wimpole Street*. Fox terriers also soared to the top in the '30s as a result of a remarkable string of victories in the

Westminster Kennel Club Show in New York City and because they went well with the mannish fashions women then wore.

German shepherds became a rage in the '20s because of a pair of screen heroes named Rin-Tin-Tin and Strongheart. Then came the Depression and breeds with big appetites hit the skids. Now they're popular again because of the need for guard and guide dogs.

Saint Bernards, Great Danes and mastiffs—among other large breeds—are also popular today because people believe their sheer size terrorizes burglars.

Scotties were popular during Franklin Roosevelt's administration because of the presence in the White House of a dog named Fala. Weimaraners were made a hit by the breeders' clever policy of charging sky-high prices for them, and boxers were put across by a loud and misleading publicity campaign.

On the other hand, a number of once-popular breeds have lost favor because they have been so overbred that they are full of mental and physical woes. Just the other day a woman said to me with a sigh, "Well, that's the end of that breed. It used to be great until the fanciers latched on to it. But whenever that happens, you soon get so many poor specimens in circulation that the whole breed is ruined."

What are breed standards? Where do I look them up?
Breed standards give the ideal for each breed: size, weight, appearance, gait, temperament, etc. They will also include disqualifications. They are set by each breed club and approved by the members.

In the case of breeds registered by the AKC, the standards must also be approved by the AKC. They are then printed in *The Complete Dog Book* published by the AKC.

Dog World magazine also has an annual issue containing the standards for all AKC breeds as well as a number of others.

Why do American-bred dogs hold their tails high when hunting while English-bred dogs hold theirs straight out?
They've been bred differently and belong to different strains. Comparable differences are found in other breeds.

Which mature earlier, big dogs or little?
Little. They often mature long before they're a year old, whereas giant breeds occasionally are not mature at two years.
The average age at maturity is—very roughly—one year.

My pup is only four months old and he's already acting very precocious sexually. Is that normal?
Quite normal. It's all part of growing up. Dogs follow no timetable in this respect; some start earlier than others.

When does a male dog start lifting his leg to urinate?
When he reaches the age of puberty. Small breeds start at about six months; large breeds at about a year. Dogs that are castrated early in life never lift their legs.

How young can a male be to sire a litter?
The male is not fully capable of siring a litter until he is seven months old, but you will be wise to wait until he is a year old because it is thought that the litter will be stronger.

I have a five-year-old male. He has never been bred. Can he sire a litter of puppies?
There is no physical reason why he cannot be a fine sire, but he may need patience, assistance and encouragement. If he has not run free very often he may have no sexual experience at all and simply may not understand what he's supposed to do. But try him; give him time; and if the bitch is ready, you may have a successful breeding.

What is a cryptorchid?
A male dog with testicles which have not descended into the scrotum. The dog is sterile but otherwise unimpaired. The AKC rules that such dogs may not be shown in the show ring.

What is monorchidism?
This is the name given a congenital defect in which one testicle has not descended into the scrotum. In occasional cases, hormones may help the testicle to descend. But whether it does

or not, the dog should not be bred because he may pass the defect on to his offspring. AKC rules state that monorchids are ineligible for showing.

Should a dog ever be castrated?
Although most people have a natural aversion to castration, you might resort to it if your dog is forever roaming far and wide looking for females in heat or if he is too rambunctious or ill-tempered. The operation may calm him down and curb his wandering tendencies. But it won't affect him otherwise.

What are the disadvantages of castration?
You may later regret that your male cannot be bred. In addition, under AKC rules he cannot compete in dog shows.

If a male dog is castrated, will it keep him from wandering?
Not necessarily. If your male wanders solely because there is a female in season in the neighborhood, he will no longer have this urge. But if he wanders because he is left alone a great deal and is lonely, he may continue to wander.

Will castration or spaying stop a dog from being vicious?
Don't count on it. Putting him to death is the only sure answer.

If we decide to have our male castrated, when should it be done?
Preferably at six months. But it can be done at any later time.

Does a dog that is raised in an apartment become frustrated because he cannot get out and chase females?
If canines could be psychoanalyzed they might tell us the answer is yes. But as far as a human can tell, neither a male nor female dog is bothered by incarceration that keeps him away from the opposite sex.

How does a bitch compare to a male in temperament?
It is usually conceded that a female is less stubborn and easier

to train, will wander less as she does not have a constant sexual urge, and shares her affection with each member of the family rather than doting on one single member. I do think that females are often more nervous and excitable while a male will tend to ignore odd noises, storms, gunshots, etc.

Is a female as good as a male for hunting?
That depends a great deal on the individual dog. But as a rule, hunters prefer the male for his untiring stamina, steady nerves and temperament.

Are females used as guard dogs?
Yes, but males are preferred as they have greater strength, stamina and size.

When does a bitch have her first heat?
On the average, the first heat will occur sometime between the seventh and the twelfth month, but many females in the larger breeds may not have their first heat until after they are a year old. This delay in no way affects their ability to be bred and to produce fine puppies.

How often is a bitch in heat?
Normally every six months; but it is not unusual for some dogs to have a seven- or eight-month cycle. A few breeds—the basenji for example—have just one heat period a year.

How long does a period of heat or estrum last?
Twenty-one days is the usual length of time. If the period is prolonged, there may be some abnormality that should be checked by a veterinarian.

Is the bitch attractive to males for the entire three weeks?
Unfortunately, yes. In fact, males are likely to know she is in heat before you have any visual signs of it. Although she is not fertile for more than four days, the country is full of unexpected pups because owners didn't know which days to keep their

females secure from roving males. So lock her up for the full twenty-one days and you won't have a mongrel litter.

I can't afford to board my female twice a year when she is in heat. What are the problems if I keep her at home?
You must make certain that you can provide absolute safety from roaming dogs. An outdoor pen should have a fence at least eight feet high and set in concrete to stop dogs from digging underneath. If you have many neighborhood dogs, they may surround the pen and fight and howl for ten days to two weeks. In a closely built-up area this will be highly annoying both to you and your neighbors. Obviously the annoyance is reduced in open country with fewer dogs and fewer neighbors.

If you decide to keep the female in your house, you should shut her in a locked room or basement lest someone inadvertently leaves a door open so she can escape. You will be wise to have her use newspapers to relieve herself, although this will be hard on a house-trained dog. The alternative is to *carry* her to an area away from the house, because if you walk her there on a leash she will leave a scent that will bring dogs from miles around.

Staining caused by the discharge may or may not be profuse. Some females keep themselves clean; others don't. In either case, since your rugs and furnishings can be badly soiled, you may want your bitch to wear a sanitary napkin. However, she will *not* want to wear it and you may have to have her wear the Elizabethan collar (see page 153) to prevent her from tearing it off. A lot simpler to have her confined in a boarding kennel.

I had my female bred to a carefully chosen male. Unfortunately, before she could be returned to the boarding kennel, she escaped and was mated to a mongrel. Will this unplanned breeding affect the arranged breeding?
Unfortunately, yes. A female ovulates for several days and can be bred to numerous males during this period. Obviously a mixed litter will result. Since no one can determine the sire of an individual puppy, no pedigree can be given.

It is of the utmost importance that a female in heat be kept under lock and key in a secure kennel at all times for the full three weeks.

Is it true that when a bitch has a mongrel or unplanned litter she will never be able to produce a purebred litter?
This is a very old belief and there is not a vestige of truth in it. One litter has no bearing whatsoever on succeeding litters.

I have a young female puppy. Even though she is registered with the AKC and beautiful, we don't plan to raise puppies. Should we spay her?
If you are absolutely certain that you will *never* want to raise a litter, then you should spay your female. But remember the decision is irreversible, because the ovaries and uterus will be surgically removed. You must be certain, too, that you will not want to show her. Spayed females are not eligible in the show ring. They may, however, be shown in obedience trials.

There are many advantages in spaying a female: You never have to worry about unwanted puppies. She doesn't have to be confined in a boarding kennel or at home for three weeks twice a year for the rest of her life. License fees are lower for spayed females. And she does not develop breast tumors and uterine infections.

Will spaying change a female's personality? Will she become fat and sluggish?
Spaying may have a calming effect, but it won't make a bitch sluggish. She will not gain weight just because of spaying *provided* you are wise about her diet, don't overfeed her, and see that she gets enough exercise.

When should a female be spayed?
Ideally, it should be done before her first heat when she is four to six months of age. It is wise not to delay it beyond three to four years. Few, if any, veterinarians will consider spaying a female over six.

Are there hormones that can keep a female from coming into heat?

No longer. These have been removed from use as they proved to be extremely dangerous.

What is false pregnancy?

It is not unusual for even a maiden bitch to begin showing all signs of pregnancy thirty days or more after she has been in heat. Her abdomen will swell, her teats will secrete some milk, she will be broody one day and restless the next. And she will dig holes and make nests of anything available. Usually this is due to a hormone imbalance, and though some females return to normal without help, hormone injections will speed up the process.

Why do females sometimes mount other dogs as if they were males?

I don't know why. They just do. Don't let it upset you.

My four-month-old female is house-trained but often dribbles. What can be done about this?

This is a common problem with females, especially the very young or the very old. If not caused by any physical ailment, it is due to shyness or nervousness. Don't treat it as a behavior problem, because it's something she cannot control. Scoldings and punishment will only make matters worse. If dribbling occurs when you speak sharply, try a gentler tone. If it occurs when she greets a roomful of guests, let her meet them outside.

With patience and affection, you can help her get over the problem eventually.

2
Buying a Dog

We have never had a dog, but now that we've moved to the country we want one. What type of dog do you suggest?

The choice of a dog for a family must be made by the family itself. If you have no special interest in or knowledge of any breed, visit one of the many all-breed dog shows. Here you will be able to see the best representatives of a great many breeds, watch their behavior with people and observe the general attitude and personality of each—whether they're sluggish, restless, of good or bad temper, alert, etc. The owners will be happy to talk to you and answer your questions. Then try to see the breed that appeals to you in a family atmosphere. Find out how much space the dog requires, if he is easy to train, if he is dependable with children, if he will adapt well to the country, if he needs an unusual amount of grooming. Good breeders will be interested in helping, for it is to their advantage to see that each pup is placed in the right atmosphere.

What is the right breed for a city family?

Choosing the right dog for the family is as important as deciding that it is the time to have a dog. There are 166 breeds and Section II describes each breed—its appearance, its personality—at some length. If you live in a city apartment you would be wise to choose one of the toy breeds or one of the quiet spaniels, although some large breeds adapt well to city living. You will give any dog daily walks but the larger breeds should have a good run in open space and not just a quiet turn around the block on the end of a leash. Among the small breeds, choose one that is quiet, not too excitable or nervous and that will adapt easily and be a happy companion to your children. Some small breeds are definitely not good with children. Among the larger breeds that adapt well to the city are the standard poodle, Afghans, and the springer spaniel. Beware of over-excitable terriers that bark at every noise every hour of the day or night. They will not endear you to the neighbors.

> *What kind of puppy should we get for our five-year-old son?*

Let's get one thing straight: People think they are buying puppies for their children. And many of them really do believe that their children are going to take care of the dogs. But they are simply having pipe dreams.

Buy any kind of puppy for your five-year-old you like. It's you—not he—who's going to love it and take care of it.

> *How early should you let a child have his or her very own dog?*

That really depends entirely on the child and how much responsibility he shows. Generally, you don't find the sense of commitment that a dog deserves from its master in children under ten years of age.

> *We are giving our young children a puppy for Christmas. Will we have any problems?*

Not if you take some precautions. The children must be taught that the pup is essentially an infant and like all infants must have ample time to sleep, eat quietly, be alone, play, and to be held gently and loved. If this regimen is adhered to and all playing with the pup is under the supervision of an adult, you will avoid problems. A pup cannot be expected patiently to endure continual harassment, poking, prodding, being picked up, put down, dropped, dressed up, dragged around by a leash, etc. If he turns to growling, snapping or biting, it is his only defense.

BUYING A DOG / 43

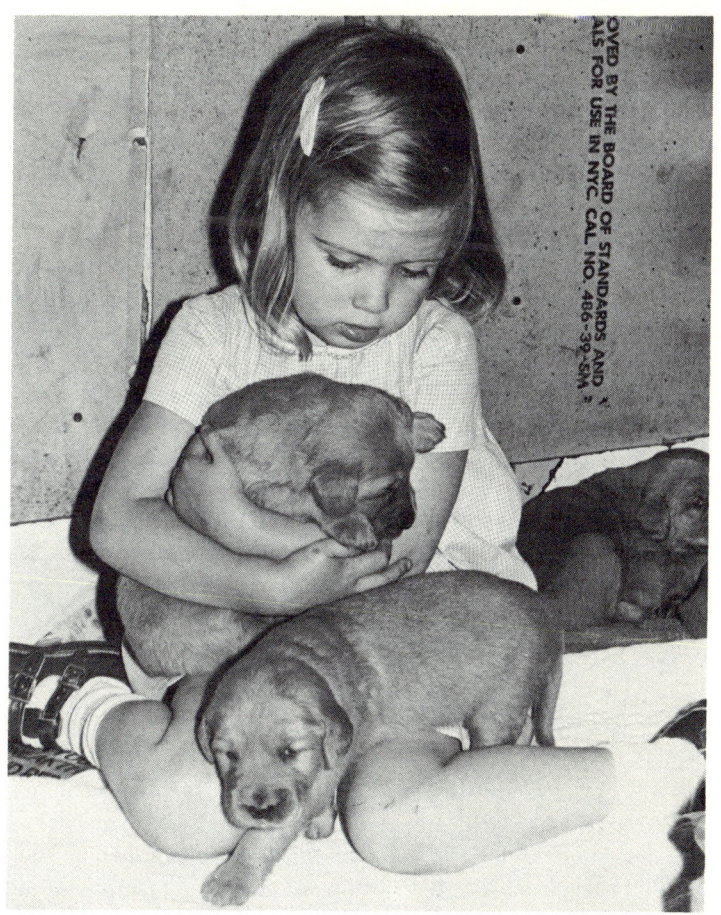

A puppy needs love and gentle care from the day he is born.

It is up to responsible parents to teach young children thoughtful care of a small creature. If they can't, they should not give a child a puppy.

> *I am finding it difficult to deny my young children the companionship of a dog and yet I am very unenthusiastic about owning one. We live on a pleasant suburban*

street and the large yard is fenced. I dislike the thought of the yard littered with animal messes, bushes broken and holes dug. Am I just being selfish? Should every family have a dog?

To have a dog or not should really be the enthusiastic decision of *all* the family members. Even devoted dog lovers admit that dogs do bring in dirt, do dig holes and do mess up lawns. But training can help to prevent many of the problems. The dog can be confined to one area of the yard for his outdoor needs and the area can be cleaned up as necessary. A towel kept handy by the kitchen door will take care of muddy feet and dirt and the dog can be taught to stay in dog-proof areas.

A dog in the family can bring fun, protection, and deep and loyal affection, but unless you are convinced that this can offset the problems and expenses of food and medical care, you would be wise to join numerous other families who are quite content without a dog.

Is it wise for an active woman in her seventies to buy a puppy?

That depends on how active she really is or likes to be. Everyone must realize that a young puppy is as demanding and needs as much care as a two-year-old child; and even when grown, he still must be given a lot of attention.

To be blunt about it, a dog is a burden. He ties you down. This is true when you're in your twenties and even truer when you're seventy and without any family responsibilities.

The other thing that worries me about elderly people taking on puppies is that puppies get underfoot and often cause falls that may break old bones.

In short, I never encourage a person of retirement age to buy a puppy; and in some cases I discourage it. But if the person recognizes the disadvantages and still wants a pup, then, of course, she should have one—the companionship outweighs everything else.

P.S. The best buy for the elderly person is a mature dog that doesn't need frequent feedings, housebreaking and training, and that isn't so likely to trip you up.

Is it possible for a lame person to have a dog?
Certainly, but select a quiet or even sedentary breed that won't jump on you and knock you down, that won't get underfoot and trip you up, and that isn't forever demanding to be let outdoors. I'd also recommend that you buy an adult dog that doesn't present all the teaching problems of a puppy.

Some of the breeds I favor for handicapped individuals are English bulldogs, golden retrievers, English setters, Welsh springer spaniels and pugs.

Is there such a thing as a dog that would be suitable for people with bad allergies?
The claim is made that the poodle is the "only" non-allergenic dog. While it's true that there are people with hay fever and asthma who live very happily with poodles, the claim is not only too sweeping but also lacking in conclusive scientific support. Keeping the poodle well clipped and brushed free of dust are additional safeguards.

Both my husband and I work five days a week, but we have a small house in the suburbs and long for a puppy. What kind do you recommend?
Don't buy a dog of any breed until you're able to be at home. You cannot properly train a pet if you have to leave it shut up all day on papers or outdoors all day in a pen. A puppy is like a two-year-old child. He must have companionship, training and constant care. Without this, he will be miserable and so will you because he will be almost totally untrainable.

In buying a dog for our family, we can't decide between a male or a female. Is one preferable to the other as a general all-round family pet?
Many pet owners feel that the female of any breed makes a better family pet: she is less likely to wander; somewhat less stubborn and therefore easier to train; less likely to devote herself to one person, and instead spreads her affection to the entire family group. However, there are many people who just as firmly insist that a male is always the first choice.

> *Isn't it true that most people prefer male dogs to females? Why?*

I do not find this true any longer. People are showing a preference for the female. But there are many dog owners who say stoutly, "I have never owned a female." Their reasons are somewhat nebulous: They think having a female in heat will be difficult. They worry that a female will always be pursued by males and be more nervous and delicate. They are sure a male is a more impressive and better protector of the family. They like a male's independent, self-reliant air.

> *Would I be making a mistake to buy the runt of a litter?*

Runt simply means undersized, and there's nothing wrong with buying a pup that is somewhat smaller than his brothers and sisters as long as you realize that he probably won't be as large as they when fully grown and that he won't be a winner in the show ring. You should also recognize the fact that just because he's small doesn't make him exceptionally smart—as some people believe.

The only thing basically wrong with a runt is that he *may* not be healthy. I acted one time as intermediary between a breeder and a distant friend who wanted a golden retriever. The pup the breeder offered me was pathetic. As the breeder said, he was as cute as a button. But he was half the normal size for his age; and the longer I looked at him, the more obvious it became that he was totally lacking in the physical and mental vitality we all want in a pup.

You must examine a runt in the same way yourself. Take lots and lots of time. Make sure he's healthy, lively, alert and perky. And if he's a great deal smaller than his peers, forget him.

> *When looking for a dog for a family pet, should we look only at AKC pedigreed breeds? What is wrong with taking a puppy of unknown parentage that is being given away free? The papers are full of such ads.*

Many a pup of unknown parentage makes a good family pet. But if you decide to give a home to one of them do try to see his mother and find out something about where he was raised. It is not just his parentage that is "unknown" but also his entire background. Is he free of worms and fleas? Has he been wisely fed? What about any inoculations? If the family took such poor care of his mother and allowed her to have an unwanted litter, it may be assumed that they have done little to insure the future health of the pup. Before you agree to take such a puppy, have him checked over by a veterinarian.

Is a mongrel puppy a better pet for children than a purebred dog?

A mongrel puppy is such a mixture of breeds it is hard to judge what his talents, instincts and temperament may be. You may well be lucky, but then again you may not be.

However, if you have a puppy of two purebred dogs that are not of the same breed, he can be a fine choice, for you know his parentage and have a pretty good clue as to his probable temperament and appearance.

Is it true that a mongrel puppy is healthier than a purebred puppy?

This long-held belief stems from the fact that unwanted, mongrel litters have to struggle for survival. Those that make it are hardy because they battled against all odds.

This doesn't mean, however, that just any mongrel will be healthier than a purebred dog.

Isn't a mongrel usually smarter than a purebred dog?

Of course not. Some may be; others are not. There's a natural tendency to assign to a mongrel a superior intelligence or cleverness because, deep down, we're a little sorry for him and admire him for the way he has made his way in the world. We do much the same thing with people. We admire the man who made it from rags to riches; downgrade the other who was born rich. Yet the latter may be the smarter of the two.

Are two dogs in a family better than one?

I give a most emphatic yes. A dog is a very sociable beast and though he gives his heart to humans, he thoroughly enjoys having another dog to romp with, chase squirrels with, lean on for a cozy nap, etc. We have always had two dogs and now we have three; and never have we seen any sign of jealousy, rivalry or even hurt feelings. They have violent mock battles, play a real game of hide-and-seek, thoroughly enjoy one another and cuddle up in a clump at the end of the day. Some might think that a group of dogs in a family would be very independent and less interested in the human side of things. It just isn't so. When Joshua joins us for some activity, he alerts the others. When Jennifer knocks on the door to come in, they all troop in, because they're devoted to one another, yes, but mainly because they are deeply interested in everything we do. And when in the past we have lost a dear companion to old age, it has been a wonderfully warming comfort to have a consoling four-footed friend still beside us.

We have two grown female dogs and want to buy a three-month-old male. Will our females be upset?
They may be very ungracious about welcoming a frisky young pup, male or female, to their home. But see to it that the pup is not allowed to pester them, nip their heels, pull their ears, eat from their dish, usurp their bed or sleeping area. Above all, don't lavish affection and attention on him and ignore the adult dogs. Give them just as much of your time and care as you always did and within a few days they will be vying to care for the pup in true maternal fashion.

Will there be trouble if you bring a new female into a home with an established female?
There must be some truth in the widespread belief that two females don't get along together as well as two males; but I have never had a particle of trouble of this kind. In my experience, if the new female is a pup, the older one will accept her (after she has taught the youngster her manners) and they will eventually be like mother and daughter.

Once I know the breed I want, how do I find a puppy?
Write the American Kennel Club and the United Kennel Club

BUYING A DOG / 49

for a list of the people who raise your chosen breed in your area. Watch the newspaper ads. Call the breeders whose dogs appealed to you at the dog shows in the area. Ask owners of that breed where they found their dog. Call veterinarians in your area for information on any recent litters by reputable breeders. Then make a list of the most promising places and pay them a visit.

What are "referral services"?
They are services set up in some parts of the country by breeders to assist potential dog buyers and thus help themselves. The services run advertisements in local newspapers offering to help people locate top-quality, registered dogs of any breed. The services are free.

How do I go about buying a dog once I have found a reliable source?
Call the owner of the litter and make an appointment. Go at the stated time and ask to see all the puppies available as well as the dam (and sire, if available). Are the puppies alert and clean? Are they bright-eyed and healthy looking? Is the breeder pleasantly affectionate and gentle with the pups? Are the adult dogs glad to see him or do they cower away when he steps into the runs? Does he willingly answer all your questions? Is he interested in you and the kind of home and care you will offer the pup? Good care of a litter by a kindly breeder helps to assure that you are acquiring a fine, healthy pup.

When you make your decision and choose the pup you want, a deposit will be asked, and the date for getting the pup will be set.

What papers should the breeder give me when I buy a puppy?
He should supply you with the following:
1. The dog's registration paper showing that the litter has been registered. The breeder must sign this certificate to prove that the puppy has been sold to you.
2. The breeder may or may not give you the dog's three- or

50 / THE DOG LOVER'S ANSWER BOOK

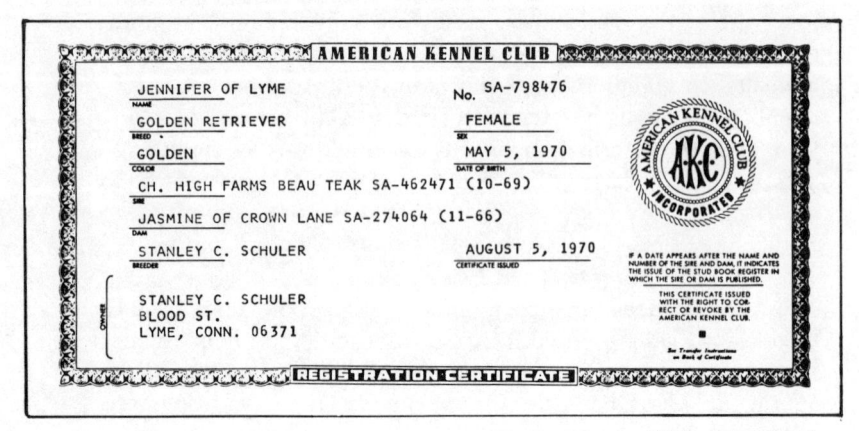

AMERICAN KENNEL CLUB

NAME JENNIFER OF LYME
BREED GOLDEN RETRIEVER
COLOR GOLDEN
SIRE CH. HIGH FARMS BEAU TEAK SA-462471 (10-69)
DAM JASMINE OF CROWN LANE SA-274064 (11-66)
BREEDER STANLEY C. SCHULER
OWNER STANLEY C. SCHULER
BLOOD ST.
LYME, CONN. 06371

No. SA-798476
SEX FEMALE
DATE OF BIRTH MAY 5, 1970
CERTIFICATE ISSUED AUGUST 5, 1970

IF A DATE APPEARS AFTER THE NAME AND NUMBER OF THE SIRE AND DAM, IT INDICATES THE ISSUE OF THE STUD BOOK REGISTER IN WHICH THE SIRE OR DAM IS PUBLISHED.

THIS CERTIFICATE ISSUED WITH THE RIGHT TO CORRECT OR REVOKE BY THE AMERICAN KENNEL CLUB.

REGISTRATION CERTIFICATE

AKC registration.

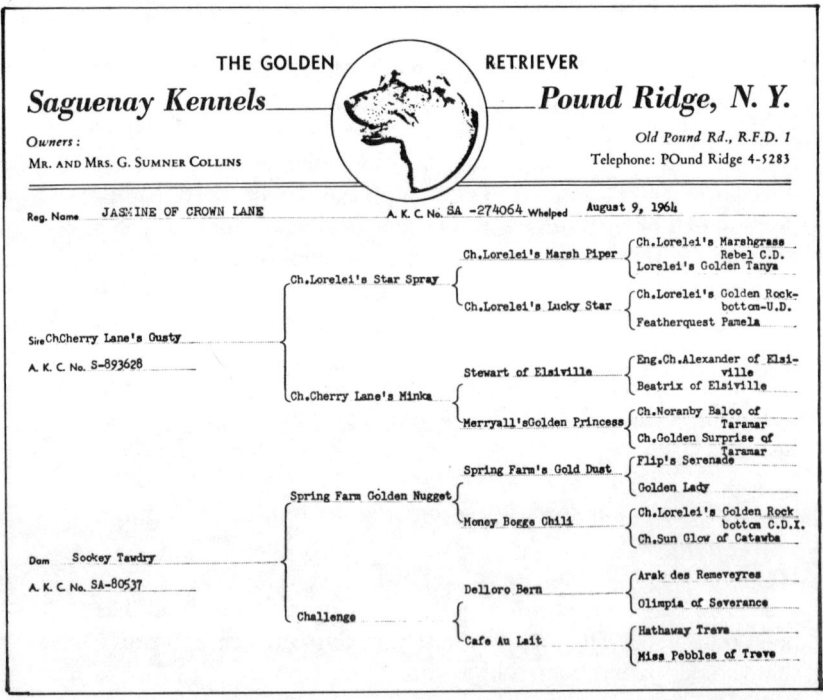

THE GOLDEN RETRIEVER
Saguenay Kennels — **Pound Ridge, N. Y.**

Owners:
MR. AND MRS. G. SUMNER COLLINS

Old Pound Rd., R.F.D. 1
Telephone: POund Ridge 4-5283

Reg. Name JASMINE OF CROWN LANE   A. K. C. No. SA -274064 Whelped August 9, 1964

Sire ChCherry Lane's Ousty
A. K. C. No. S-893628

- Ch.Cherry Lane's Minka
  - Ch.Lorelei's Star Spray
    - Ch.Lorelei's Marsh Piper
      - Ch.Lorelei's Marshgrass Rebel C.D.
      - Lorelei's Golden Tanya
    - Ch.Lorelei's Lucky Star
      - Ch.Lorelei's Golden Rockbottom-U.D.
      - Featherquest Pamela
  - Stewart of Elsiville
    - Eng.Ch.Alexander of Elsiville
    - Beatrix of Elsiville
  - Merryall'sGolden Princess
    - Ch.Noranby Baloo of Taramar
    - Ch.Golden Surprise of Taramar

Dam Sookey Tawdry
A. K. C. No. SA-80537

- Spring Farm Golden Nugget
  - Spring Farm's Gold Dust
    - Flip's Serenade
    - Golden Lady
  - Money Bogge Chili
    - Ch.Lorelei's Golden Rockbottom C.D.X.
    - Ch.Sun Glow of Catawba
- Challenge
  - Delloro Bern
    - Arak des Remeveyres
    - Olimpia of Severance
  - Cafe Au Lait
    - Hathaway Treve
    - Miss Pebbles of Treve

AKC four-generation pedigree.

four-generation pedigree. If he does not, you can obtain this through the AKC by sending them all information about your pup as shown on the litter registration. The cost at present is $5.00.

3. The feeding schedule for the puppy and the recommended diet.

4. A certificate of inoculation against distemper, leptospirosis and hepatitis; including the date each inoculation was given, what was given, and when it must be repeated.

5. Information on when the puppy was wormed and what type of worms were found.

6. Instructions on how the puppy should be cared for and trained.

7. Certificates showing that the sire and dam were judged normal and free of hip dysplasia.

What are the advantages of buying a dog from a kennel rather than a pet shop?

A kennel specializes in one or more breeds. The owner knows the background of each pup, and will show you the dam and perhaps the sire. A well-run kennel takes pride in raising and selling good, sturdy pups because its future depends on the quality of its stock.

There are many well-run, experienced pet shops offering a variety of puppies. But you cannot see the parent stock. Since the pet shop owner handles so many different breeds, as well as kittens, rabbits, birds, etc., he cannot be as knowledgeable about one breed as a kennel that raises that particular breed.

If a dog is purchased from a pet shop, how can you be sure he's healthy?

Unfortunately you can't be. Many pups sold in pet shops are bred in quantity in the Midwest where costs are lower, then shipped to large cities and sold in shops. A rather hard road for a young pup; often hazardous to his health and shattering to his nerves. If you do choose to buy a pup from a pet shop, look over the shop carefully for cleanliness. Check to see if the chosen pup's skin is clean and if his ears are free of parasites and are clean-smelling. Is he alert and clear-eyed? If the pup has been shipped in across the state lines, ask to see the health certificate issued by the state from which he was shipped. The majority of states require that puppies from another state be accompanied by such a certificate; and in many cases the certificate must show that the dog has been inoculated against rabies. Then ask if the pup has been inoculated for distemper. If you are satisfied to this point, you should then ask for a five-day written guarantee of health. You then must take the pup to a qualified veterinarian for examination. In addition, the shop should give you a thirty-day extended guarantee against distemper, hepatitis and congenital defects. If the animal proves to be ill, the shop should then give you another pup in exchange. If difficulties are encountered, consult your local Better Business Bureau.

What is the best age to purchase a puppy?
Six weeks is quite acceptable, especially in the larger breeds. Eight weeks is excellent. (In Connecticut a puppy must be, by law, eight weeks old.) A puppy left too long in the kennel is far harder to train because he has already developed ingrained habits that are hard to change.

What points should be considered in selecting a puppy?
All young puppies may be charming and appealing, but when you are about to purchase one take your time and be certain you select a pup as free of problems as possible.

Given a choice, don't pick the pup that backs away from you in fright or shyness, or the one that is overly aggressive, knocking aside the others as he struggles to get to you. Do select the pup that comes trotting happily to you and welcomes your petting but doesn't claw or tear at you when you stop.

Watch out for the overly fat pup. You want a pup that is well-rounded, not pig-like; bright-eyed and frisky, not restless and nervous.

His coat should be shiny and clean; the skin clean, healthy in color and free of bites and parasites.

Is it hard to train a kennel-raised dog?
This depends on the type of kennel, for some give a good deal of affectionate care to the young pups while others do not. Many a pup has little close contact with humans. He sees only the kennel man who keeps his quarters clean and provides his meals.

We bought a two-month-old puppy some years ago. She was pretty, healthy and fine in every way except that she was totally unused to people. She actually quivered when I held her, and when released in our kitchen, she scuttled around in abject terror. When I put a small dish of food down for her, she panicked completely. I knew she had not been mistreated; she had just not been treated at all. It took days to gain her confidence. I babied her, snuggled her, patted and praised, crooned and cuddled and soon she realized that we were concerned only with loving her. The change was sudden and startling. Never was a puppy so eager to please or so quick to learn. She became a fine dog but we missed out on many weeks while she was becoming "humanized."

In contrast, the well-run smaller kennel that says its puppies are home-raised has already accustomed its litters to handling and close attention. Those pups move easily into a new home and adapt quickly. Frequently they are already paper-trained and know to come to your voice or whistle.

We have a three-year-old boy and a six-month-old baby. We now want to buy a dog. Should we get a puppy or look for an older dog?
You would be wise to look for a grown dog that has lived in a home and knows children. Children are not always gentle; and rough, thoughtless treatment can be very painful for a young pup. He may resort to biting in his own defense and this will not bring about the mutual trust and happy companionship you are seeking. An older animal has the tolerance that comes with maturity or the wisdom simply to escape when the treatment gets rough.

In any case, choose a breed known to be gentle and calm with children. Avoid the small toy and terrier breeds that may be snappish even when mature. Setters, spaniels and retrievers are well known for steadiness and tolerance.

Where does one buy a guard dog?
If you want a dog for protection, you probably don't want to wait for it to be trained; instead, you want it ready to go to work for you right now. It follows that you need an older dog that is fully trained, and the best source of this kind of animal is a reputable training kennel. (See page 222.)

Seeing Eye dogs should be purchased in the same way. So should hunting dogs if you want to go hunting, in effect, tomorrow.

I'm thinking of buying a beautiful year-old male who has always been in a commercial kennel. Can he become a well-behaved house dog?
I had just such a dog and it took a long time to make him understand what we expected of him. The first week I despaired of housebreaking him. But at the end of the week I caught him in the act and spanked him. The punishment followed the transgression so closely that he understood what all the fuss was about and he didn't misbehave again.

It was not so simple teaching him to tolerate being shut in an enclosure. He had been penned up all his life and evidently had spent much of his time trying to dig and claw his way out. The day I shut him in the kitchen he literally took the door frame apart in small pieces. There was no use in punishing him; I knew I could not change this deeply embedded feeling. So when restraint was needed I put him on a trolley (see page 77) and he was content because he felt free.

I could go on and on in the same vein. Buying an adult dog calls for understanding and patience. But the ultimate reward justifies the effort.

We have a chance of being given a fine ten-month-old spaniel. Can a family take a dog at that age and have him fit into the household easily?
It may work out very well, and it may not because the dog has ingrained faults. Try to ascertain from the owner just why he's

giving up the dog. If the answer is that he's vicious, chases cars or roams, you may not want him. On the other hand, if the dog is rough with children, can't stand being penned up in the city or won't ride in an automobile, that may not bother you in the slightest. Canine faults which annoy one person don't always annoy another; and even if they do, it should be remembered that some faults are cleared up by a simple change in environment while others can be corrected by patience and training.

I know a young male who was thought to be such a hopeless wanderer that when he was a year old his unhappy owners found him a new home. He has not wandered since. The answer: the new home had three young children, two cats and a young mother who loved all creatures. The former owner had no children, was not very fond of dogs and until the husband came home at night the dog was lonesome. So he wandered in search of companionship.

Another year-old male was in deep disgrace because he had bitten a teenage boy in the neighborhood. It was not entirely his fault; the big boys thought it great fun to ride him like a pony. He was a big dog, but the boys were bigger. Riding hurt his back and in defense he did the only thing he knew. But while his owners understood, they felt they could not risk his biting again. So they found a home in the country where there were few children to torment him. He has given no trouble since.

But I don't want to give the impression that all gift dogs work out beautifully, because they certainly do not. Offhand I can think of one dog that had such a bad upbringing he was constantly transferred from one home to another; an inveterate car-chaser who eventually was killed chasing a car on a country road; a nervous wreck who stayed a nervous wreck her entire life, even though she had three understanding owners.

In other words, while you shouldn't look a gift horse in the mouth, you shouldn't be too eager to accept his offerings either. Find out all you can about the dog's background; study him well. If you're on the fence, accept him only on a one-week trial basis.

Is it wise to take a dog from a pound?
If you have known and owned dogs over a long time, you may be experienced enough to choose a dog from the pound. Your judgment will have to take the place of the information about breeding, background, health and temperament that you usually get from a breeder. Some very fine dogs arrive at pounds for obscure reasons. You may be lucky enough to find one of these. Surely it is a humane thing to give a home to a dog that may lose his life in a gas chamber. But don't count on being able to register the dog.

What about a dog from a humane society kennel?
Same answer.

How do you go about naming a dog?
First you pick out the pet name he will answer to; then his registered name.

I read in a book recently that a dog should always be given a one-syllable name because it's easier to say and call. But that's just nonsense. And it's also nonsense to use the same hackneyed dog names that people have been pinning on dogs since heaven knows when. I like original names that may or may not have some point; they add to the dog's distinction. There are thousands of marvelous names you can steal from humans, mythology, the plant world, geography, etc. A few of the names I have liked are Hawkins, Rufus, Chincoteague, Solomon, Nugget, Jason, Arthur, Blitz and Janus.

The registered name is the name by which a dog is officially listed by the AKC or other registry. It need not have any connection with the pet name, although there is no reason why it cannot include the pet name. For example, I had one dog with the registered name of Falconridge Otter who was actually known as Jason. On the other hand, my present male answers to the name Joshua and is also registered as Joshua of Lyme.

There are several rules for selecting a registered name: First, it must contain no more than twenty-five letters. Second, you must file a first choice and a second choice just in case your first has been used by someone else. If you want to use the dog's pet name in his registered name—as in the case of my

Joshua—just add something to make it unique. However, a registered name cannot include such terms as champ, champion, sire, dog, dam, bitch, hound, etc. A name may not include Roman numerals; may not be pornographic or derogatory to the dog. Names of prominent living persons may not be used. Avoiding the use of trite, hackneyed names will make registration easier.

The puppy I bought was given a pet name and a registered name by the breeder. Can I change them?

You can change the pet name; but if the registered name has been accepted and recorded by the AKC, or other registry, the dog is stuck with it for the rest of his life.

Some breeders—like the one who sold you your pup—assign registered names which incorporate the name of the kennel to every pup they sell. Thus, if the dog is later a winner in the show ring or obedience trials, he gains extra prominence for his breeder.

Other breeders leave the choice of registered name up to the buyer of each puppy.

If you buy or are given a grown dog that already knows his name, can you change the name and still have him come to you?

Yes, it isn't a difficult transition. Use the two names together at first, and then gradually phase out his original name.

There's no point in having a dog saddled for the rest of time with a name you dislike. If people can change their names, so can dogs.

Why should I register my new pup with the AKC?

If you don't, none of the dog's descendants can ever be registered, and neither they nor your dog may compete in AKC dog shows. A fine dog deserves to be fully registered.

Of course you know you can register a dog with the AKC only if he's a purebred belonging to a breed recognized by that organization.

Purebred dogs are also registered with several other organizations. (See page 28.)

58 / THE DOG LOVER'S ANSWER BOOK

How do you register a new dog with the AKC?
If the litter was registered by the owner, he should give you at the time of purchase a blue application form for registering the dog with the AKC. Make certain that this paper has been signed by the owner of the dam. If there is a co-owner he must sign, too. All signatures must be handwritten; typing will not be accepted. Now this application for registration is ready to be completed by you. Give two choices for the pup's formal name, fill in your name and address, enclose the $4.00 fee (subject to change) and mail it to the American Kennel Club, 51 Madison Avenue, New York, New York 10010. In about three weeks you will receive a purple-edged certificate of registration giving your name as owner, the new registered name of your dog, his registration number, his sire and dam and their registered numbers and the date the litter was whelped. Keep this paper safe because it is a lengthy process to have it replaced.

If the person selling the dog does not supply you with the registration application form properly filled out, you must demand a written bill of sale, signed by the seller, giving the dog's full breeding particulars including breed, sex and color; date of whelping; registered names and numbers of the sire and dam, and the name of the breeder and owner. If there is a co-owner, this bill of sale must be signed by him also. Contact the AKC to acquire the necessary registration application. Do not complete the purchase of the dog until you are assured that the seller has the legal right to transfer ownership to you and AKC registration can be completed.

Where do you get the pedigree for a registered dog?
If it is not available from the breeder, send the dog's registered name and number to the AKC, and ask for either his three-generation pedigree (fee: $5.00) or four-generation pedigree (fee: $10.00).

Should I buy a dog from outside the U.S.?
If you are considering this, first ask the AKC which foreign countries produce dogs that can be registered in the U.S. Many

countries do not register dogs at all; and dogs from other countries that do may not be accepted for registration here.

We're moving and must give up our five-year-old dog. How do we go about finding a home for him?

A five-year-old dog won't take as kindly to a new home as a one-year-old, but he will react a lot better than a ten-year-old. I think giving away a really old dog who has had a happy life with one family ranks high in cruelty—putting him to sleep is kinder. As a matter of fact, no dog that's been loved by a family is going to find the transition easy.

Probably the best home you can find for a dog is with a relative or friend who knows him and likes him. Otherwise, you must let the word get out—through the grapevine or by advertising—that the dog's available; and then you owe it to the dog to screen the offers you receive very, very carefully. You want to find out not only whether the people have a good, clean home for the dog, but also whether they are going to give the dog the attention he's had in the past. And though it's awful to say, you'd better be on the lookout for men who want the dog solely for illegal professional dog fighting.

If there is someone you trust who will take the dog, be grateful and don't try to make money out of the deal. On the contrary, if you know the dog is due for his next rabies shot in another month, take him to the vet and pay for it yourself. If you have a case of food left over, give it to the new owner. You're lucky to have found him.

Many dogs are given to animal shelters; but before you do this, you should investigate local shelters to determine whether they'll take the dog—and when. With many, you must make an appointment at least a month in advance. Even more important is their policy about the animals they shelter: Will they keep your dog till someone asks for him, or will they destroy him after a certain time?

When you finally send your dog away, by all means send his blanket and favorite playthings with him.

3 General Care and Handling of Dogs

There was quite an uproar when it came out in the papers that President Johnson lifted his dogs by their ears. How should you lift a dog?
Put both hands under his chest; hold tight, and lift. This doesn't work if you're trying to lift a large dog several feet, because he drags his hind legs and pushes away from the bench, etc., you want to put him on. With him, you must bend your knees, wrap your arms around his four legs and lift with a straight back.

How do you show a dog you love him?
Stroke the top of his head. Scratch him where he likes to be scratched. Put an arm or arms around him and hug him to you.

What are the favorite scratching points on most dogs?
Behind the ears, on the throat, on the stomach (when he's on his back), and at the very top of the tail where it joins the body.

Should you let a dog lick your face?
No particular harm is done. But I draw the line at his licking near your mouth. People carry germs; so do dogs.

Is it all right to roughhouse with a dog?
Of course. He'll love it once he gets used to the game (that

doesn't take long), provided you don't get too rough. But if you get bitten or ripped by a claw, don't blame him. And I suppose you do run some risk—though I never found this to be the case—that he will turn into a nipper or will be too aggressive with a child who wants to play.

How do you stop a dog fight?
Avoid trying to pull the dogs apart by their collars because you're likely to get badly bitten unless you have a helper who can grasp one dog while you grasp your own. The better procedure is to grab your dog's tail or, if he doesn't have a tail, his hind legs; give a mighty heave and toss him as far from the battle scene as possible.

Belaboring the fighters with a stick is likely not to have any effect—in the heat of battle, a swat across the rear end doesn't seem to make much impression. Water, however, is a first-rate fight stopper—probably the best there is if it happens to be handy. Turn a hose on the combatants or hit them with a bucketful of water.

If all else fails, grab your dog's collar and twist it until he breaks off the fight for lack of air.

Do male and female dogs fight?
Rarely. But a female who's not in heat often gives a strange male the devil when he approaches her. That's just to keep him in his place.

Fights are usually between two or more males or two or more females.

But if a male and female have the same home, the female will wade in to help the male when he gets into a fight with a second male. One of my most vivid memories is of a fight between my first male golden and the boxer from down the road. The golden was an unusually rough, tough fellow and he was holding his own. But what really did the boxer in was my young female golden. She grabbed the boxer's stub of a tail and pulled until I thought it would snap in two. Evidently the boxer thought so too, because he broke off the battle and fled.

Is there a special secret to finding a lost dog?
If he often plays with other dogs or children in the neighborhood, ask if their families have seen him. If he loves a swim, go to the nearby pond or brook. If he loves a romp with children, visit the nearest school playground. If your local radio station has a lost pet service, give them a description of the dog and have it announced on the air. Call your police station or dog warden in case they get a report he has been seen or injured.

Of course, it is essential that all dogs that are allowed to run loose wear collars with their dog licenses attached. Anyone finding a lost dog can soon track down the owner from the license. Identification tags bearing the name, address and phone number of the owner produce even faster results; but unfortunately most of these are made of such flimsy metal that they fall off dog collars in a matter of months.

What is the right way to approach a strange dog?
Approach quietly, speak to him in soft tones and do not reach out to him for he may mistake your gesture. Keep looking at him, make no sudden moves and don't turn your back to him. He is probably not vicious but he may well be curious about you, so allay his fears by moving along at a normal pace. If you feel fear, don't show it.

When he seems ready to accept you—starts to sniff your shoes or wag his tail—you can put out your hand, palm down. This isn't as frightening or threatening as a hand held palm up. If he approves this goodwill gesture, you have passed muster and can start letting down the bars—but gradually. If he backs off from your hand, however, continue on your way.

How do you make a dog enter an elevator?
Some dogs don't have to be "made" to enter, they just walk right in. Others need to be coaxed, pulled, or even carried. Whatever the case may be, the dog should precede—not follow—you, because he will be scared out of his wits, and perhaps hurt, if the automatic doors suddenly close on him or on the leash.

My grandchildren love to pretend that my large retriever is a pony and want to ride on his back. Is this harmful? They are very little and my dog is large and strong.

It seems a mild sort of play idea, but don't ever allow children of any size to ride on a dog. His back is not for such use.

Is there any way to stop dogs from beating a definite trail across lawns and through other plantings?

Put a barrier of wire mesh across the trail so they are forced to make a detour. The mesh needn't be more than fifteen inches high because the dogs will find it easier to go around it rather than over it. But unfortunately, if you ever remove the mesh, the dogs will probably go right back to the old trail.

In other words, there is no real solution to the problem, just partial solutions. For example, don't draw up plans for a lawn or garden until you have determined the locations of the trails made by your own and neighboring dogs. Then plant the lawn or garden to one side of the trail.

Another partial solution is to put in plants that dogs can't trample down. These would include not only the shrubs and trees that grow too tall to be trampled but also various very tough prostrate plants, such as the creeping junipers. But of course, this might not be the kind of plant you want for a particular location.

How can I stop dogs from ruining certain plants?

It's not attractive, but if you surround the plants with loose collars of wire mesh, there won't be any more damage.

The only other solution is to hide in waiting for the dogs to sidle up to the plants and then douse them with a pail of water or shoot a mild household ammonia solution into their faces.

Can you keep a dog out of a vegetable garden with an electric fence?

If you make certain he touches the fence when it's installed, he'll stay well away from the garden. Of course, if he should learn that he can safely jump the fence (which need be only twelve to eighteen inches high, depending on the height of the dog), you may have trouble from him again; but the chances of his learning this are fairly small, unless he has a sudden compelling incentive to get into the garden.

What's the secret to taking good pictures of a dog?
Patience. Dogs are the most uncooperative photo subjects I know of.

1. Use a fixed-focus camera; otherwise get far enough away from the dog so you can set your camera at infinity. Most dogs don't give you enough time to focus and then shoot.
2. Place the dog against a solid background.
3. Try to shoot in bright shade rather than sunlight.
4. Shoot the pictures just after the dog has eaten, when he's feeling fat and content.
5. If the dog is frightened of a flash, aim a bright light at him and turn it on and off several times. Pat him or give him a treat after each flash.
6. Get down on the floor and shoot from the dog's level.
7. When taking pictures of young puppies, put them on a bench or table; they won't dare to move.
8. Keep trying.

If you want to take pictures of young puppies, place them on a table or bench—they won't dare to jump off.

Another way to pose puppies for a photograph.

How do you get dog hair off car seats?
A slightly dampened sponge picks it up easily.

How are urine, excrement, and vomit removed from carpeting and upholstery?
Lift off as much matter as possible with paper towels. Wipe the surface with more toweling, preferably cloth, working from the outer edges in so you don't widen the stain. Then saturate the spot with bottled soda water. Let this stand, blot it up and repeat as needed. Finally blot dry with a clean towel. Success is not always certain, but the quicker the treatment, the better your chances.

Why did my dog eat a hole out of one of our rugs?
I'm willing to bet that he threw up, then ate the vomit and, to get rid of all evidence, also ate that portion of the rug.

Fortunately, this doesn't always happen when a dog vomits. But just in case, waste no time in getting up the mess and thoroughly cleaning the carpet.

Must a dog wear a collar?
Of course not. And if you live out in the country where he can run, he's actually safer without a collar, which sometimes gets hung up on branches and fence wire.

A collar serves two purposes which are primarily to the owner's advantage: First, it is something you can leash or hang on to. Second, it holds his license, name tag and rabies tag—and if a dog warden catches him off your property without these, he's in serious trouble.

What is the best kind of a collar?
For general use, a round or flat leather or nylon collar. It should be neither loose nor tight. As long as it doesn't slip easily over a dog's ears it's about right. Check it frequently to be sure the fit is comfortable.

What is a choke collar and when is it used?
A choke collar is a steel chain designed so that, once it is fastened around a dog's neck, the dog's handler can easily tighten it simply by giving it a tug, loosen it by relaxing pressure. The collar is used in obedience training.

Choke collars are made of light-weight and medium-weight stainless-steel chains. They must be put on a dog properly so that they will release easily after the dog has been corrected. Hold the small ring in front of the dog's right shoulder; bring the chain across under his neck, then up and over the top. Slip the large ring in that end of the chain over the small ring; and attach your leash to the small ring.

A well-fitted choke collar has no more than three inches hanging at the loose (small-ring) end.

Is it true that a dog should not wear a choke collar except when in training?
I do not like to have dogs running free in the country wearing a chain collar, because the dangling end can easily become caught on low shrubs and the dog can be choked to death. Use the chain collar for all training sessions, but substitute a smooth, flat leather collar or a round leather collar at all other times.

Are shock collars good for training dogs? What are they?
They are special collars with electrodes. When the handler pushes a button on a sort of walkie-talkie device, the dog receives a very brief, harmless shock.

The collars are used primarily by people who train lots of dogs, not just one, because they are fairly expensive. But they are also said to be quite effective in making a dog give up bad habits and obey commands.

Which is better—a harness or a collar?
You have more control over a dog wearing a collar. If you use a collar from the beginning, he will be easier to train and easier to handle ever after. However, once a dog is well trained, there's no reason why he shouldn't wear a harness if it makes you or him any happier (which I doubt).

What kind of a leash should I use?
I prefer a steel link leash over leather or nylon because it's durable and easy to keep clean, won't snap under a straining dog, and can't be chewed in two. The weight should be proportionate to that of the dog.

Many people, however, prefer leather or nylon leashes to steel because they're lighter and easier to handle.

What type of leash is used in obedience training?
An inch-wide leash of cotton webbing. It is usually five or six feet long.

Should a dog wear a coat in the winter?
If a dog lives in an overheated apartment and goes out on occasional walks in windy, cold weather he should have a coat or sweater. Dogs are susceptible to colds and pneumonia and a coat that covers his chest and stomach is a wise safeguard. However, large sturdy dogs that are outside as much as they are in adjust well to low temperature and do not need added protection or pampering.

Is tattooing of dogs really valuable in case of loss?
Having your pet tattooed gives extra protection against loss or theft. The tattoo used is your social security number and it will last his lifetime. You must register this number, your name, address and telephone number with the National Dog Registry, 227 Stebbins Road, Carmel, New York 10512, for full protection. The charge at present is $15.00 per animal. Note, however, that if you sell or give your tattooed dog to someone else, the tattooed number has to be given an additional digit or initials and be registered again with the new owner's name and address.

How is a dog tattooed and who does it?
Veterinarians, kennel clubs and humane societies will do tattooing. It is a simple procedure and painless. The hair is clipped on the inside of the dog's rear right upper leg. Thereafter you should keep this area clean of hair. The fee varies from one area to another, but the average is $5.00 per dog.

Which is better: to put a dog in a kennel when you go away, take him to the home of a relative or friend, or leave him in your house and ask a neighbor to take care of him?
The safest procedure is to put him in a kennel, because that way you are certain that he can't run away or be stolen. But the cost is fairly high and the dog won't like it very much.

Sending a dog to a relative's home is asking a lot of the relative and the dog; but if they are fond of each other and know each other well, it may work out nicely.

GENERAL CARE AND HANDLING OF DOGS / 69

It's also quite a lot to ask a neighbor to watch over a dog left at your own home. But if the dog isn't a wanderer or can be confined, he will probably be happiest at home, and perhaps help to protect the house against intruders.

When it's necessary to board a dog, is it better to use a veterinarian's kennel or an ordinary boarding kennel?
One is as good as another. Not all veterinarians, however, are willing to board dogs. Boarding kennels, on the other hand, are not always as clean as they might be. In fact, I wouldn't use one without inspecting it first.

I'm going on a trip and must put my two dogs in a kennel. Should I ask that they be kept in the same run?
They will be a lot happier if they are.

Which is the better place to carry a dog in a car—on the seat or on the floor?
On the floor in back, away from the heater, where he can't stir around so much. If you suddenly apply the brakes, he won't be hurled forward over the back of the front seat or against the dashboard. And if he gets sick, you won't have such an awful job cleaning up the mess.

Should you let a dog ride in an automobile with his head stuck out the window?
Some dogs love the feel of the wind on their faces, but it's wise to deny them this pleasure. I've seen some big dogs with their heads stuck out so far that they're in danger of being sideswiped. In addition, all dogs may be pelted in the eyes and ears by dirt and larger foreign objects. The best place for the dog is on the floor in the rear of the car.

Isn't it inhumane to transport a dog in the trunk of a car?
Inhumane and dangerous. Even if the trunk lid is propped open slightly, the dog may suffocate from the accumulated heat or be killed by carbon monoxide fumes. If you have to use

the trunk, it should be equipped with a specially designed ventilator that brings in air from the top or from the car itself.

How about carrying dogs in small, enclosed trailers?
These can get just as hot as an auto trunk, and carbon monoxide can seep in from the car's exhaust. Here again, you need a special ventilator in the roof. If possible, it's best to keep the dog facing the rear of the trailer during the trip.

I take my dog with me in the car wherever I go, even though he is a very restless traveler, forever jumping around. Are those grilles you put up behind the seat any good?
A grille will certainly keep the dog from jumping over into the driver's seat, although it won't make him any calmer or quieter. Most grilles are designed for installation in station wagons, but you should be able to adapt one to a sedan.

We're thinking of taking our dog on a vacation trip. Are there many hotels, motels and campgrounds where he will be allowed? Where do I find out beforehand which will take him?
There are plenty of places where dogs are allowed. Check the automobile clubs for listings. The Gaines Dog Research Center, 250 Park Avenue, New York, New York 10017, also has a list. Send 25 cents and ask for the booklet *Touring with Towser*. Also highly recommended is the book *Travel with Your Pet* by Paula Weideiger and Geraldine Thorsten, published by Simon and Schuster.

Is a dog allowed into federal and state parks?
Check the regulations. Even where allowed, he must be kept confined.

How should a dog be prepared for a trip by air?
Make sure he is in good health. He must not be an unusually nervous animal. Don't feed him within six hours of flight time;

GENERAL CARE AND HANDLING OF DOGS / 71

and except on a very hot day, don't give him water within two hours of flight time. Exercise him just before takeoff.

He should probably also have a tranquilizer, because even though he may be a good traveler in an automobile, a long trip with strangers in a strange vehicle will upset him. Talk to your veterinarian about this.

How can you make sure a dog will get safely to his destination?

Fasten a tag listing your name, address, and the dog's destination to his collar.

Attach the same information on the outside of the crate. Include the dog's name so the attendants can talk to him. If he bites, add that fact, too.

Put a water bowl in the crate and attach it so that the attendants can get it out without being bitten. If the trip will exceed 24 hours, attach dry food to the outside of the crate with simple instructions about when to give it.

Give the dog something soft to lie on and a couple of beloved toys.

Arrange for the dog to be picked up promptly when he reaches his destination.

Must a reservation be made for a dog to travel by air?

Yes, especially if he's going into the cargo hold, because space for animals is limited. You will pay the freight rate for a dog shipped as cargo. Excess baggage rate is charged for a dog accompanying you in the cabin.

Do all domestic airlines allow small dogs to be taken into the cabin of the plane with their owners?

No. Check the airline first. Even those that do permit it require that the dog be kept in a carrier which is small enough to fit under a seat. Guide dogs are the exception.

What sort of a crate should a dog be shipped in on an airplane?

It must be sturdy, well ventilated, with a leak-proof bottom and an escape-proof feeding hatch. It should be big enough for the dog to lie down, stand and turn around.

Carriers may be bought from a pet shop, department store or the airline.

> *Are the baggage compartments in which dogs are shipped on airplanes pressurized?*

Yes. And they have the same oxygen supply as the passenger cabin. But they are not air-conditioned and temperatures may range from zero to over a hundred degrees.

> *Can a dog travel by train?*

He *may* be able to travel in a compartment with you, but baggage cars have pretty well disappeared so you can't put him in these. Railway Express still ships dogs by rail, however.

In sum, train travel is even more uncertain than air travel these days; so unless your dog can accompany you, it's unkind to ship him this way.

> *Are dogs allowed on buses?*

Except for guide dogs, no.

> *How feasible is it to take a dog abroad?*

Physically it's as easy as taking a dog into another state. But other nations have a rather bewildering array of regulations about dogs crossing their borders, and you should check these carefully before you make a decision. Write to the American Society for the Prevention of Cruelty to Animals, 441 East 92nd Street, New York, New York 10028, and ask for its booklet, *Traveling with Your Pet*. Send 60 cents.

> *We are moving to another city and I am worried that our dog will be upset and run away. Is there any way to prevent this except by keeping him tied up?*

It will take some effort on your part because your dog won't be very happy about all his new surroundings; you must therefore do all you can to make them as much like the old as possible. As soon as convenient, put his bed in a place similar to what he had; its comforting smells will help immensely. Bring his favorite toys. Put his water dish and feeding bowl in as nearly the same location as before—by the back door, near the refrigerator, etc. All this will help. But you will have to keep him tied or penned for the first few weeks. The confusion of moving, the new sights and strange neighboring dogs will all be distracting and interesting.

Do register your dog immediately with the dog license bureau and throw away the previous license tag. If your dog should escape, the finder must have a way of notifying you.

It is advisable, too, to locate a veterinarian. Don't wait for an emergency. Go visit his animal hospital and if you approve of it, tell him you are new in the area and ask if any special precautions such as heartworm protection are necessary. Have his office put your dog's name on file with your name and address and ask to be notified when it is time for annual inoculations. Inquire about boarding facilities.

> *We have been living in open country where our Labrador can run free. Now we're being transferred to a metropolitan area and will be living in an apartment. Will we be able to make this dog adjust to walking on a leash and giving up all outdoor freedom, or should we find him a home in the country?*

Any dog who is used to being outdoors the greater part of the day hunting, running, swimming, or just sleeping against a sunny bank may well be miserable in a confined city situation. However, if he was reasonably happy indoors, he should be able to adjust to city living. Adapting to another family is not a simple adjustment so you will have to decide whether your dog is more devoted to your family or to his outdoor activities.

4 / Housing

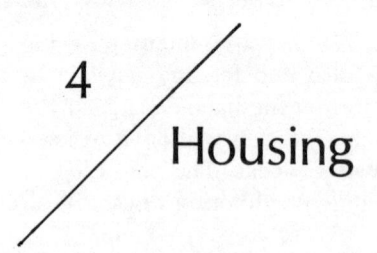

Do dogs need bedding if they sleep in the house?
Yes. Bedding has several advantages: it shows the dog where you want him to sleep; serves to keep that place clean; cushions his elbows so they won't become hardened and calloused. I use old worn bathtowels because they are fairly durable and easy to keep clean.

At what age can a puppy live outside?
Puppies of the large, sturdy breeds may live outside at eight weeks in summer. In winter, not until three or four months old. The small breeds should never live outdoors.

Regardless of breed or age or season, all puppies must be provided with a good shelter against wind, rain, damp, cold, and hot sun.

If I decide to have my two-month-old pup live outdoors, what kind of housing and equipment should he have?
Housing need not be elaborate or costly, but it absolutely must provide protection for your puppy from every variation of weather. Even rugged outdoor breeds must not be left without shelter from sun, rain and snow. Many breeds suffer just as much from excessive heat as from excessive cold. All must be shielded from harsh winds.

The doghouse should be large enough for your pup when full grown to lie down easily. The door must be big enough for easy access, but not so large that winds and rain can enter.

A good doghouse with the door to one side provides protection for the dog to sleep out of rain and drafts.

Place the door in a corner to provide a draft-free place at the other side. See illustration. In severe winter weather tack a piece of heavy canvas inside the doorway. A roof with a wide overhang will provide a shady spot for the dog when he sleeps outside. Hinge the roof so it can be opened for cleaning the house and spraying for ticks and fleas. In hot climates, a louvered roof is advisable to prevent heat from building up in the house. Using white roofing material also helps to keep the house cool. A solid wood floor raised off the ground a couple of inches keeps the house warm and dry.

Provide bedding that will be easy to clean and that will keep the dog comfortable. I prefer a zippered bag of sturdy washable material filled with cedar shavings. While the cover is being washed, the shavings can be transferred to a second cover. The shavings keep the dog warm; insulate him against dampness in the ground; and discourage buildup of fleas. Cleanliness of outdoor housing is important.

> *We want our puppy to live outdoors. What kind of run should we have?*

The size of the pen depends on the size of the dog when full grown. An average size pen is 4 feet wide, 10 to 20 feet long, and 6 to 8 feet high. The most popular fencing material is chain-link or somewhat lighter steel mesh. Both are sturdy and durable. Metal or 4 x 4-inch wood posts should be set 30 inches deep in the ground and surrounded with concrete. Set the fencing 6 inches below the surface, or pour a strip of concrete about 4 inches wide and 6 inches deep around the buried edges. This deters dogs from digging underneath.

One problem with all steel mesh fences is that some dogs develop an amazing facility for climbing up over them. If you run into this problem, a narrow strip of fencing that slants in toward the run should be added at the top of the fence.

Install a gate that swings inward, so it is not so easy for the dog to escape when you enter and leave.

The floor surface may be grass, dirt, gravel, concrete or blacktop. None of these is perfect. Grass has to be cut; dirt turns into mud; gravel scatters and becomes littered with twigs; concrete and blacktop must be hosed down regularly. Concrete is the most durable and the least trouble. Blacktop is somewhat less durable and becomes uncomfortably hot in the summer sun, but is warmer and drier in winter.

Placing the run is very important. There should be some protection (not necessarily complete) from the sun at all times of the day, yet there must not be such heavy shade that the area stays damp; the run should also have protection from prevailing winds; and be visible from the house (though it need not be adjacent to the house).

Is there any way of putting up a temporary run for a bitch in heat or any other dog that might require safe, temporary restraint?

The easiest way is to buy one. Sears, for example, has several runs or exercise pens made of stout wire-mesh panels. The 4-foot-long by 3½-foot-high side panels are linked together by rods which are driven into the ground. (One of the panels has a door.) Similar panels cover the top. You can even get canvas covers for the top and sides to protect the dog against rain and sun.

These are very good arrangements, but you cannot count on

them to stop a dog from digging underneath. And to keep a whole gang of rambunctious males from getting at a bitch in heat, you must brace the sides with 2 x 4s driven deep into the ground.

Is it wrong to keep a dog in a kennel run?
There are disadvantages, but most can be partially offset. You will lose out on companionship, fun and affection if your dog is always confined to the pen. He should have periods of freedom in the house, the affection of the family and frequent walks on a leash. His bored wandering up and down in the run cannot take the place of a good brisk walk with you or a romp with the children. It should be obvious, too, that your dog cannot be very useful as a protector for your home or children if he's confined to a pen.

What is the safest way to keep a dog tied or restrained short of building a dog pen?
My preference is to install a trolley. This is a heavy (No. 9 gauge) galvanized steel wire stretched between two posts or

When you are bored, you just dig holes. Norwegian elkhound pup.

two trees, or from the house to a tree or post. The wire must be taut and high enough to be above an average adult's head and should be placed so that it is easy to reach in all kinds of weather. Choose a place that is free of entangling small shrubs and visible from the house.

Buy a steel chain long enough to reach the dog easily, but not so long that it drags along the ground and becomes snarled in any nearby growth. One end snaps around the wire; the other is attached to the dog's collar. Your pet will feel free but is safely restrained. Shelter must be provided from rain, sun and snow if he is to be kept on the trolley for any length of time. Keep a water bowl within the trolley area and keep it always filled with fresh water.

How do you discourage a dog that's tethered to a tree or post from getting wrapped around it?

That's one thing I don't think you can teach. The best solution is to get a tether he can't snarl. One of these is a heavy steel "post" which is driven into the ground like a drill bit. It has a swivel at the top to which a long chain is attached. Another device, resembling a retractable clothesline, consists of a spring-tension reel with a steel cable which automatically extends and retracts as the dog exercises. It is mounted either on a stake driven into the ground or on the side of a building.

In both cases, of course, the central post must be placed in an open area free of entangling trees, shrubs, etc.

Does tying up a dog for long lengths of time affect his personality?

It tends to make him more aggressive because he can't retreat when anything representing possible danger approaches him; so he learns to attack.

What kind of fencing is best for enclosing an entire yard in which a dog is confined?

Most people put in a 4-foot-high chain-link fence regardless of the fact that it totally spoils the appearance of the yard. Picket, solid board fences, or masonry walls are infinitely more attractive; and although the wood fences require more maintenance than chain-link, no dog can climb over them (chain-link is easily climbed by some dogs).

Of course, for a big dog, no 4-foot fence is an effective barrier. If he can't sail over it like a high-hurdler, he can hook his paws over the top and pull himself up. In such cases, if your building code allows, the height of the fence should be increased to 6 or 8 feet.

Is there any kind of door a dog can use to let himself in and out of the house?

There are a couple which can be installed in an opening cut in an exterior wall or door of a house. The better of the two has a rigid, one-piece swinging door that is weatherstripped to keep out drafts and can be locked on the inside.

Both doors are suitable for small and medium-sized dogs. For a big dog, make your own.

5 / Feeding

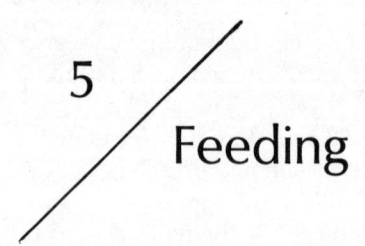

How often should a dog be fed?
Puppies from weaning to six weeks, three or four times a day.
Puppies from six weeks to five months, three times a day.
Growing dogs from five months to one year, twice a day.
Adult dogs over one year, one meal daily, or two small meals.
Lactating and pregnant females, two to three times a day.

If a dog is fed just one meal a day, should he be fed in the morning or evening?
Morning feeding is preferred because he will feel content while he is awake and active; and if outdoors he won't be so interested in investigating trash cans. Feeding at night can send a dog to bed on a too-full stomach, which may lead to gas or the more serious bloat.

What is the best feeding dish for a dog?
Get a good-quality dish that's durable, easy to clean, and shaped so it won't tip over. For breeds with long ears, get a very narrow deep dish; it will help to keep his ears out of the food. Toy breeds should have a small, low dish.

Why does my spaniel eat almost as much as my Labrador, even though he weighs about one-fourth as much?
This is not unusual. A small dog eats proportionally more than a large dog if the two are equally active. And if the small dog

is unusually active, he may eat more than a large dog of quieter nature.

Is a purebred dog fed the same diet as a mongrel?
Although their heritage may be miles apart, each has the same needs when it comes to nutrition.

What is the correct diet for an average-sized adult dog?
There is no pat answer. Many diets are excellent. The "correct" diet is a balanced one containing all basic nutrients—vitamins, fats, proteins, minerals and carbohydrates—in the proper amounts. (See the next question and answer.)

You may decide to feed your dog a canned meat product with filler added; prepared dry meal moistened with water; a canned all-meat product mixed with moistened kibbles, or you may prefer the semi-moist patties.

The best test of a good diet is the dog himself. He should be well filled out and not fat. His coat should be healthy looking. And he should eat with enthusiasm and stay content until the next feeding.

What should you feed a dog?
The market is full of excellent choices:
1. Canned food with cereal added
2. Semi-moist prepared patties
3. Canned all-beef
4. Canned horsemeat
5. Dry food in small, medium or large chunks
6. Dry meal
7. Fresh ground meat

Each type of food has its adherents, and there are many dog owners like me who use a mixture (in my case, it's canned all-beef mixed with a medium-sized kibbled dry food). You can't say that one type is a great deal better than any other, provided each gives all the nutrients a dog requires.

Once you find the food your own dog likes and thrives on, give it to him daily.

How do you stop a dog from getting overweight?
If a dog is overweight, it's because you're overfeeding him, he's raiding garbage cans or getting handouts from your neighbors. See what you can do about eliminating the latter two sources of food. Then give the dog only enough to maintain his weight as it should be. Don't overfeed and don't underexercise. Your pet will be far healthier and live longer if fed properly.

How can I tell how much to feed my dog?
There is no easy rule of thumb for how much food a dog requires daily. Some dog-food manufacturers suggest that a grown dog needs 3 to 4 ounces of food per 15 pounds of body weight. That may suit dogs that are moderately active, but may not be sufficient for the working and hunting breeds. A fair test is to watch your dog and his eating habits. If he quickly consumes all the food offered, appears content all day and does not beg for scraps, you are probably giving him the right amount. If he leaves part of the food, you may be giving too much. On the other hand, if he continually returns to the dish and seems restless, you may not be giving enough. However, all dogs differ. I feed my three retrievers one meal a day. Each gets a 1-pound can of all-beef, filler-less dog food mixed with 1½ cups of moistened, enriched kibbles. I add fat, up to a half tablespoon daily, *if* their coats show a need for it. My five-year-old, 75-pound, active, energetic male is content, healthy, and does not gain. My four-year-old, 65-pound female, who is even more active, responds in the same way. But my ten-year-old, 65-pound female—a much less active dog—is never content with the same amount and gains weight even so. In other words, diets and amounts have to be based on the individual dog, his appearance, and the life he leads.

The young growing puppy needs nearly as much and often more food daily than the mature adult dog. A human baby only triples his weight in a year whereas a puppy in the larger breeds may go from one to seventy pounds in the same time. His food requirements must be based on his growth. Again, feed what he consumes quickly and notice whether he stays content until the next feeding.

How do I cut down the rations of my overweight, always-hungry dog?

If you are certain his is just an overweight problem, start cutting down on the amount of carbohydrates you have been giving. Make this gradual and be assured the dog will not starve; he can live on that stored-up fat for some time. If you have been giving him a can of all-meat mixed with two cups of kibbled crackers once daily, reduce the amount of the crackers a quarter cup every three days until you are giving one cup only with the meat. If you find the dog is not content with this, divide his feeding into two meals daily. This bridges the long hungry wait and he will be more content. Do not give any in-between snacks and make sure he gets outdoor exercise.

There are excellent prescription diets—tested and proven canned foods—available from your veterinarian. These are more expensive than the usual prepared foods but well worth the cost if there is a need for them.

My dog prefers to stay in the house, is not very active and is always hungry. How can I keep her from being fat and lazy?

Give her a good protein diet and no snacks. And whether she likes it or not, take her for a walk.

Why does my dog occasionally refuse to eat? What do I do? She has just one meal a day.

If she appears healthy and is full of her usual pep and spirit, she may have a simple case of hurt feelings. A happy, healthy dog should eat all that you offer without hesitation, lick the dish sparkling clean and be content until the next meal. If the dog seems suddenly out of sorts and uninterested, take the food away after 15 minutes—*never leave food around all day*—and do not offer any more until the next day. At that meal give her half her usual portion. She will probably eat it with her usual relish. If not, remove it and offer nothing. Make certain she is not constipated and take her temperature. If there are no symptoms of any illness, continue to offer half her usual meal, removing it after a reasonable length of time. No dog will starve when food is readily available.

Does adding garlic to a dog's food make a non-eater eat better?

This is not entirely proven; but if you have a finicky eater it will not do any harm to try a little.

Does garlic prevent worms?

Definitely not. There has never been the least amount of proof for this oft-told tale.

How do I feed a bitch after she has whelped and raised a large litter? The last time we had a litter, she looked like a lot of rags and bones.

See that her diet is rich in protein for nourishment and fats for her coat. Continue her vitamins. The average adult dog

Mother, looking lean after nursing a large litter, cleans up a puppy pan while the pups go after their favorite source of food.

needs a diet of 10 to 20 percent protein. For the brood bitch, this can be doubled until she regains her former appearance and weight.

> *My dog eats well and looks healthy, but am I right to give him the same food every day? Doesn't he need some variety?*

Dogs do far better on the same diet given at the same time each day. You can add a bit of broth or some leftovers whenever they are available, but your dog is quite content without any such additions.

> *Is it wise to give just dry food without any meat to a dog?*

Many kennels and dog owners feed their dogs nothing but dry-meal food moistened with water. Such products are well balanced, nutritious and economical, and most dogs do very well on them.

> *Can I feed my dog just table scraps?*

Not if you want him to flourish. Scraps should not make up more than a fourth of his daily diet.

> *Does a dog need vitamins when he is fed mostly table scraps?*

If your dog lives mainly on table scraps, the nutrition he gets is hit or miss—too much starch, too little meat, etc. Give a good vitamin supplement daily.

> *Is there any human food a dog should not eat?*

Raw egg white, raw potatoes, and raw grains such as cornmeal. I don't recommend the various vegetables in the cabbage family as they create gas. You would be wise also never to give your dog poultry or fish unless you have carefully removed every vestige of bone.

> *What are prescription diets?*

They are canned foods developed for specific dietary needs and come under the following labels: K/D, for the older dog with kidney trouble; H/D, for dogs with heart trouble; P/D, for puppies and lactating bitches; R/D, a low-calorie food for the overweight dog; and L/D, for dogs requiring a bland diet.

Prescription diets are more expensive than ordinary canned foods and available only through veterinarians.

Does a dog need meat?
Not if he is getting the equivalent nutriment from other sources.

Can I give my dog raw meat?
Certainly, if he likes it. It saves you a little work and contains more vitamins than cooked meat. Serve it at room temperature, not ice cold.

Is fresh meat better than canned?
Fresh meat is not better than many of the well-balanced canned meats on the market. If you use it, make sure it contains a good percentage of fat.

It really is not important whether meat is fresh, frozen or canned as long as the dog has a balanced, nutritious diet daily.

Are vegetables good for dogs?
Vegetables abound in vitamin C. But since dogs on a balanced diet get enough of this vitamin, vegetables are not necessary. There's nothing wrong with giving them to dogs, however.

Should a dog be fed nothing but meat?
No. Meat will not supply the vitamins and minerals he needs. He must have a well-rounded diet containing cereals, fats and vitamins.

Does it do any harm—or good—to give a dog fruit?
It will not do any harm if your dog likes fruits. Our three retrievers delight in eating peaches and pears that fall in the orchard, but I don't suggest that fruit is necessary. Dogs have been found to manufacture their own supply of vitamin C.

Is it all right to give a dog potatoes?
If the potatoes are cooked and your dog is not overweight, it is all right. But you are adding calories he may not need.

Should a dog have eggs?
Not necessarily. Actually whole raw eggs are inadvisable since they may cause diarrhea. The raw white interferes with the absorption of minerals, and the cooked whites are of no value whatsoever.

On the other hand, yolks, either raw or cooked, add protein to the diet—if additional protein is needed.

What vitamins does a dog require?
If your dog is eating a good brand of dog food, he is getting all the vitamins he needs. If not, his diet is deficient in the necessary vitamins and his health will suffer. He needs the following:

Vitamin A—for growth, digestion, coat, sight, appetite, resistance to infection

Vitamin B complex—a group comprised of riboflavin, thiamine, pyridoxine. These are necessary for good skin, blood, and growth

Vitamin C—this is manufactured by the dog himself, so it is needed only to correct an imbalance

Vitamin D—for good bones and teeth and growth in the young puppy

Vitamin E—necessary for fertility and nursing bitches

May I give my dog the same vitamins we give our family?
If you do, you must scale down the dosage, which is based on weight. For example, a dog weighing 20 pounds would need a fifth or less of the dose recommended for an adult woman.

It's much easier and better to buy one of several vitamin products produced especially for dogs. These are available at pet supply counters in drugstores and groceries, as well as from your veterinarian.

Does a dog need minerals as well as vitamins?
The list of minerals he needs includes calcium, copper, cobalt, iron, zinc, potassium, phosphorus, chlorine, iodine, and sodium. Most of these are supplied in every well-balanced dog food. If you are not using such a food, then the minerals must be supplied separately.

Should a dog have fat as a daily supplement?
Most of the recommended nutritious dog foods contain sufficient fat for the average dog. Add fat only when his coat seems dry. There are excellent coat conditioners on the pet supply counters; follow directions on the bottle. Cooking fats may be given, from ¼ teaspoon to 1½ teaspoons daily, depending on the size of the dog. Do not overdo it.

What kind of bones should I give my dog?
It's far wiser not to give him bones of any kind. Dogs do not need bones if their diet is well balanced. Also, bits of bone can be broken off by a determined dog and, if swallowed, can lodge in the intestines and cause an obstruction or lacerations. Bones may also lodge between a dog's teeth, across the roof of his mouth, or in his throat.

Is it all right to give a dog candy?
An occasional piece can do no harm, but it doesn't do any good either. Candy is heavy in calories your dog does not need, since a fat dog has a short lifespan. If you must give a treat now and then, give him a small-sized dog biscuit. This will make a dog just as happy as candy and is far better for his teeth.

Is there any harm in giving our dogs some of our crackers at cocktail time?
No, but dog snacks are just as welcome and may help your dogs to beg less when you have a party.

Is it good for a dog to eat grass?
This is an old story without any foundation in fact. Eating

grass can make a dog ill; and now that grass is treated with so many chemicals, it is better to stop the habit—if you can. But, if not, do not worry about it.

How can I stop my neighbors from giving my dog table scraps?
Tell them your dog is on a restricted diet and that he cannot eat scraps, as they make him violently ill. No one should ever give food or bones or anything to any dog but his own.

I must confess, however, that it is awfully hard to convince some people that you mean what you say.

My dog has a most unpleasant habit of giving off foul gas. How do I prevent this?
First consider what he is eating; a too large intake of proteins often brings on an accumulation of gas. Reduce the amount of meat in his diet and do not give him cottage cheese or hard-boiled eggs. Avoid any vegetables in the cabbage family. Give him a small dose of milk of magnesia (1 teaspoon for every 20 pounds of weight). If the gas emissions persist, consult your veterinarian.

How often should you change the water in a dog's water bowl?
Dogs aren't finicky about what they drink or eat. They seem to like the water in a mud puddle or a toilet bowl just as much as that from a crystal-clear spring. From a practical standpoint, therefore, you don't have to worry about their water bowls until they're empty. You yourself will be happier, however, if you change the water every day. If this does nothing else for your dog, it will at least force you to keep the bowl full.

6 Grooming

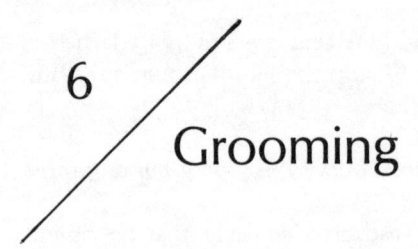

What care does a dog's coat require?
This depends to some extent on whether he has short, medium or long hair; crisp or silky hair. Directions for taking care of breeds with unusual requirements are given in the breed section of this book. But all breeds should be combed and brushed several times a week. Make these sessions pleasant. Don't pull the hair or scrape the skin. If you're reasonably gentle and toss in some compliments along the way, your dog will learn to stand patiently and enjoy it all.

You need a good bristle brush and a sturdy comb. Choose them to suit the type of coat. Stand the dog on a table or bench and comb thoroughly through the entire coat.

If he has small mats of hair that cannot be combed out, remove them with scissors. Don't cut straight across as that will leave an odd blunt look; rather, work up through the mat toward the skin in close cuts. Then you can comb out the small bits of mat without leaving an ugly mark on the coat.

Finish off with the brush. It is used mostly to add a shine to the coat.

Should I have my dog clipped in hot summer weather?
Years ago most dogs with heavy coats were clipped because their owners thought they would be more comfortable. But this is now a discredited theory. The clipped coat is scratchy; the dog is no cooler; and many animals are obviously embarrassed by their nakedness.

What is stripping?
Stripping is the removal of dead hair on a heavily coated dog. It is done with a stripping comb obtainable at any kennel supply place. This is more like a saw than a comb—a steel cutting blade with small teeth. Watch a professional before trying to use the tool. A badly done job will not improve your dog's appearance.

How is a dog plucked?
This grooming method is most unusual—reserved for the ultra-neat care of show dogs. Just grasp the hairs to be removed between thumb and forefinger and pull. Dusting with powdered chalk improves the grip.

Can an amateur learn to clip and trim a poodle?
Of course. But either take some lessons from a professional first, or buy a book strictly about grooming or about poodles and study that.

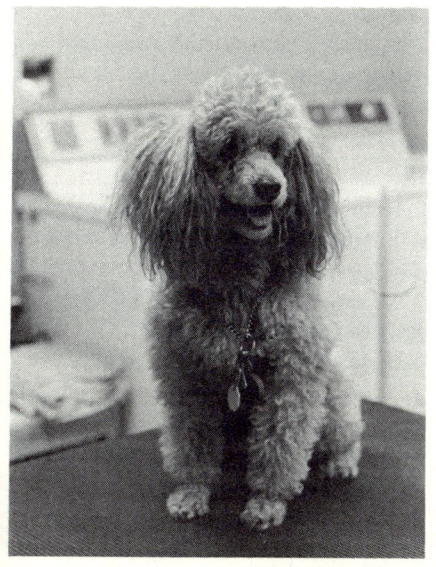

A miniature poodle before and after clipping and trimming.

What is a hound glove?
A square mitten that is put on the hand and used to polish the coat of short-haired dogs. It has a rough-textured palm.

The glove is used after you have brushed the dog thoroughly. Always polish the coat with the grain.

My boxer may be a short-haired dog but he sheds terribly in almost every month of the year. Why, and what can I do about it?
Few people realize that a dog has a thick winter coat to protect him from the cold and that this is shed in the spring and replaced by a lighter coat, which in turn will be shed in the fall. However, if you keep your pet in a heated house he will not need a winter coat and you will find that he sheds heavily all year 'round. Short walks in cold air will not have much effect, and unless he stays outside for longer periods he will continue to shed. You can assist by brushing him daily. The addition of an oil coat conditioner will help to offset the dryness of his skin due to house heat.

What is bloom?
The shine of a dog's coat when it is in top condition.

How do you get rid of the doggy odor in dogs?
The natural odor given off by a dog is so slight that it bothers only a few people. It is quite inoffensive. The rather strong doggy odor which is thought to be characteristic of dogs is caused primarily by the dirt they pick up. To eliminate or prevent such an odor, therefore, you must simply keep the dog clean. Brush and comb him daily. Sponge off stuck-on dirt. Give him a dry shampoo occasionally and bathe him only when the dirt and odor seem to be beyond control.

How do you remove tar from a dog's coat?
Rub small areas with vaseline or baby oil or cut the hair away with scissors. Under no circumstances use kerosene or any chemical tar remover since it may burn the skin.

One of my spaniels always has great mats or knots of fur behind her ears and on her back legs. How can I stop this?
Some dogs have the type of hair that will develop these unsightly mats. The only way to prevent this is to comb her daily or as frequently as possible, giving special attention to those trouble areas.

How are burrs removed from a dog's coat?
You can simply pick most of them out with your fingers or comb them out. But some, such as cockleburrs, are more difficult. Just recently one of my retrievers came home so stuck up that even she quit trying to pull them out with her teeth. I finally got rid of most of them by using a coarse comb, and by crumbling and working them out with my fingers. In an exercise like this, remember to grasp the hair behind the burrs so you don't hurt the dog as you pull.

How often should I bathe my dog?
It is not advisable to bathe a dog unless it is totally unavoidable. Frequent brushing is usually sufficient, but occasionally you should use one of the many dry shampoos available at any pet counter. These spray on, look sudsy, have a pleasant odor and do a very good job. They do not chill a dog as a bath does.

When you must bathe a dog in water, keep him in a warm, draft-free room until he is thoroughly dry. Do not let him get chilled.

How do you bathe a grown dog?
This isn't an easy job but is often unavoidable. Buy a bottle of good dog shampoo—one that will kill any fleas and ticks. Corral several big bath towels and a small hand sprayer that attaches to a faucet or a large plastic cup.

Half-fill a bathtub with lukewarm water and coax or lift the dog into it. Pour a little water from the cup or sprayer down his back and drizzle on some shampoo, talking reassuringly all the time. Keep a firm hold, for though many dogs love a dip in a swamp they object to a bath in a clean tub. Rub in the shampoo all over his body, but take care not to get soap or water in his eyes or ears.

When the dog is well sudsed, start letting the dirty water out of the tub. Let in fresh water; increase your hold for he will be ready to flee, and dip clean water over him until every bit of suds is gone. Let the water get as high as his hips to help remove the suds and make sure his stomach is clean and rinsed. If he will consent to lie down, the job is simpler. We had one golden who was so amiable he would lie on his back basking in all the attention, but this is unusual.

Now let out all the water, rub off as much water as you can from the dog's coat, and cover him with a towel. The most important thing now is to get him dry—bone dry if it is cold weather. Rub him hard while keeping him covered with a towel, for he will shake and drench you and the entire area. Keep him in the house as long as possible. Finish the job with a grand brushing and combing.

My dog's coat is very dry. I have been told to add oil or fat. What is the recommended dosage?

If the dog's coat is of average dryness, give oil or fat as follows:

Dog's Weight	Daily Dosage
1 to 10 lbs.	¼ teaspoon
10 to 20 lbs.	½ teaspoon
20 to 50 lbs.	1 teaspoon
over 60 lbs.	1½ teaspoons

For severe dryness, consult your veterinarian.

Is one oil or fat as good as another for a dog's coat?

You can use any cooking oil, any animal fat. You can also buy a number of good prepared coat and skin conditioners. If using the latter, follow the directions on the label.

How often should a dog's toenails be cut? What do I use?

A small puppy needs his nails cut frequently, but as the dog matures and goes outdoors, the nails are worn down on sidewalks, country roads, etc. However, they should be looked at regularly for if neglected they may grow inwards, giving your pet a great deal of discomfort. In addition, they are hard on your floors, clothing and furnishings.

For puppies, use your own nail clippers or scissors. For a grown dog, buy special animal clippers. Sit in a good light, hold his paw firmly and talk reassuringly, because he may well be frightened. Using the clippers, cut only the transparent part of the nail. It's better to cut twice than to cut too deeply. If your dog's nails are too pigmented to have a visible quick, cut just the hooklike extension of the nail. If you chance to cut into the quick, hold a piece of gauze against it to stop the bleeding. Don't overlook the dewclaws; they should also be cut regularly.

Should I clean my dog's eyes?

You rarely need to do anything here, but if there is moist matter in the inner corners, wipe it out with a piece of clean cotton. If it looks yellow or infected, take your pet to the veterinarian. Dogs have a third or inner eyelid and small particles often become lodged in this fold; only a veterinarian should treat this condition.

Is it necessary to clean a dog's teeth?

If your dog has a bad-breath problem, cleaning his teeth may help. Simply rub them every week with cotton dipped in milk of magnesia or wet baking soda. If tartar accumulation is giving trouble, however, ask your veterinarian about removing it. Generally this must be done under anesthetic.

Incidentally, if you want to pamper your dog, you might try a beef-flavored toothpaste recently developed just for dogs. But no matter what the flavor of toothpaste, brushing a dog's teeth is no fun for you or him.

How do you control fleas on dogs and in the house?

The following is taken from a publication of the Connecticut Agricultural Experiment Station at New Haven:

"The most prevalent flea is the dog flea. This species breeds both on cats and dogs and does not occur in large numbers unless a dog or cat is or has been present. Adult fleas are small and brown, with legs well developed for jumping. They live in the hairs of the host and pierce the skin to feed by sucking blood. Eggs are deposited among the hairs, but are not attached and usually are shaken off. Large numbers of eggs accumulate where the animals sleep. The white worm-like larvae feed on organic matter in lint and dust and on bits of skin, hair and dried blood. They pupate in a cocoon and emerge in about a week.

"Very large infestations develop when a house in which a cat or dog lives is closed for some time. The larvae continue to hatch from the eggs, feed to maturity, then emerge. When the house is reopened there may be hundreds of fleas ready to bite the people as well as pets. The severity of such infestations might be reduced by thorough cleaning before the house is vacated, destroying or spraying the animal bedding, and spraying the floors of all rooms used by the pet.

"Except for these large infestations, control of fleas seldom requires spraying. It is usually sufficient to control the fleas on the pet by use of a suitable product and to keep the pet's bed clean. The product selected should be labeled specifically for use on the type of pet involved.

"Space sprays (containing pyrethrum, naled, Malathion or ronnel) are adequate for control of fleas when needed. Since the fleas are on or near the floor, the spraying is done by standing in the center of the room and directing the spray toward the wall and parallel to the floor. Spraying should also be done under large pieces of furniture."

How good are flea collars?

Very good. But they must be replaced every three months. And if they are frequently wet, they need to be replaced at shorter intervals. Some dogs are allergic to them.

You can buy the collars in several sizes. Keep them in their tight plastic wrappings until you use them. Cut off the ends about an inch or two beyond the buckle. They should fit securely but not too snugly around the dog's neck. Since they tend to loosen, you must tighten them occasionally after you put them on.

How do you remove ticks from a dog?
First moisten the tick and adjacent skin with vegetable oil. This will paralyze the tick and asphyxiate it. Then grasp the body with tweezers and remove it with a slow but firm tug. Pull straight; don't twist. Make certain you don't leave the head embedded in the skin, for it will continue to cause irritation and possibly infection. Either burn the tick or flush it down a toilet. Dab the dog's skin with iodine.

Check your dog frequently—daily when ticks are on a rampage. Look especially at the dog's ears, between the pads of his feet, and along his backbone.

Are there any sprays or dips which rid a dog of ticks and prevent their return?
There are several such things on the market. I think I have tried most of them and found none truly effective. Admittedly, they stop an infestation for a few days if you really saturate the dog and then tie him up (so he won't go swimming) until he is dry. But in no time the ticks are back.

If you want to make your own dip, mix 1 ounce of mild soapflakes and 3 to 4 ounces of derris powder in a gallon of water. But this doesn't have any lasting effect either.

Never use ordinary household or garden insecticides. They rarely faze ticks. Worse, they're likely to be harmful to the dog's skin.

Incidentally, if you do dip or spray a dog, it's wise to wash or spray his bedding at the same time. Spray or wash down his doghouse or kennel area, too.

Are flea collars effective against ticks?
To some extent, especially when new. I've had pretty good luck with them as long as I replaced them every few months.

When are ticks most prevalent?
Generally in summer during damp weather (they die in a very

dry environment). But if they get loose in a house, they can be troublesome all year 'round.

How do I stop an infestation of ticks in my home?
The tick is one of the hardest—if not *the* hardest—pests to get rid of. It hides in cracks, moldings, wallpaper seams, inside walls and under floors—anywhere; and it reproduces itself in vast numbers. You can try picking and scraping off all you can find and burning them. You can try spraying with an insecticide effective against ticks. But the only sure solution is to call in an exterminator.

Can ticks do serious harm to dogs?
Their bites may become infected. But far worse, they sometimes cause paralysis or malignant jaundice. They may drain so much blood from a dog that he becomes listless. And they have even been known to remove so much blood that dogs have died.

Are ticks that attack dogs harmful to humans?
There are about 400 species of ticks, but only three give much trouble. These are the Rocky Mountain spotted fever tick, the American dog tick (also called the Eastern wood tick), and the brown dog tick. Because Americans—and their dogs—move so frequently from one part of the country to another, these may be found almost anywhere. The first two have white marks on their backs; the last has none.

The Rocky Mountain spotted fever tick is most feared because it is the carrier of Rocky Mountain spotted fever, tularemia, Colorado tick fever and tick paralysis. The American dog tick is also a carrier, though less versatile. The brown dog tick is not so feared because it rarely bites people, but it is also suspected of carrying Rocky Mountain spotted fever and tularemia.

If a dog swims a lot, will he have ticks?
Yes. Ticks survive long immersion in water.

Part of my property is an open meadow. Will it help to control ticks if I keep this mowed?
Yes. Ticks congregate in tall grass, waiting for dogs to come by. But while keeping the grass cut may reduce the number of ticks, it won't eliminate them because they also infest other plants.

I think my dog has lice. How can I get rid of them?
You could be wrong, for lice are so minute—smaller than the head of a pin—they are hard to see; and they dig into the skin. However, if your dog scratches determinedly and you can detect no other reason, lice may well be present. Waste no time in giving the dog a bath with Hilo Dip Concentrate, dissolved according to directions. This will kill lice, fleas and ticks. At the same time, clean his bedding, and spray his kennel area with a good insecticide. Lice multiply so rapidly you must get rid of them as soon as possible.

Keeping the dog well groomed is the best way to prevent a reinfestation of the parasites.

7 / Training

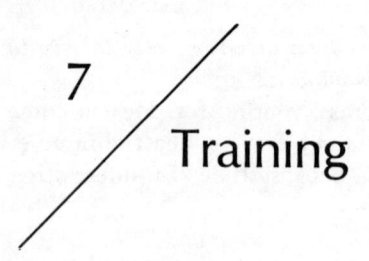

How early can you start training a pup?
The day you bring him home.

One of the most important things to do after purchasing a puppy is to learn to understand him and begin simple training. A shy, quivering pup needs a different approach than a boisterous, stubborn pup. But regardless of temperament, the sooner you start training, the happier you both will be.

Ignore the so-called authorities who proclaim that you cannot teach a pup anything before four months. If you wait that long you will surely have a difficult time teaching him anything at all. Let your pup know from the very first encounter that you love him and expect him to please you. Show him what pleases you and make your approval clear; also let him know what does not please you and what will not be tolerated. Every pup yearns for praise and approval. It's your responsibility to make him understand what elicits this response and what does not.

Will a dog obedience school help me to train my dog?
You certainly will find professional training helpful both to you and your dog. But don't wait weeks until your dog is eligible for a school (some won't accept a dog under six months). Give the dog all the home training you can; then when he finally joins a class, obedience will be easier and more exacting demands more quickly learned.

These training classes may vary in type, but generally all

are well organized. A dog actually enjoys the fun of working with you in a group; and you will benefit by seeing how other dogs respond to commands. However, such training is worthwhile only if you continue the regimen at home. School may be over, but the learning and training must go on. The most valuable lesson to be learned is how to understand your dog and how to train him yourself. The right approach brings the greatest success.

Will a dog learn more quickly if made fearful of punishment?

Definitely not; you will end up with a cowering, unhappy, puzzled animal. Make him think of the rewards for following commands rather than fear of being punished. Keep training sessions brief, happy and clear. As a child's attention span is short, so is a puppy's. If you are not making your commands clear and are not having any success, stop for the day and try another day when you are relaxed and he is more eager to try. Continuing only raises your temper and lowers your patience, and success is impossible. You have to make the pup know that you love him, think he is a great little guy and believe he will do better tomorrow.

How do you punish a grown dog?

The main thing is to punish him immediately after he has done wrong, while he is aware of what he did. If you procrastinate (for whatever reason) he will only wonder why you are being so mean to him. Even if you wave his mistakes before his nose, he may not connect himself with them.

The punishment should be mild. Hold your anger in check (and if you're simply furious, go outside and cool off). Often a few harsh words in a strong tone of voice are enough. But if the misdemeanor is flagrant (and fresh in mind), give the dog a couple of firm swats on his well-padded rump. Use your hand. Or if it won't waste time while you go after it, use a folded newspaper—it's easier on you and makes more noise. But never use a belt or leash or anything else that can really hurt the dog.

After he's been punished, let him dwell on his misdeeds for a little while. But don't overdo it. A dog's memory of punishment is short. What he really wants to remember is that you love him. So tell him.

Is it correct that I should be very gentle and make few demands on my German shepherd puppy because punishment will make him vicious?
German shepherds are no more likely to become vicious than other breeds. So you will be making a very serious mistake if you do not immediately establish with a new shepherd—or any other pup—that you are his master, albeit a kindly one, and that you don't tolerate certain behavior. You need not battle with him or use heavy chastisement; but gently, firmly set him straight from the moment he comes home with you what you want him to learn. Teach him just as you would a pup of any other breed. Delaying will only make him harder to teach as he grows bigger and possibly belligerent.

How do you reward a dog?
Many professional dog trainers hand out small treats, biscuits, meat tidbits, etc., as a reward for good behavior. This works very well. However, a dog always nuzzling in your pockets for an accustomed treat can be a nuisance. It is often just as rewarding to the dog for you to talk to him happily, rub his ears, pat him affectionately, and let him know clearly that you really think he is just great. Praise given in a firm, affectionate tone of voice can be just as welcome as tidbits.

How can you stop a little puppy from crying at night?
From the moment you bring him home, give him a place he can call his own. It can be a small laundry room, a lavatory, a carton turned on its side—any place that's small, warm, cozy, and reasonably confining so he can't wander afield, and not too far from you. Avoid just turning him loose in a dark, vast basement or garage. Put down something soft and clean for him to lie on, and leave him.

Introduce the pup to his special corner as early as possible after he first enters the house; and go back every once in a while to give him a pat. But pay no attention when he wails, otherwise, like a human baby, he'll wail simply to bring you to his side. As long as he knows that he is not completely alone or forgotten, he will soon settle down and go through the night without a sound.

Another thing that helps to stop a puppy from wailing at night is to insist that he spend some time in his quarters during the day. This familiarizes him with his surroundings so that they are less frightening when darkness falls.

How do you paper-train a young puppy?
There are many experts who say it is hopeless to try before a pup is at least three months old. However, the litters I have raised are always on newspapers and they are so used to them that they trot over and use the paper in their new homes at eight weeks old. In fact, some know their lesson so well that new owners have told me they dared not drop the evening paper on the floor! So worry not. You can teach a puppy as early as you wish as long as you are patient about mistakes and full of praise for successful attempts.

Confine the puppy to a small area or the kitchen. Put a paper down about 3 feet away from his blanket—it is very rare that a pup will puddle in his bed or close to it—and show him the paper. When you see him get up from a nap and start wandering around, pick him up, put him on the paper and wait. He will cooperate instantly. Tell him what a good boy he is, pat him and hope for the best next time. He will need help: pups do not plan ahead, so you must think for them. Put him on the paper after every meal and every time he wakes up. Always be lavish with praise when he is right, scold when he makes a mistake, but never destroy his infant dignity by rubbing his nose in the mess.

How is a new puppy housebroken?
A young puppy must be put outside the first thing in the morning and the last thing at night, immediately after each meal, each nap, and after a good rousing romp. Stay with him

when you take him out, praise him when he responds; then rush him back into the house. Taking him to the same place each time is very helpful.

When you are in the house, keep him in sight so you'll be able to avert mistakes. If he suddenly becomes restless, starts circling, or has a look of dazed concentration, rush him outdoors at once. When mistakes do occur, scold him clearly and say, "Bad, bad, bad," with great emphasis, then give his rear one firm spank, and rush him outside to the usual spot. Having erred, he may not now follow through as he should. But give him time. Then bring him back into the house, give him an affectionate pat and show him that you are no longer displeased.

Don't expect a young pup to go through the night without trouble. He simply does not have the capacity. Cover the floor with papers, put him out just as the household retires, then again the first thing in the morning. As his understanding of proper behavior increases, so does his ability to wait; and by three months he is usually able to keep his quarters clean.

If you take time to concentrate on housetraining a pup, not just when it suits you but from the moment you buy him, you will find he learns quickly. Always keep in mind that scoldings must be firm, yet gentle and immediate, and that praise must be as emphatic as scolding.

> *My young puppy learned paper-training easily and quickly but now, no matter what, he will not use the outdoors but returns to the house and uses the paper. What can I do?*

There are a good many breeds that seem unable to give up this paper-training in favor of using outdoor areas. You have to resort to a bit of trickery, but it works. Put a paper down outdoors in the area you want him to use and firmly suggest that he use it. Be patient and wait until he cooperates. Do *not* have any papers in the house in his usual area, and if he makes a mistake, scold him. When he looks restless, take him outside to the paper. After he has succeeded a time or two, offer half the size paper the next time. After a few more suc-ceases, reduce the size of the paper again, and again, and again, until it's a postage stamp and he no longer needs it.

Should a puppy be punished for mistakes?
Definitely. He cannot know what behavior you expect unless you make it clear that a puddle in the house is very bad and merits a scolding, while instant cooperation when you take him out is worthy of high praise. Your tone of voice more than what you say is well understood; and since the puppy yearns for your happy approval, he will do his best to win it.

When a puppy must be punished, many authorities recommend spanking with a folded newspaper; but I find this very impractical as I rarely have one handy. I feel all punishment should be administered instantly, so I give a firm spank with my hand on his solid rear—never on his head or on his face. I never whip, and if you patiently emphasize good behavior, you should never have to resort to whipping.

How long can a dog hold his urine?
Don't trust puppies for more than two hours. You can pretty well count on them to urinate very soon after they drink and eat and wake up from a nap.

Mature dogs are hard to judge. I know for a fact that my females can on occasion wait for 18 hours; but I seriously doubt whether anyone has made a study of dogs in general. You just sort of learn how long every dog you own can hold out, and you shouldn't try to push him any further.

Why does a dog lift his leg in a strange house? How can I stop this?
In my experience, this happens only when there's a dog living in that house. Your dog is marking off territory as his—staking his claim, so to speak.

To stop him, keep him on a short leash and watch him steadily. If he begins to sniff around, give his leash a sharp jerk and say, "No," firmly. If you are too late and he does misbehave, give him a firm swat on his rump and leave immediately. Next time leave him at home.

How do you teach a puppy to come to you when you call?

A puppy is eager to come when you whistle or call his name as long as you make the experience pleasant for him. Never call a puppy to you to punish him. Make it a pleasant encounter. Pat him, tweak his ears, toss a ball and play with him for a while. Of course, whatever enticement you provide will have to be equal to all the other things that lure a puppy.

The stubborn dog that comes only when he chooses should be put on a long rope. Then call him, and tug on the rope. When he comes, reward him by word and even with a tidbit. I don't like to drag a puppy just to get a lesson across, so try to make the tugs definite, but short of dragging. Dragging him may only make him fearful and cowering. If all fails, give the exercise up for the time being because he may just get more obstinate and you will get impatient—and nothing is accomplished by bad temper.

Is a so-called silent whistle any better than an ordinary whistle for calling a dog?

A dog can be taught to respond to one as well as the other. The advantage of a silent, or Galton, whistle is that your dog can hear it but your neighbors can't, so you don't have to worry about waking them up when Rover decides at midnight he'd rather stay outdoors.

How early can I teach my puppy to sit and how do I go about it?

I have had great success teaching six-week-old pups not only how to sit but also how to do other things. It all depends on how you go about it.

When you are sitting down, call the puppy to you. His first inclination will be to climb up and put his feet in your lap. Firmly say, "No, I want you to sit." Push him off your lap, press down on his rump and continue to say "sit" in a pleasant, cajoling tone of voice. He will sit—he almost can't avoid it. Then say, "Good boy, good," and pat him. He will be pleased at your approval and soon find that sitting by your feet is very pleasant and companionable. You can reward him with tidbits if you wish, but such rewards get to be a nuisance.

After the dog has learned to sit down while you're sitting, teach him how to sit when you're walking with him in a busy area. Put him on a leash, and after walking a few paces give the command to sit. No other words are needed—just "sit." If he does not respond immediately, push his hindquarters down as you pull up on the leash and he will sit. Remember that he will be puzzled that you are now standing and obviously ready for a pleasant walk and not sitting quietly beside him. Repeat the exercise several times and be lavish with your praise as he responds. Then repeat the whole procedure without the leash. When response is slow, replace the leash and he will soon get the point.

As the pup learns to respond quickly, raise your hand as you say, "Sit." This is the visual signal for the command. When you make a habit of using the signal every time you give the command, the dog will soon learn to sit whether he is near enough to hear you or not.

How can I teach my puppy to walk on a leash?

Just like a skittish colt that must be broken to a bridle, a pup must be taught to accept a leash. Start out determined to make it a pleasant idea; never drag him around no matter how stubborn he may be about being led. Attach the leash and let him wander around the house with it until he loses any fear of it. Do not try this outside as he may get entangled or be choked. He certainly would be terrified.

When he appears to accept the leash, call him to you in a cheerful tone of voice and say, "Let's go for a walk." He may not understand the words but he will guess that something pleasant is in store. And by all means, make it pleasant. Give a mild tug, talk happily, urge him to come. He will sit, struggle, jump around and complain bitterly, but coax him along, pat him, and when he does trot along for a few paces, tell him he is a good boy. Let him lead you a little; he can wait a bit to learn about proper heeling, just take time for him to get accustomed to walking on a leash. In a few days he will realize that, when he wears the leash, he is off for a pleasant walk with you, and acceptance is easy.

How do I teach my dog to heel?
Attach a leash to the dog's collar. Place him at your left side, and hold the leash in your left hand about a foot from him to give you firm control. Now start walking quickly and firmly, saying, "Heel." Make it sound like a happy excursion, using a pleasant but firm tone of voice. The dog will resort to various schemes to change such a pattern—leap up on you, dash in front of your feet, sit down or even lie down with his feet in the air—to show he would rather play informally than learn anything. But be not dismayed and don't get angry. Pull him back to the heel position, pat him affectionately and start again. It will not go easily, but even if you take only a few strides with your dog at heel, praise him and keep trying. Keep the training sessions brief, however. A happy, hopeful five minutes are far better than a ten-minute session that ends up with an angry owner and a bewildered dog. Make your wishes clear and your praise sincere.

When the dog does understand and walks nicely beside you, drop the leash, say, "Heel," and keep walking. Although he may be startled, urge him on, and reward him with tidbits if you wish. It will take a good many sessions, but several short ones every day will bring success in a fairly brief period.

I have found it easy to teach my dog to sit, but how can I make him stand quietly on command?
When you are walking with your dog on a leash, stop suddenly and say, "Stand." Place your hand against his face or nose so that he cannot move ahead of you and repeat, "Stand." He will be puzzled at this new idea; his legs will droop and he will either go into a sit position or lie down in obvious dismay. Place your hand under his hindquarters and lift him to a standing position or a close facsimile and repeat the order to stand. Smile at him, pat him, let him know that all is well, but keep him upright. Now go on walking for a bit and repeat.

How do I teach my dog to sit-stay?
After your pet has learned to sit, the next command is logically the sit-stay. Attach the leash, give the command to sit and then, holding your upraised palm toward the dog, say, "Stay." He will be very puzzled but restrain him firmly and hold him in a sitting position for a few minutes. As he begins to respond, add a long cord to the leash and try giving the command a bit farther away from the dog. If he stands, rush back to him, say, "No," and start again, moving a few feet away at each successful stay.

It will take time, but if you're patient, show your appreciation, and reward him now and then, you will soon be able to order the sit-stay and leave the room for a moment. But again, keep all training sessions short and pleasant. Nothing will be gained by impatience. If the dog seems slow to understand, it may be that you have not made your wishes clear.

How do you teach your dog not to do something?
Teach him the meaning of the word "No" from the day his ears open.

Of course, it takes more than a No to train a dog not to do certain things. But if he learns to associate the word with all misdeeds, you'll be able to stop many of them at the outset.

How do you break bad habits?
Just don't let any habit get started that you will later find hard to accept. A young puppy may look charming lying on the damask loveseat, but he will not be so charming when he grows up and wants to lie on the same loveseat in his wet and muddy coat. Sleeping in your bed may seem cute and cuddly, but will it really be so cute when he is fully grown? So when the youngster tries to get on the furniture just say, "No, down," and pat the floor by your feet. He will be almost as content to nap there with his head across your foot.

In other words, stop any habit that may be annoying before it gets to be a habit. The dog that learns to fetch and return a ball can also learn to stop when you are weary of the game. The cocktail canape beggar can also learn that he may have one or two treats and "That is all, lie down now." Or take the easier course and never give any tidbits.

What can be done about incessant barking?

We are grateful when a dog raises an alarm by barking; understanding when he barks at a strange dog that comes onto the property. But incessant barking or howling without apparent reason is not a pleasant habit.

Barking is often a nervous trait of some of the small high-strung breeds. They bark from boredom, lack of exercise, or just to get attention. But many members of all breeds will get into this annoying habit, so stop it as soon as it begins. Try to understand why the dog barks. If he is confined to a dog yard, small apartment or kitchen, he may well be bored or lonely. Give him more companionship; see that he has sufficient exercise. When he starts to bark, scold him immediately, and each time he starts again scold him firmly. He really would rather please you than distress you, so be adamant. Do not simply tie him to a trolley and leave him all day in bored loneliness; if you do, his annoying barking is strictly your fault. If you must be away from the house, try leaving for shorter periods, return suddenly and if you find him howling away, scold him firmly. Repeat this as often as possible. Barking is not an easy habit to cure, so try to stop it with emphasis at the outset. If all else fails, there is a collar device on the market that gives a mild electric shock whenever the dog howls or barks. Advertised in dog magazines, it might be worth trying as a *last* resort.

How do you keep a dog from chewing?

This is one of the most difficult habits to stop, but waste no time in taking steps about it. Many a pup rolls back a rug and chews happily on the fibrous rug cushion. It does not dismay him that you are right there; it feels great to chew something so spongy and how can he know that he's being destructive unless you say so? Tell him very firmly, "Stop that, it's bad, bad, bad," and when he persists, spank him. He will shortly find that rug-cushion chewing is not so pleasant after all. But don't let down your guard because he will then probably investigate the taste of an electric cord. Repeat the same process and give him one of his own toys. Keep alert and stop him instantly if he returns to either rug or cord.

Outdoors the enticements are greater in range and the destruction harder to prevent. Every puppy is often outside alone and often just plain bored. I have never raised a pup that did not consider an azalea bush just the tastiest food ever offered, and it is not possible always to catch the pup in the act. So try to avoid trouble by ringing your shrubs with wire or keeping the pup in an area without prized shrubs. Mousetraps set under a shrub will work wonders and cannot injure the puppy but will make a clear impression that a bush is terrifying.

Doormats of almost any material are also choice morsels and become minute morsels in very short order. A mousetrap here is also helpful. Or you may simply give up the struggle and remove the mat until he outgrows the early chewing period.

There are deterring sprays on the market, but I have never found them effective, mainly because rains reduce the deterring odor. The best solution to the problem is simply eternal vigilance on your part and removal or protection of favorite chewing targets.

> *I have an eight-month-old puppy that is terribly destructive. She has literally torn our upholstery to shreds. Since I work, she is alone all day. Is there anything I can do?*

The dog is bitterly lonely and she feels by destroying something of yours she will make you understand. No young dog can be expected to behave well all day alone. The only thing to do is to lock her in some dog-proof place or find her a home where she will have the companionship you can't give her.

> *How can I break my puppy of the nipping habit?*

Nipping usually starts when a pup is teething. Don't encourage it—as many people do—by letting him chew on your fingers or nip at your hands. Tell him, "No," very firmly when he tries. And give him something hard and durable to chew on—a sturdy rawhide toy, for example.

What can be done to stop dogs from scratching the door to come in?

This annoying, destructive habit must be stopped the day it starts. First of all, when the dog scratches, open the door but do not let him in. Instead, give him a resounding scolding, go back inside and shut the door in his face. Repeat as necessary. When he does stop scratching and is lying quietly, ask him in. People insist that dogs do not reason, but when he realizes that scratching brings a sound scolding and you do not let him in, he will eventually give it up.

For the stubborn dog, try another tack. Go quietly out another door, come up behind him and just as he flails away again at the door, give him a firm spank. Even the most muleheaded dog will catch on that the scratching makes you angry and does not bring him the desired result. Do not give up.

It should be mentioned that you can avoid much distress if you are alert to your pet's needs. Don't leave him out for long hours—especially if the weather is inclement. Remember that he, too, prefers to be indoors. So ask him in before he gets desperately lonely or chilled.

How do you stop a dog from begging?

You shouldn't have allowed the habit to get started. Always feed your dog from his bowl at his regular mealtime; never give him anything between meals. Then he won't expect handouts and won't become a beggar.

To break the habit, firmly say, "No," every time he starts to beg. He'll get discouraged after a while. If you put on his leash before his usual begging time, and give him a jerk when he starts to beg, that will help to reinforce the No and produce somewhat faster results.

Can I stop a dog from "talking back" when I give an order?

You shouldn't tolerate talking back because it undermines

obedience and may lead to aggressiveness. To stop the habit, jerk him with his leash and say, "No," every time he barks at you after an order.

How do you stop a dog from jumping up on people?
If it's a puppy, just as he starts to leap, give him enough of a nudge with your foot so it knocks him off balance. If it's a grown dog, bring your knee up into his chest as he leaps. In both cases, say, "No."

I have often heard it suggested that you should step on a dog's toes as he is about to start to jump. I'm sure it's a good idea, but I haven't yet figured out just how to do it!

Of course, you must be consistent about stopping a dog from jumping up. If you encourage it one day and object the next, you'll never win the battle.

How do I stop my dog from pawing at people when they're seated? He ruins women's stockings.
In some dogs this seems to be a natural habit; others pick it up after they have been taught to shake hands. In either case, it's annoying. But it can be stopped if, every time the dog raises his paw, you firmly grasp it, put it on the floor and say, "No."

How can I prevent my dog from sniffing under women's dresses?
You won't want to go through the embarrassment of correcting him the next time you have a party, so get an understanding friend to help you. When the dog approaches her, say, "No," and jerk his leash.

Why do some dogs slobber and others don't? How can you stop it?
Slobbering is another individual mannerism for which there is no clear explanation except that the dog is excited by the appearance of food and the hope that he may enjoy it. You can't stop it.

> *How can I stop my dog from dashing out the door the instant it's opened? I'm afraid that one of these days he'll run right in front of a car.*

Teach him first of all to sit-stay (see page 109). Then when you take him to the door, always make him sit and stay before you open it. The first few times, of course, he will jump up and dash forward when you open the door. To stop this, leash him; tell him to sit-stay; open the door; then when he dashes through the opening, give him a sharp jerk on the leash and say "No." Then praise him for following orders.

Keep at this until he learns not to move. You must then teach him to walk at heel with you through the door.

> *My dog has the embarrassing habit of mounting other dogs, children and even the legs of adults. How do I put a stop to this?*

For one thing he may need more exercise to dissipate some of his sexual desire. But you will probably also have to put him on a leash and then give him a really hard jerk, accompanied by the order "No," every time he starts to mount.

> *My dog is big enough to give most intruders pause, but I'm afraid he's never going to be a watchdog. Isn't there some way I can get some protective value out of him?*

Insist that he go to the door with you when the doorbell rings, and teach him to stand or lie beside you, watching, as you open the door. Just having him there will make an evil-intentioned caller think twice before trying to force his way in.

> *We picked up our dog in the East and drove to Michigan, taking two long days for the trip. Now I cannot get him into the car for any reason. Why?*

Not all dogs like being confined in a car and now he fears any ride will again last an eternity.

Insist on his going with you frequently and make each trip a short ten-minute errand that's pleasant; for example, to take the children to school—not a trip to the vet's. It will take patience and perhaps time, but eventually he'll look forward to riding in the car.

Not every dog likes to ride in a car. This hesitant Great Dane has just been adopted from the pound.

Is it possible to teach a dog not to chase cars?
Possible, yes, but not easy, and you will need someone to assist you. Usually it is only certain cars that make the laziest of dogs a car chaser. For example, whenever the yellow station wagon of one of my friends drives away from my house, my three calm goldens go berserk and chase him all the way down the driveway. It's rather hopeless to catch them, and by the time they return feeling pleased that they have won a battle with an intruder, my scoldings only surprise them. (In all fairness to the dogs, they developed this bad habit when my friend came around with his own dog in the car. But they're still at it even when the "enemy" dog is left at home. On the other hand, they never chase his second car.)

To stop a dog from chasing a particular car, ask the harassed driver to drive up and down the drive while you hold the dog firmly on a leash. As he lunges to chase the car, jerk the leash firmly—even if it knocks him off balance. Give a sharp slap on his rump and scold him. He will not like displeasing you. Neither will he like the indignity of being tossed flat, and in time he will decide that car chasing is not so pleasant. The same treatment can be used for dogs that chase cars indiscriminately. But in this case, if you can't get a friend to work with you, just take the dog out to the street and give him a jerk whenever he sets out after a passing car.

An older method frequently suggested is to have a friend drive a car while you sit poised in the back seat with a water pistol filled with a mild ammonia solution that is shot into the dog's face.

If your dog has a habit of even occasionally chasing your own car when you drive away, take immediate action. Stop the car on the spot, leap out in real or simulated anger, and spank the dog if he is within reach. Then point firmly to the house and order him to go home at once. Remain standing there until he does. Repeat this process every time he makes a misstep. He will shortly discover you are *not* happy to have his offered companionship and he will return to the doorstep to wait and greet you on your return.

One additional point should be emphasized: Remember that a dog has a very short memory. So when you come back home after he has chased your car, don't bring up his past misdeed, but greet him with happy affection.

> *What can we do to teach a dog not to chase and bark at children on bicycles?*

The barking and chasing of bicycles is attributable in large part to fear. Cars follow a rather steady pattern and most dogs are not concerned about them. But when a group of children rides by on bikes, shouting to each other, dogs are annoyed by the noise, give chase, and the children retaliate with more shouts and threats and bikes become a fixed target for hatred. You can, however, eliminate the problem as soon as it shows signs of starting by riding a bike in your driveway or on the road with your dog alongside. Having you on the bike and not a shouting youngster helps to allay his fears.

How can I keep my dog from chasing the neighbor's cat?

You can't do much short of locking him up. Leave it to the cat; a few stabs from her claws and the dog will soon settle for a truce. They may never be friends, but will learn to keep their distance.

My dog has started to wander—just vanishes for hours. Is there any way of stopping this new problem?

If a dog has not always been a wanderer, there is usually some reason why he suddenly leaves home. Generally he's just plain lonely and wants companionship. One dog I knew became a vagrant after five years. The children he had loved had gone off to college, so he would wait at the school and go home with any child.

Try keeping your dog in the house, pay him a lot of attention, lavish affection on him, take him with you in the car when possible. Don't leave him alone all day bored and lonely.

Of course, male dogs often wander when they discover that a bitch is in heat. Unhappily, this can become a pretty steady habit if you live in a neighborhood with a lot of females that are not properly confined when they are in season. The only possible way to stop wandering in this case is to keep your dog locked up.

Is there any way to keep a dog from running with a pack? There is a group of dogs in my neighborhood, and when my dog joins it he is gone for hours or even days and comes home exhausted. What can I do?

I'm afraid this is a pretty hopeless problem. Once a dog has savored the taste of freedom and fun with a group, he will not get over it easily. Put him in a fenced yard or on a trolley. He will have to give up all freedom for a long time—or possibly permanently.

My two-year-old dog has suddenly become terrified of thunderstorms. How can I cure or relieve her fear?

Unfortunately, there is not a great deal you can do. Even

though her fear may have come upon her suddenly, it is usually firmly fixed. But you can comfort her somewhat if you put her in a hallway without windows or another quiet place where the storm is less visible and possibly less audible. Sitting with her offering sympathy does little good; tears always seem to flow more readily if someone is there to witness one's misery.

However, if there are other dogs in the family, take firm measures now to keep them away from your storm-sensitive dog, for they may be quickly influenced by her and become terrified too.

> *We have just put up a large ship's bell to call the children but our dogs cower in terror every time we use it. How can we teach them to tolerate it?*

Loud sudden noises usually do terrify animals—mostly because they do not understand them. Let them learn to associate the noise with something pleasant and their terror will soon disappear. Call your dogs, show them a handful of dog crackers, then ring the bell gently. They will probably run off a short distance; but call them back, give each a cracker and ring the bell again. They will soon decide that the sound is announcing something pleasant.

I don't advocate snacks every time you ring the bell. Switch to rubbing their ears. Soon you can give up all rewards.

> *How can I teach my dogs not to chase after and bark at horses being ridden down our road?*

This is an extremely difficult lesson to teach. A horse is so big and his hooves make such a clatter that most dogs are frightened and will give chase. If you know when riders are out, confine the dog. Or if the owner of one of the horses is tolerant and helpful, take your dog on a leash and introduce him to the horse yourself. Possibly seeing you patting the horse may take some of the terror out of it for your dog. Certainly there are farm dogs that are so accustomed to horses they pay them no attention at all. Familiarity does ease fear in most cases.

We have a year-old Norwich terrier who is our constant companion. We want to live on our cabin cruiser for the entire summer. Can we teach our dog to live on a boat?

There's no reason why not if you take a little time to show him the hazards. Your main problem will be to keep him from being swept overboard in rough weather, but he can be leashed in the cabin a great part of the time and always when rough weather threatens. If you are likely to be at sea for long periods, he will have to go back to paper-training. He may need long walks and romps on the grass when you are ashore, but the Norwich is a most adaptable dog and will certainly be happier with you than kenneled on shore.

What tricks can I teach my dog?

The possibilities are limited only by your imagination and patience and your dog's intelligence. Some tricks are amusing, some useful and some rather silly. I doubt if it ever did any dog any good to learn to say his prayers, but that has been on all the dog-trick lists—along with "roll over and play dead" and "shaking hands"—for generations. I doubt whether some of the following tricks are a great deal more useful, but at least they are not insulting to the dog's intelligence.

Catching a small cracker
Catching a ball
Retrieving a ball, etc.
Rolling a ball down a stairway for you to catch and toss back
Go fetch the newspaper
Go upstairs and find Stanley
Go upstairs and stay; I'm cleaning
Diving in not-too-deep water for sunken objects

8
Obedience Trials

What is the difference between obedience training and advanced training?
In advanced training the dog is off the leash, hand signals are used, and in some exercises the handler leaves the ring for a stated period of time. Tests are rigid, requirements high, and a dog who wins his C.D.X.—Companion Dog Excellent—has a great deal to be proud of.

Who holds obedience schools?
Any group of dog owners can hold classes in obedience; all you have to do is hire a hall and get an instructor. Many instructors give obedience training to individual dogs on a daily basis. Other instructors with continuing training programs board the dogs and put them through rigid daily programs.

How far do obedience schools go in training a dog?
There is no limit. They will teach as much as your dog is ready to learn.

If you have a dog who is already obedient and a decent member of the family, what is to be gained by sending him to obedience school?
Obedience schools challenge your dog, make him more responsive, help him to develop mentally and physically.

What are obedience trials?
Dogs of all breeds compete against one another in a series of

selected and clearly defined exercises. The requirements of obedience trials are published by the AKC in a pamphlet titled *Regulations and Standards for Obedience Trials.* This may be obtained through the AKC. There is no charge.

Where are obedience trials held?
Obedience trials are frequently held in conjunction with all-breed AKC licensed point shows and are listed in the premium lists. In addition, many sanctioned match shows offer obedience trials. These are excellent for training in show procedure but do not give obedience credits. You will also find obedience trials held separately by obedience clubs and groups that sponsor training dogs in obedience.

Can a handicapped person show a dog in obedience trials?
If a handler is able to follow the exercises and can move about the ring without assistance from another person, he is eligible to show his dog. The judge is allowed to make some modification in the regulations for the handler, but the dog must perform all parts of each exercise.

Do dogs enjoy performing in obedience trials?
A dog that is firmly trained and given a great deal of praise and affection by his owner or handler truly enjoys performing because he understands it brings pleasure to the person he is devoted to. But thoughtless handling, long exhausting training and shouted commands only bring results through bullying. A dog so trained may perform but he does not enjoy it.

What classes are offered in obedience trials?
There are five: Novice Class A, Novice Class B, Open Class A, Open Class B, and Utility Class. The two novice classes require the same exercises, but in the A class the dog must be handled by his owner or a member of the family, while in the B class he may be handled by a professional. Both A and B classes are open to dogs that have not yet won their Companion Dog title (C.D.). Open classes are for dogs that have attained their

C.D. degree and are seeking the next award—Companion Dog Excellent (C.D.X.). Dogs are also eligible that have already won this award as well as the next award of Utility (U.D.). And again, in the A group the dog must be handled by his owner or a member of the family, whereas in the B group he may be handled by a professional.

What do the letters C.D. mean in my dog's pedigree?
This means that he has earned his Companion Dog title. To do this he must win a score of 170 points or better at three obedience trials under three different judges.

What are the exercises a dog must pass to earn his C.D., and how are they scored?
As a beginner a dog must compete in the novice classes. The six exercises are:

1. Heel on leash	35 points
2. Stand for examination off leash	30 points
3. Heel off leash	45 points
4. Recall	30 points
5. Long sit (1 minute)	30 points
6. Long down (3 minutes)	30 points

A dog will be scored zero for any exercise he fails to perform on the first command.

1. Dog walks close to the handler's left side, without crowding. At the judge's command to halt, the handler stops; the dog must sit straight in the heel position until the command "Forward" is given. The leash must be loose, and no signaling or assistance is given by the handler to the dog.

2. At the judge's order, the handler gives a command to the dog to stay, then walks six feet away from the dog and stands facing him. The judge will touch the dog on the head, body and hindquarters, then order, "Back to your dog." The handler returns to the heel position. The dog must remain standing until the order "Exercise finished" is given.

3. The same exercise as No. 1 but the dog is off the leash.

4. When the judge orders, "Leave your dog," the dog is given the command to stay in a sitting position. The handler then walks 35 feet from the dog, turns around and faces the

dog. On the order "Call your dog," the dog must go on command of the judge. The dog is to be sitting at the far end of the ring when the order is given.

5. When ordered by the judge, the handlers command their dogs to sit. On second order from the judge to "Leave your dogs," the handlers hand-signal or command their dogs to stay, then walk to the far side of the ring, turn and stand facing their dogs. One minute after leaving their dogs the handlers are ordered "Back to your dogs." On this order each handler returns, walks around his dog and goes to the heel position. During this time the dogs do not move until the signal "Exercise finished" is given.

6. Similar to the above "Long sit" exercise, the dogs are ordered to lie down on command or hand-signal by their handlers. The dogs are not touched by the handlers and must maintain the down position for three minutes. The judge then orders the handlers back to their dogs, and the dogs do not move until the judge says, "Exercise finished."

What do the letters C.D.X. mean?
This means that a dog with the title of C.D. (Companion Dog) entered open obedience classes and won the title of Companion Dog Excellent (C.D.X.).

What are the requirements for the C.D.X. title? How are they scored?
A dog qualifies for this title by winning at least 170 points in each of three open obedience trials. He must win half the points allowed in each exercise and is marked zero if he fails to perform on the first command in each exercise.

The open exercises and scores are as follows:
1. Heel free   40 points
2. Drop on recall   30 points
3. Retrieve on the flat   25 points
4. Retrieve over high jump 35 points
5. Broad jump   20 points
6. Long sit   25 points
7. Long down   25 points

1. The unleashed dog walks by the handler's left side and obeys all given orders—"Right turn," "Slow," "Forward," "Stop." He is expected to go through the figure-eight exercise, following his handler as he walks the course.

2. The handler leaves his dog and walks to a spot 35 feet away. On order from the judge, he calls the dog, who must come straight toward him. At a designated spot the dog must drop instantly to a "down" position on command from the handler. Then on signal, the dog completes the exercise by returning to his handler.

3. The handler stands with his dog sitting in the heel position. On command from the judge, the handler throws a dumbbell. When the order is given to retrieve, the dog must go swiftly, pick up the dumbbell and return to sit facing his handler. After the handler takes the dumbbell, the dog then goes to sit in the heel position.

4. This exercise is done in the same manner, but the dog must leap over a high jump to retrieve, and jump again as he returns.

5. The dog is commanded to clear a broad jump consisting of four evenly spaced hurdles. After completing the jump, the dog returns to the heel position.

6. The handlers stand with their dogs until the judge gives the command for them to leave. The dogs are ordered to sit while the handlers go out of the ring and out of sight of their dogs. The dogs remain in the sitting position for three minutes. On order from the judge, the handlers return.

7. The dogs are ordered to take the down position. The handlers leave the ring and remain out of sight of the dogs until called back by the judge after five minutes.

What do the letters U.D. mean?

It means that a dog with a C.D.X. competed in the Utility Class and won a total of at least 170 points at each of three obedience trials. There must be at least three dogs entered for each trial.

The exericses are:

1. Scent discrimination   60 points

2. Directed retrieve   30 points
3. Signal exercise   35 points
4. Directed jumping   40 points
5. Group examination   35 points

1. Out of a group of five identical leather articles and five identical metal objects, the dog must locate and retrieve the one in each group that was handled by his trainer.

2. At the judge's command, the dog is ordered by his trainer to retrieve one of three gloves placed to the right, center and left at the end of the ring.

3. The dog is required to obey signals rather than commands. Orders are given in any sequence to stay, lie down, go slow, fast, turn, etc.

4. The dog is ordered by signal or command to jump over one of two jumps—a bar jump or high jump. Both jumps are ordered and either one may be first. After jumping, the dog is required to return directly to his handler and sit in front of the handler's feet. On signal from the judge to finish, the dog goes to the heel position and sits.

5. Handlers stand with their dogs in the heel position. On order from the judge to "Stand your dogs," the dogs are posed. On the second order from the judge to "Leave your dogs," the handlers order their dogs to stay and then go to the opposite side of the ring and stand, facing their dogs. They remain there at least three minutes. The judge goes to each dog, examines him with his hands, then orders the handlers back to their dogs to stand at the heel position. Each dog remains standing until the judge orders "Exercise finished."

What does the title U.D.T. mean?

After a dog has won his U.D., he must be approved by two accredited judges to compete against at least three other dogs. The test is given outdoors and requires the dog to follow a person's trail for at least a quarter mile. If passed, he is then given the title U.D.T. (Utility Dog Tracker). This is the highest obedience title a dog can win.

9 Medical Care

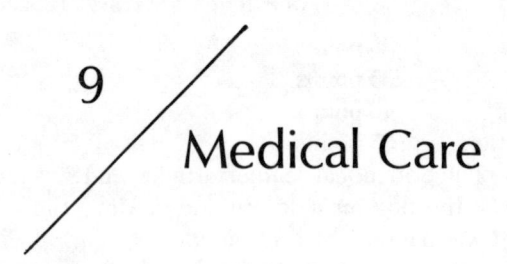

How do you choose a veterinarian?
The same way you select a doctor for yourself. Get recommendations from people who obviously love their dogs and take good care of them. Go to see the veterinarians and take a look at their treatment rooms and kennels. By all means ask them for their fee schedules before you have reason to go to them. Forget any who refuse to give this to you.

Modern veterinarians are not just "horse doctors" (although many of the old "horse doctors" were extremely fine veterinarians). They have been through veterinary schools and they must have a license to practice. They love animals.

One thing you should ascertain is whether they make house calls. Many do; others don't. I've always favored the former; yet today I go to one who works only in his own quarters and I have had no reason to regret my decision. I can always get my dogs to him; and in an emergency, this usually saves time. But of course, if you don't have an automobile you can jump into at any time, you would be quite correct in favoring a vet who will come to you.

Should you try to treat a sick dog yourself?
Most people do a pretty poor job of treating their own ailments; so it's obvious they can't do any better treating an animal whose body they don't understand and who isn't capable of telling them where he feels bad.

Obviously, there are minor dog ailments almost anyone can

treat. But if minor ailments persist, or if a dog is very sick, call a veterinarian.

> *My eight-year-old poodle has to have an operation. She is spoiled and pampered and will be miserable in a hospital. Could I care for her at home?*

A dog requiring surgery needs hospital care until recovery is well along; only then will she be likely to benefit from returning home to her own accustomed care and comforts.

You will have to provide a safe, quiet place—a small pen or large box—where your dog can be confined so that her activities are held to a minimum. Follow the vet's orders to the letter; take the dog's temperature daily; feed her what she's supposed to have and no more.

> *How can you tell if a dog is sick? Does his nose always become hot?*

Even if there are no definite symptoms, such as diarrhea or runny eyes, it's just as easy to tell there's something wrong with a dog as with a person. He goes off his food; becomes listless; wanders around with hung head and dull eyes.

Contrary to general belief, his nose tells you nothing. It can be hot or cold.

> *How do you feed an ill dog that doesn't want to eat?*

Don't, unless the veterinarian says the dog must take food. In that case, call up all your patience. Don't show exasperation. Make the dog know that you sympathize with him, understand his problems and want very much to help.

Feed him frequently in very small doses. Give him food he especially likes. If he's on a solid diet, make little meatballs mixed with beef broth, and let him eat them one by one out of your hand. If he's on a liquid diet, feed him a teaspoon of broth at a time. If necessary, pour the broth into a pouch formed by pulling the corner of his mouth away from his gums. To make him swallow, whether the food is liquid, soft or solid, stroke his throat gently.

How do I give my dog a pill?

Press the hinge of the dog's jaw on either side to make him open his mouth. Place the pill as far back on his tongue as you can. Snap the dog's mouth closed and stroke his throat. If he spits out the pill, place it on the back of his tongue, hold his jaws closed and blow into his face.

How do I make my dog swallow a liquid medicine?

Hold his head up, pull out a portion of his cheek and pour the liquid into this small pocket. Pour slowly and keep his head held up until he swallows. Talk encouragingly while giving the medicine; he will sense you are trying to help.

How do you take a dog's temperature?

Smear vaseline on a rectal thermometer and insert it for about half its length into the dog's rectum for two minutes. Keep the dog still. Normal is 101.5° for most breeds; 102° for very small breeds. If a dog's temperature goes one or two degrees above normal or drops below 98°, he's definitely sick and needs attention.

How do I give a dog an enema?

First be certain the dog needs an enema—not just a dose of magnesia. Use a small syringe for toy breeds; an ordinary household enema bag for all others. Fill it with lukewarm water and a very mild soap, such as Liquid Ivory, to make it bubbly. Now tie the dog so he won't break away and urge him to lie down, grease the tip of the nozzle with vaseline, and insert in the rectum. Let the solution flow slowly; if it comes too fast, it will upset the dog and he will release too early. Talk gently and reassuringly to keep him calm. The longer he retains the fluid, the more effective it will be. Repeat as necessary.

Should my dog be vaccinated against rabies?

Definitely. He may never be infected, but this is a protection you must provide for all those who come into contact with your dog. Rabies outbreaks are becoming fewer because of widespread use of the vaccine. Every dog should be vaccinated at six months and revaccinated every two years. (Check your state laws. Florida, for example, requires a revaccination yearly.)

What are the symptoms of rabies?

Rabies strikes the nervous system in a dog and is carried by the nerve sheaths to the brain. The course of the disease is varied; some dogs are struck with "dumb" rabies, others have the "furious" type. With the "dumb" strain, the afflicted animal is quiet, hides from people, is obviously dejected and miserable, becomes paralyzed and dies. The "furious" strain affects the animal quite differently; he races around, bites anything in sight, is obviously frenzied. In both cases the dog craves water but is unable to swallow since the virus paralyzes the throat. There may or may not be foaming at the mouth. As the disease progresses it reaches the brain and the animal eventually dies.

How is rabies transmitted?

The disease is transmitted by one infected animal biting another. The virus is carried by the saliva to the nerves and from the nerves to the brain. The incubation period has a wide range—from three weeks to six months.

I have been bitten by a neighbor's dog—not seriously, but the skin was broken. What precautions should I take?

You are lucky that you know the owner of the dog, for it is essential to find out if the dog has been vaccinated for rabies. Even if vaccinated, the dog must be kept in quarantine for ten days; in a few rare cases rabies could develop. If the dog survives the ten days you are safe. However, if he is proven to have rabies, you must immediately start the series of rabies vaccine.

What is distemper?

It's a dreadful disease that has killed many dogs or led indirectly to their death. But it is a disease you should never have to worry about if you inoculate your puppy against it and give him annual booster shots thereafter.

The disease is a virus infection which is easily spread (but not to people). It is most common in fall, winter and early spring. When a dog comes down with it, there is no question that he's very ill. He doesn't eat, he may vomit or have diarrhea, and he has a fever. His eyes run and are sensitive to bright light. He sleeps and sleeps. And toward the end, his nervous system is affected and he twitches and champs his jaws.

If your dog should come down with distemper, don't waste any time in calling the vet. Treatment isn't easy or sure. If he does survive, he is likely to have so little resistance that he may come down with something else. On the other hand, many a dog has been nursed back to health, so don't give up on yours.

Is there a disease called hard pad?

Yes, this is an extremely dangerous form of distemper; so called because one of the first noticeable symptoms is the clicking as a dog walks across the bare floor—the pads become very hard. The dog will have difficulty walking, frequently stumbling and falling. The course of the disease is swift, attacking the nervous system and finally the brain itself. It is usually fatal.

What is hepatitis and how is it spread?

Canine hepatitis (which is different from human hepatitis, so don't worry about contracting it) is a very serious, very infectious, widespread disease attacking all dogs, but primarily puppies. It mainly affects the liver and the intestinal tract.

A dog can pick it up from an infected dog or from an infected dog's urine or stools. After about a week's incubation, the dog's temperature skyrockets, he becomes extremely listless, he vomits and has diarrhea, and he rubs his stomach on the floor and humps his back for relief.

Get him to the vet's at once, because the progress of the

disease is swift. If he survives, he will be immune for life, though he can spread the disease to other dogs for a short time after he is cured.

The best way to cope with hepatitis in dogs is to prevent it. This is easily done by having them inoculated when they are puppies and by giving them booster shots regularly thereafter. The vaccine used provides immunity not only against hepatitis, but also against distemper and leptospirosis.

How can you tell leptospirosis from distemper?

The symptoms of the two diseases are very similar. So are the symptoms of leptospirosis and hepatitis. Some of the distinctive signs of leptospirosis are: The dog's temperature shoots up suddenly to about 105°, then comes down just as suddenly. His urine has an offensive odor and is almost orange. He doesn't rise from a sitting position.

This is another very serious disease that is easily transmitted from rats to dogs, dogs to dogs, and in rare cases, from dogs to humans. It affects the liver and kidneys. Cure is difficult and must be left in the hands of a veterinarian.

But, happily, the disease is easily prevented by inoculating all puppies and giving them booster shots throughout their lives.

What is hip dysplasia?

Hip dysplasia is a deformity of the hip joint characterized by a shallow hip socket and a flattening of the head of the leg bone. This prevents a close fit in the hip socket. The condition shows up at any time from eight to 20 weeks of age, but definite diagnosis can be made only through an X-ray examination when the animal is at least 12 months old.

How is hip dysplasia transmitted?

Hip dysplasia is an inherited weakness which may be compounded by environment; that is, a fast-growing, over-active pup is more likely to develop hip dysplasia than the lean, less active pup.

Is hip dysplasia found in all breeds?
To date, no breed is consistently free of hip dysplasia other than the American greyhound. There is greater incidence in the large breeds; less in breeds that mature at less than 25 pounds.

How can I find out if my dog has hip dysplasia?
Except in the extreme case where difficulty in walking is evident, positive diagnosis can be made only by having the dog anesthetized and X-rayed by a veterinarian.

Can any veterinarian X-ray and diagnose hip dysplasia?
Any veterinarian with the proper equipment can make an X-ray examination of your dog's hips and tell you if there is any degree of hip dysplasia.

How do I have my dog certified free of hip dysplasia?
Write to the Hip Dysplasia Control Registry at the Orthopedic Foundation for Animals, 817 Virginia Avenue, Columbia, Missouri 65201, and ask them to send you application forms for certification, all necessary radiograph material, and instructions. When you receive this, make an appointment with your veterinarian for an X-ray examination of your dog.

Fill out the forms, and make certain the dog's registration number is entered on the negative. Return the material to the Control Registry with your check for $10.00.

The negative is judged by a panel of experts. You will receive a certificate grading your dog's hips A, if normal; B, if near-normal; C, if borderline; D, if dysplastic; E, if severely dysplastic.

At what age can a dog be X-rayed for hip dysplasia?
Severe hip dysplasia can be diagnosed at 12 weeks, but in most cases you would be wise to wait until the dog is at least 12 months old. The disease usually shows up clearly then. There will be some instances, however, when final judgment is better delayed until the dog is 18 to 24 months old.

Is there anything I can do to lessen the possibility of a litter of puppies developing hip dysplasia? The sire and dam are both certified free.

Even with parent stock that is certified free of hip dysplasia, dysplasia can occur in the next generation. To lessen the possibility, keep your puppies on the lean side; unnecessary weight puts too great a burden on the developing hip joints. Caution new owners against running a young puppy for long periods. The soft cartilaginous hip joint does not become strong bone until after six months.

How can I lower the incidence of hip dysplasia in my breeding stock?

Breed only those animals that are certified free of hip dysplasia by the OFA (Orthopedic Foundation for Animals); keep your pups on a slow growth and gain program and have every member of each litter X-rayed at 12 months old. Following such a program takes great patience, but the occurrence of dysplasia can be reduced and hopefully eliminated from a breeding kennel.

Should I spay my year-old female who has been X-rayed and found to be afflicted with hip dysplasia? She does not seem to be bothered by it, but the X ray clearly shows a poorly formed hip socket.

A dysplastic female should not be allowed to have puppies. To make certain she does not, you would be wise to spay her.

I was planning to use my unusually fine male as a stud dog. Now at one year old he has been X-rayed and found to have a slight case of hip dysplasia. If I breed him to a female certified free of dysplasia, wouldn't the litter be all right?

To breed a dog, male or female, that is found to have hip dysplasia in any degree is wrong. Dysplasia has become a problem in every breed because too many breeders have felt that just a mild case of dysplasia would not be harmful. This is simply not true. It follows that, if you breed your male, you might perpetuate his weakness, not only in his puppies but also in some or all of those sired or whelped from any one of his puppies. Only by careful breeding of certified hip dysplasia-free males and females will this serious disease be wiped out.

If I breed two dogs certified free of hip dysplasia by the OFA (Orthopedic Foundation for Animals), can I be certain that the litter will all have normal hips?

Unfortunately, no. In breeds with a high rate of hip dysplasia, the condition may appear in some of the pups in the litter. This is because the disease sometimes skips one generation only to appear in the next.

Do dogs suffer from many inherited ailments like hip dysplasia?

I am sorry to say that there has been so much inbreeding and injudicious use of poor stock by some breeders that the list of inherited ailments is growing longer and longer. Here are some of the more common:

Achondroplasia—Malformation of the legs. Common in bassets, dachshunds, Dandie Dinmonts, Pekingese and Welsh corgis.

Aseptic necrosis of the femoral head—Resembles hip dysplasia but occurs only in one hip in breeds under 20 pounds.

Cancer

Cataracts

Colitis—A problem in boxers that causes loose stools.

Diabetes mellitus—Similar to diabetes in humans.

Elbow dysplasia—Similar to hip dysplasia but affecting the elbows of the hind legs.

Entropion—A condition where the eyelid is inverted, causing painful eye irritation.

Epilepsy

Glaucoma

Hemophilia—The same inherited defect that plagues man.

Intervertebral disluxation—A very serious disease of the spine; seen frequently in dachshunds.

Osteogenesis imperfecta—Causes misshapen bones.
Progressive retinal atrophy—Starts as night blindness, progresses to total blindness.
Retinal detachment—Another ailment leading to blindness, occurs in Bedlingtons, collies and shelties.
Tetany—Causes muscle spasms in scotties.

We bought a puppy and now discover that he is deaf. What shall we do? Can we raise him successfully?

A deaf puppy presents a great many problems in training since he cannot understand your commands unless he can see you. When he is at a distance he will not come readily, but this can be overcome by keeping him leashed. He will need more protection from automobiles; but again, if he is leashed he will be safe. With great understanding and affection you can raise him successfully.

I urge you to alert the breeder to the deafness defect for only by knowing of it can he eliminate this fault in her puppies. It is an inherited weakness, especially common in Dalmatians.

How often should grown dogs be checked for worms?

Every six months or when your dogs show signs they may be infested: they are listless; rub their bottoms on the ground; have diarrhea; either lose their appetite or are ravenous; appear bloated. Occasionally their coats dry out or they lose weight.

Take a stool sample to your veterinarian for analysis.

Do dog worms also infest people?

They can. Roundworms and hookworms are among the worst. Make sure that if your dog has worms your children are not permitted to go near his excrement.

What are hookworms?

Hookworms are often found in young puppies, and an infestation can cause severe anemia and death if not treated quickly. The worm is minute and white, and has a hooklike mouth which it attaches to the lining of the intestine. A dog with hookworms is tired, listless and anemic. His gums look pale. Blood transfusions may be needed before he can be treated to eliminate the worms.

What do roundworms look like?

Roundworms usually infect young puppies. Even though the mother was wormed, the litter may be born with roundworms. They are passed frequently in the stool, and look like coiled pieces of white kitchen string as much as three inches long. Puppies infested with them have voracious appetites, look too fat, and often have diarrhea.

Take a stool sample to your vet. He will prescribe the proper treatment and dosage.

What are whipworms?

These round, tapered worms are usually found in older dogs and can be very difficult to eradicate. They settle in the colon, but often lay siege to the cecum, a small blind pocket which is not easily reached by medicine. An infected dog looks in poor condition and has occasional diarrhea.

How can I tell if my dog has tapeworms?

If your dog is unusually hungry but is visibly losing weight and looks in poor condition, you should suspect worms. Then, if you see small white particles like grains of rice around the anal area, this is a good indication that tapeworms are present.

Since the head of a tapeworm is attached deep within the intestine, it must be dislodged by special medicine; otherwise it will continue to grow. Several treatments may be required.

Why does my dog frequently drag his rear along the ground?

There are two possible reasons: he may have worms, or he may have an accumulation in the anal glands. Take a stool sample to the vet to be checked for worms, and ask the vet to check the anal pouches.

Are diet additives designed to control worms of any value?
There is no universal medicine that successfully treats or prevents all types of worms. Never give a dog any worm medicine until you know which worms are present. There's a wide variety and each must be treated differently. Take a stool sample to your vet. If worms are present, they will be identified and you will be given the right medicine and proper dosage for your dog. This can be administered at home, or treatment can be given at the hospital.

Can anemia be caused by an infestation of worms?
Definitely. Hookworms and whipworms can bring on anemia. Examine your dog's gums; they should be a healthy pink. If not, have him checked for worms at once.

How do you worm a grown dog?
The same way you would worm a puppy (see page 194). The exact method and amount of dosage varies with the medicine given. Your veterinarian will give you precise directions.

What causes little circular patches of bare skin on a dog?
If the patches are concentrated more or less in definite areas, they are caused by ringworm (the hair falls out and the skin in the patches looks scaly). A positive identification must be made by your veterinarian.

Treatment generally consists of washing and softening the scabs and applying an ointment. A medicated bath and/or injections may also be necessary. Whatever is done, do not touch the dog with your bare hands; and if you wear rubber gloves, don't touch your skin with them. Ringworm is highly infectious and can be passed on to humans.

What is heartworm disease and is it serious?
The disease is caused by a parasitic worm named *Dirofilaria immitis*. It is transmitted by mosquitoes.

When a dog is bitten by an infected mosquito, larvae are released into the bloodstream. As these develop into adult worms during a period of six to seven months, they settle into the heart and multiply rapidly. Adult worms reach a length of 6 to 12 inches. Permanent damage to the lungs, liver and kidneys follows, due to the interference with normal blood pressure caused by the presence of the worms. Death may follow.

These adult worms give off microfilariae into the bloodstream and it is through detection of these that diagnosis of the disease is made.

What are the symptoms of heartworm?
Symptoms do not appear until the infestation of the larvae in the dog is well advanced. A dog will appear listless, cough, tire easily and lose weight. He may even die before you are aware he has the disease.

The only sure way to determine if he is infected is through a blood test given by your veterinarian. It is highly recommended that this test be given every six months in areas where mosquitoes are abundant the year 'round; once a year in the regions where frosts keep down the mosquito population.

How is heartworm disease spread and where is it found?
It is spread by mosquitoes that ingest the microscopic microfilariae (the name given dirofilaria when young) when they bite an infected dog. These develop into infectious larvae and are passed on to the next dog to be bitten by the mosquito. Just one bite from an infected mosquito will give a dog or cat heartworm disease unless he is taking the proper preventive medicine. It is obvious that an epidemic can develop as long as thousands of animals remain untreated.

The disease is most prevalent in areas where mosquitoes abound the year 'round. With the increasing trend of families moving from one part of the country to another, taking their untreated dogs with them, no area can be considered safe from heartworm infestation.

Can heartworm be transmitted from one dog to another?
No, it is transmitted only by a mosquito which bites an in-

fected dog. The mosquito is the host for the larvae, which are passed into another dog after a 10- to 12-day period of development.

What can I do to protect my dog from heartworm?
Have your veterinarian give your dog a blood test in early spring—every year. If you live in a warm climate, have the test done every six months. If the dog is free from any sign of heartworm the vet will then prescribe the medication that he feels is best. It may either be a liquid or a pill, with the dosage based on the weight of your pet. It is of great importance that you give the medication daily, without fail, for the entire time ordered.

Should all dogs be tested for heartworm?
If your pet is rarely outdoors or exposed to mosquitoes, you may be safe from worry; but the risk is great and the test easy. I suggest you take no chances.

What do you advise for dogs that live in warm, humid Southern climates with mosquitoes often in evidence the year 'round?
Dogs in such areas need protection the year 'round.

What can be done if a dog is proven to be infected with heartworm?
The drug used is an organic arsenic compound. Before starting treatment, your veterinarian will make careful tests of the dog to determine the condition of his vital organs, for if kidney or liver function is poor, the dog may not be able to eliminate the poison and the worm accumulation.

If the dog can be treated, he is given intravenous injections of the arsenic. During this time he must be kept under careful medical supervision and his activity must be severely restricted. About eight days after the treatments, the dead worms are swept from the heart into the pulmonary blood vessels. The dog must continue to be kept quiet to prevent the dead worms from remaining in vital blood vessels.

After the adult worms are cleared out, microfilariae still remain in the bloodstream and are treated with Diahiazinine iodide, the most effective drug to date, but also a poison that is dangerous to the kidneys. This treatment covers a period of about a week. The blood is then tested, and if any microfilariae remain, the treatment is repeated. Again, careful supervision by your veterinarian is essential. If all microfilariae are not destroyed, they will develop into adult worms, and the whole cycle starts again. In addition, they may be picked up by a mosquito which may then infect another dog.

One point must be emphasized: Even though some dogs seem to respond quickly to the treatment, they must not be allowed to resume their normal activities until all the worms and microfilariae are proven by test to be eliminated.

My dog had heartworm last year, was treated and recovered. Is he now immune to heartworm?
Unfortunately, no. As long as mosquitoes abound, every dog must have a blood test annually in early spring and be given protective medication daily from the time mosquitoes appear until 15 days after the first killing frost in the fall.

Can heartworm be transmitted to humans?
No. This is the only good thing about it.

My poodle has occasional attacks of diarrhea. Is there a home remedy for this condition?
If the diarrhea seems to result from a mild stomach upset, you can try 1 tablespoon Kaopectate for every 20 pounds of dog weight. Do not feed him a soft fluid diet, but add cooked rice. If the diarrhea persists more than a day or two, or other symptoms appear, take him to your vet.

My dog often suffers from constipation. What is the best treatment?
Give him milk of magnesia—1 teaspoon for every 10 pounds of

body weight. If trouble persists, give an enema of mild soap and warm water.

If constipation is a regular problem, the dog may need a change of diet. Try a different brand of meat, add leafy vegetables, give him less dry food. Be sure he has sufficient water and exercise. In an old dog the problem may be due to an enlarged prostate, so if constipation is a steady problem, consult your veterinarian.

Never experiment with laxatives which are prescribed for humans. Some are lethal for animals.

> *What is "bloat"?*

Bloat is a sudden accumulation of gas in a dog's stomach. It comes on so rapidly that you can actually see him swelling up; and if you don't take him to a veterinarian immediately, it can kill him within hours. Though not entirely understood, it is sometimes caused by eating spoiled garbage or by too violent exercise right after eating.

> *My dog hasn't been acting right. He often gets down on his forelegs as if he were praying. I've seen him do that when he was stretching, but now he's not stretching. What's wrong?*

He may have an inflammation of the intestine, called enteritis. If mucus or worms appear in his stools, that's reasonably sure evidence that this is the trouble. Have him treated by a veterinarian.

> *Is there any reason to worry if a dog vomits?*

I doubt if there is a dog alive that hasn't vomited many times. A dog vomits when he eats something that upsets him, and he often vomits just because he wants to. So there's no cause for worry—unless he vomits frequently after eating or more or less persistently. In those cases, see a vet.

> *How is carsickness in dogs prevented?*

Don't feed him for at least four hours before the trip. Ask

your veterinarian to prescribe a sedative. There are also motion-sickness pills available at drugstores that are effective. Ask your veterinarian for the proper dosage.

How do you handle a dog with a broken leg?
Tie his mouth shut. Treat him for shock. Wrap the leg in a bandage, clean cloth or cotton. Use anything like a board that's available for a splint, and pad it well with cloth. Then bind it firmly but not tightly to the leg, making sure it extends above and below the break.

My old dog's legs are swollen. What's wrong with him?
If the skin shows an indentation for several seconds after you press the swollen areas with your finger, it's an indication that he may have an edema. Get him to the vet as soon as possible.

Can a dog adjust to the loss of a leg?
Dog amputees are among the most amazing things I think I have ever seen. Within no time at all they are not just walking but racing around as well as they ever did.

Our collie caught the tip of her tail in a swinging door and cut it deeply. After some time it healed but she is such an exuberant tail-wagger that she keeps hitting the tail and opening the wound. Is there any permanent remedy?
The only sure solution is to have the vet remove the tip completely and suture the stub. It will not show when the tail feathers grow out again.

Do dogs have heart trouble?
Just like humans. A nine-year-old boxer I knew had a massive heart attack and died in a veterinarian's waiting room. He hadn't been well (that's why he was taken to the vet's) but he had not shown signs of heart trouble previously.

Other dogs in seemingly perfect health have heart attacks and die instantly.

MEDICAL CARE / 143

Short of having a veterinarian give a dog a thorough examination, there are no definite ways of detecting heart trouble in dogs. But you should be on the alert if he coughs sharply on frequent occasions. He may be winded quickly when he exercises. Or his heart may pound excessively.

If a dog is found to have heart trouble, a vet can treat him for it and he can go on for years.

Puppies may also have congenital heart trouble, which gives them a bluish cast (like human babies). They can be operated on, but they will never be normal.

If a dog gasps for breath after running just a little, is he having a heart attack?

Perhaps. Give him a little whiskey. A dog that suddenly develops a blue tongue or gums also needs a stimulant.

If a mature dog—say one over eight years of age—has been sedentary for a long time, should he be allowed to exercise suddenly?

Not a very wise idea. That's like letting a man who has spent his life at a desk shovel snow. It may precipitate a heart attack.

Do dogs get pneumonia?

Yes. Their noses run. They have hacking coughs. Their temperature rises. Breath is shallow. They don't want to eat.

Keep them warm and quiet. Give them soft cereal and milk. And call the veterinarian.

What is kennel cough?

A respiratory ailment characterized by rather persistent wheezing-coughing. The dog acts as if he is trying to clear his chest and throat. If it doesn't clear up pretty quickly, go to see a vet. In the meanwhile, keep the dog quiet in the house.

Kennel cough is so named because the dogs that get it are usually confined in a kennel. But non-kenneled dogs can get it, too.

What can be done for a dog that has convulsions?
Better leave him alone even though you know he has been inoculated against rabies; he may bite you. When the fit subsides, give him water and cover him with a blanket. Don't feed him. Get him to your vet as soon as possible.

Do dogs have tumors?
Frequently, and in almost any part of the body. Breast tumors in unspayed bitches are most common.

Tumors feel like little, pliable balls under the skin. Some are benign, some malignant. Take no chances. If you have an unspayed female, examine her frequently, especially around each nipple. If you notice anything unusual, let the veterinarian make an examination.

Breast tumors in spayed females are most unusual.

Does a dog that drinks enormous amounts of water have diabetes?
He may. Dogs contract two types of diabetes. One is common in old dogs; the other in middle-aged dogs—usually females.

Your veterinarian can prescribe treatment. A dog under treatment may be able to lead a fairly normal life.

What causes paralysis in dogs?
Several things: accidents to the skull or backbone, distemper, the bites of ticks carrying tick paralysis, etc. At present, probably the most common cause of paralysis is intervertebral disluxation, a congenital defect which dog breeders have brought about by their determined efforts to make the bodies of certain breeds, particularly dachshunds, unnaturally long.

In this totally unnecessary disease, lesions develop in the spinal disks which then, in many cases, become calcified. Calcified or not, the disks press on the spinal cord or spinal nerves and cause great pain. The dogs lose their freedom of movement, their hind legs become paralyzed, and they have to be put to death at an early age.

My six-year-old dog seems to walk stiffly and is often not interested in walking with me or playing with the children. What's wrong?
Your dog probably is suffering from arthritis. You can relieve his discomfort by giving him an aspirin every six hours as needed and by applying warm wet towels to the affected joint. Be sure he has a warm, dry place to sleep. Take him to the vet for treatment.

My male dog seems to have difficulty urinating and walks stiffly with his back humped. What is the trouble?
Your dog probably has stones in the bladder. Surgery is the only answer if he does not pass them. Have your veterinarian make an examination.

How do you treat a dog whose eye becomes badly inflamed?
Wash the eye with a mild boric acid solution and look for foreign objects or a scratch. If the condition doesn't clear up promptly, consult a veterinarian.

What is entropion?
This is a condition when an eyelid, either upper or lower, is turned in toward the eyeball. The irritation caused by the pricking of the eyelashes against the eyeball is intensely painful. The animal will paw at his eye, rub his face along the ground, and obviously be in great discomfort. As soon as the condition is discovered, surgery is recommended and is usually simple as well as successful. The defect is congenital.

What is a haw?
An inner fold in a dog's eye similar to the eyelid. It is a troublesome area since small bits of foreign matter can settle there causing great irritation. When this happens, treat this as for inflammation (see above). If the boric acid solution does not flush out the particle, take the dog to the veterinarian to have it removed.

What is progressive retinal atrophy?
A hereditary disease that appears as night blindness when a pup is about two months old. It gets progressively worse and the dog may finally go completely blind. There is no cure.

Which breeds have retinal atrophy?
So far it is known to affect mainly Irish, English and Gordon setters, collies, poodles and golden retrievers. There is a good question whether any breed is immune, however.

Can you detect retinal atrophy before it becomes obvious? And what do you do about a dog that has it?
Positive identification of the disease is possible only if a dog is thoroughly tested by a veterinarian specializing in ophthalmology—and there are not many of these. If a dog is found to be afflicted, you have a choice either of putting him to sleep or letting him go through life without sight. You definitely should not breed him.

Aren't eye clinics being held in some areas? What are they testing for?
Clinics are being held about every six months in the Boston area to test for progressive retinal atrophy as well as cataracts and other eye ailments. There will undoubtedly be other clinics elsewhere in the country when dog breeders realize how serious progressive retinal atrophy is.

Are cataracts common in dogs?
I can't give you exact numbers because unfortunately the dog world isn't terribly interested in statistics of this sort (on the contrary, I am afraid there is a strong tendency by many breeders to hide them). Let's just say that too many dogs have cataracts—either senile cataracts, hereditary cataracts, or cataracts induced by trauma or medication. Afflicted dogs may or may not lose all sight.

Can a dog with cataracts be operated on?
You can tell when a cataract is developing because the eye turns light blue and looks opaque. An operation is not recommended because it won't restore sight.

Can a dog with cataracts see at all?
He can see to some degree until the cataracts are fully developed—and that usually takes a very long time.

My dog has been shaking his head unnaturally for a couple of days and just now I discovered that one of the ear flaps has a large, soft swelling. What's wrong?
The swelling is a hematoma. It's common in long-eared dogs and is caused either by a blow or by violent head-shaking to get relief from ear mites or an infection. Until you can get the dog to a veterinarian, which you must do as soon as possible, cut the foot off a stocking and slip the stocking over his head to hold the ear motionless when he gives his head a shake.

The vet will draw off the blood causing the swelling; but he may have to do this several times until the condition is relieved. In some cases the area is cut open and sutured.

Have the ear examined for ear mites or an ear infection or the head-shaking will continue.

How do you remove an accumulation of wax from a dog's ear?
Drip in a little mineral oil and massage the ear very gently on the outside to soften the wax so it will fall out. There's a possibility, however, that you may injure the ear by this operation; so it may be wiser to see a vet.

My retriever's ears smell very sour and look moist and dirty inside. Is there anything I can do to clean them safely or should I take her to the vet? She shakes her head violently.
Your dog may have ear mites, minute organisms that settle in the deep crevices of the ear and cause great irritation. The dog will shake his head violently in a vain attempt to dislodge

them. When he thrashes around, he may end up with a hematoma (see page 147), so help is needed quickly.

You may relieve the situation by dipping a cotton ball into baby oil and gently removing the waxy, smelly accumulation. Remove only what you can reach easily, do not probe deeply. After the treatment, massage the base of the ear gently. Do take your dog to the vet for a more permanent removal of the mites.

Why does a dog sometimes develop a conspicuous bulge on the bridge of his muzzle just above the nostrils?

Unless you think he may have been stung by a bee, this is probably a swelling due to congestion in his nose. He may well be allergic to something. If it persists, ask your veterinarian.

Do dogs have many tooth troubles?

Very few serious troubles, and rarely do they bother the dog. They almost never have cavities; but they do lose teeth occasionally when tartar pushes back the gums and bacteria settle in. They also show worn spots along the sides of teeth (usually where the teeth overlap). And dogs that love to gnaw on bones, stones, etc., may wear their teeth down to nubs.

Have your vet check his mouth and teeth when he next sees your dog. He will pull any teeth that are giving trouble.

Is it all right to let a dog retrieve stones?

When you are out on a country walk with a dog, it's much more convenient to throw stones for him than to carry a ball. And if these are the only times you indulge your dog in this way, there is nothing wrong with the practice.

But the trouble is that many dogs get in the habit of asking you to throw stones whenever you step outdoors. After a little while, this becomes annoying. And stones will grind the dog's teeth down almost to the gums.

What can you do if a dog's teeth come in crooked? Will they disqualify him from the show ring?

Crooked teeth are fairly common in dogs with short heads

and I haven't heard of any orthodontists who have tried to straighten them. Keep your dog for a pet. You'd better not try to show him unless he is superlative in every other way (the crooked teeth won't disqualify him but will go against him). And don't breed him.

Why does a dog sometimes paw at his mouth?
Usually it's because he has something stuck in his mouth or throat (see page 154). But it may be because he has an abscessed tooth. Look for a swelling of the gums or oozing pus. Occasionally an abscess causes a swelling under the eye. The tooth must be pulled.

Sometimes my dog has terribly bad breath. Is there anything I can do about it?
If his breath is bad only occasionally, it's because he has eaten something that upset him. If the problem is on again off again rather frequently, it could be caused by a digestive ailment that calls for examination by a veterinarian.

More or less constant bad breath usually means the dog has a big build-up of tartar on his teeth. He should wear this away in time if you give him a hard rubber or rawhide toy to chew on. Or, you can have the vet anesthetize him and give his teeth a thorough cleaning.

How can you tell if a dog has mange?
Mange is not very easy to identify. One type causes a more or less general inflammation or bloody pimples. This is called demodectic mange. Sarcoptic mange is more serious and is characterized by bloody pustules that form scabs, thick, wrinkled skin, and bad loss of hair. Sarcoptic mange is very irritating to dogs, making them scratch violently, and it can be transmitted to humans.

Both types are caused by mites so small you can hardly see them.

Treatment should be given only under the direction of a veterinarian. It takes time and cannot be neglected. If your dog is long-haired, he will probably have to be clipped.

When combing my dog I found a dry, scaly, bald place on his back. He scratches it continually. What is this condition and how do I treat it?

This is probably "dry eczema." It comes on suddenly, without apparent cause, and is most prevalent in hot, humid weather. It spreads and is slow to cure. Take him to your veterinarian for treatment. There may be a dietary deficiency, though this is not proven.

My dog has suddenly developed a very red, moist, round spot on his hip. He scratches it incessantly. How do I treat it?

This is probably what is called "wet" or "moist" eczema. The cause is not clear but it comes on suddenly, especially in hot, humid weather. You may treat it with calamine lotion or with a drying, medicated powder until you can get him to a veterinarian for treatment. It will spread rapidly.

Do dogs have skin allergies?

Allergies account for far more skin ailments—almost seventy-five percent—than anything else. They are particularly prevalent among hunting dogs and others that run through fields where they pick up fungi from tall grass and weeds. Ticks picked up at the same time seem to compound the effects of the allergies.

You can relieve a dog's itch by applying a drying, medicated powder or calamine lotion. But to cure the problem is nearly impossible, though it may help if you control the ticks.

Do dogs have dandruff?

Some do, some don't. You may be able to get rid of it by careful grooming and repeated brushings. If not, you should increase the amount of fat in your dog's diet.

Six months after whelping a litter of puppies, the dam's coat is dry and very sparse, almost bare in some places. What is the trouble? Oil and vitamins have not helped.

Take your female to the vet for examination. She may have a thyroid deficiency.

My dog suffers from hard, calloused elbows. Sometimes they appear to be very painful. What can I do to relieve this problem?
This condition commonly occurs if a dog lies on hard pavement. It is also a natural sign of aging. If the areas seem painful, rub them with mineral oil or Vicks VapoRub. The latter is especially soothing. Try to persuade the dog to sleep on a rug to cushion his elbows.

What causes a swelling in a dog's abdomen?
It may be a hernia, an accumulation of fluids, or a tumor. Get him to the vet.

We live a distance from all veterinarians. What first-aid supplies should we keep on hand for our dogs?

1. Square gauze pads
2. Gauze bandaging
3. Adhesive tape
4. Sterile cotton
5. Cotton swabs
6. Boric acid
7. Hydrogen peroxide
8. Kaopectate
9. Milk of magnesia
10. Activated charcoal
11. Aromatic spirits of ammonia
12. Blunt scissors
13. Tweezers
14. Rectal thermometer

How is a cut paw treated?
Place the paw in a basin of warm water to get it clean. Examine it to be sure no foreign particles remain. Then saturate a sterile gauze pad in a mild antiseptic, press it against the cut to stop bleeding, and wrap it in clean cloth strips to hold it in place. Overwrap with adhesive tape. Keep the animal with you to prevent his tearing off the bandage. At night, put an old sock over the bandage.

If the cut is severe or deep, take the dog to the veterinarian.

What is the treatment for cuts in general?
Wash them out with boric acid or peroxide if they are slight. If large or deep, wash the cut out and then bind a thick wet compress of boric acid or peroxide over it.

If the wound is hemorrhaging, squeeze a heavy compress against it with your hand until you can get the dog to a vet. For a leg wound, apply a tourniquet. Don't worry about finding the pressure point, but release the tourniquet briefly every ten minutes.

My dog had a fight with a neighborhood cat and has a few puncture wounds. How do I treat these at home?
Cat wounds often become infected. So take the dog to a vet to have the wounds opened and cleansed. These must heal from the inside. Clean them daily thereafter with an antiseptic, removing the newly formed scab as you do so.

How do you care for a dog in shock?
Put his head lower than his body. Cover him with a warm blanket and put a heating pad against the blanket. Keep him quiet. If he's conscious, give him warm water or warm milk and sugar.

Give him stimulants—a little whiskey or warm coffee—only if he is breathing very weakly and shallowly. You may have to spoon it into his lip pouch (see page 128). If he doesn't swallow, give him whiffs of aromatic spirits of ammonia.

Above all, stay calm. Be soothing.

I saw a stray dog hit and badly injured by a car. Passersby just stood helplessly, not daring to touch the animal. What could they have done while waiting for professional help?
People are understandably reluctant to touch an injured animal. Even your own gentle pet could be so crazed with pain he might bite you. Your first step, then, is to tie some kind of restraint around the animal's jaws—a large handkerchief, belt, stocking, or rope. If the dog is vomiting, however, wait

until the seizure is over; otherwise it might make him strangle.

Now talk soothingly and try to find out how serious the injuries are. Profuse bleeding must be stopped with pressure of a clean cloth against the wound. Cover the animal with a jacket, sweater or blanket, because he is in shock. It is of utmost importance to keep him warm. Do not give him water. Get professional help as quickly as possible.

If an animal is badly injured and help doesn't come, how can I get him to a hospital safely?
Tie his mouth shut. Slide a blanket or coat under him and lift him gently into the car. Since the extent of internal injury is unknown, you must make every effort to disturb him as little as possible. If you have a helper, use the blanket as if it were a stretcher. Given a choice of vehicles to take the dog to the vet, take a station wagon or truck so you won't have to maneuver the poor animal through a narrow door.

Have someone call the vet to say you are on the way.

What can be done for a dog that may be hemorrhaging internally after an accident?
If his gums turn white, he is probably losing blood internally. Bind his chest and stomach firmly in 4-inch strips ripped from an old sheet and get him to a veterinarian at once. The bindings help to hold his organs in place.

How do you keep a dog from tearing a bandage off his front paw?
Make what is known as an Elizabethan collar. Cut a circle out of heavy cardboard or corrugated board. Cut a hole in the center just large enough to slide over your dog's head. Poke a few small holes in the collar, run string through these, then tie it to the dog's regular collar. The collar should be about 5 inches wide to prevent the dog from reaching over the edge to tear at his paw. He will not like it and probably will think he looks ridiculous (which he does), but it will allow his paw to stay bandaged and to heal properly.

Is there anything I can do to keep my dog from tearing at the stitches on his injured back leg?
This will startle you, but the newest idea really works. Get a round plastic wastebasket large enough to fit over your dog's head and deep enough to reach from his collar to three inches beyond the tip of his nose. Cut out the bottom of the bucket, poke a few holes in the sides just above the bottom, run string through those, slip the bucket over his head, and attach it to his collar. He can tolerate it. Keep it on until the wound is healed.

What is done for a dog that has something caught in his throat or mouth?
A dog in such a predicament rubs his face along the grass, shakes his head violently and paws at his mouth in a vain attempt to dislodge the problem. Open his mouth, and if you can see the object and can grasp it, pull it out carefully. If you can't extract the whole thing, take the dog to the vet immediately.

What should you do when a dog swallows a small foreign object?
Induce vomiting. This is done in two ways. Mix together equal parts of hydrogen peroxide and water and pour 1½ tablespoons per 10 pounds of body weight down his throat. Or, place 2 teaspoons of salt on the back of his tongue. If the dog does not throw up the object and is still uncomfortable or has bloody stools or diarrhea, take him to the veterinarian to be X-rayed.

What can be done for a dog that swallows poison?
Induce vomiting at once by placing 2 teaspoons of salt on the back of the tongue. Alert your nearest veterinarian that you are coming and get there fast. If you know what the poison may be, give full details. If there must be a delay in getting to the doctor and you have the poison container, give the antidote named on the label or mix 3 to 4 tablespoons of activated charcoal in a glass of water and pour it down the dog's throat. Then give the dog an enema.

My dog knocked over an open bottle of automobile antifreeze and lapped it up. He was awfully sick but recovered. What should I have done for him?
I hadn't realized it until recently, but dogs seem to like antifreeze and will lick it up on every opportunity. You were lucky. Next time, treat him for poisoning (see above).

What is the emergency treatment for a dog that eats a tranquilizer or sleeping pill?
Make him vomit by placing 2 teaspoons of salt on the back of his tongue. Give him black coffee. If he is partially knocked out, call your vet and do everything you can to keep the dog awake: roll him over; rub him; stand him up; give him a whiff of ammonia, etc.

How do you care for a dog that has a bad fall?
If a bone is broken, get him to a vet. Otherwise, keep him as quiet as possible for 36 to 48 hours. If you have trouble keeping him quiet, give him a mild sedative such as half of an aspirin.

Is there any helpful treatment for a dog that burns its paw?
If the burn is superficial, hold a wet tea bag or ice cubes against it. If the burn is deep or widespread, waste no time in getting the dog to a veterinarian.

How do you get a thorn, sliver of glass or other foreign object out of a dog's paw?
Fortunately, most such things don't penetrate deeply into a dog's tough paw, so you can usually see it and pull it out with tweezers. But if an object has penetrated deeply, don't go probing for it. Leave that job to a vet.
   Whatever the situation, tie the dog's mouth shut before you start inspecting the paw. Work in a bright light. When probing between the toes, be very gentle.

What is the treatment for a puppy that chews through an extension cord and gets a shock?

Give him a whiff of aromatic spirits of ammonia. If he is not breathing, you should, in addition, give artificial respiration. Gently press down on the upper rib cage, behind the shoulder blade, in and out about 20 times per minute. When he revives, give him a little black coffee or whiskey in water.

What do you do for a dog that is bee-stung?

Cover the sting with a thick paste made of wet baking soda to ease the discomfort. If the dog shows any difficulty in breathing, give him a spoonful of whiskey and rush him to the vet. He may need an antihistamine to counteract the poison.

Do dogs ever drown?

Yes. But if you rescue one before his heart stops beating, you may be able to save him by artificial respiration.

Hang him by his heels and let the water run out. Shake or swing him if necessary. Pull his tongue forward. Then lay him on the ground, cup your hands over his mouth and nose and breathe strongly into them until he comes around.

An alternative method is to stretch the dog out on his side and push down on his upper rib cage, behind the shoulder blade, 20 times a minute. Push down gently but suddenly; release pressure immediately.

How do you treat a dog bitten by a poisonous snake?

Snakebites that would kill a human do not always seem to be fatal to dogs. One of my cousins in Mississippi says he has seen many dogs struck by rattlesnakes and water moccasins but has never known one to die. But take no chances.

Since the bite is probably concealed in the dog's coat, and since you probably don't carry a snakebite kit, the only thing you can do is to get the dog to a vet as fast as you can.

If you can find the bite, make an X-shaped cut about ¼ inch deep over each fang mark, and squeeze out the blood. If the bite is on a leg, apply a tourniquet.

How do you help a dog that brushes with a porcupine?
Take him to a veterinarian immediately. But if none is nearby, clip off the ends of the quills with scissors and then pull them out with pliers. Remove those from the mouth and eye area first. Prevent shock by keeping the dog wrapped in blankets. Quills that are deeply embedded should be removed when the dog is under anesthesia, so let those wait until you can get him to a vet.

How do you de-skunk a dog?
Wash out his eyes as soon as possible with a boric acid solution. Put on rubber gloves and pour tomato juice all over the dog's coat. Rub it in well and let it dry on the coat. If tomato juice is not available, use straight vinegar. Repeat as necessary. Then wash with a good dog shampoo.

10
Breeding and Whelping

Won't I get more nearly perfect puppies if the best features of the sire complement the best features of the bitch?

There is a common belief that when two dogs are bred, their puppies acquire half their looks from one and half their looks from the other and come out as an average of the two. According to this thinking, for example, if you breed a female with a large head to a male with a small head, the pups will have medium-sized heads. But this isn't what happens. On the contrary, you wind up with some puppies with big heads and some with small heads. The exact number with big heads depends on whether the breed normally has big heads or, to use more scientific language, on whether the gene which produces big heads is dominant or recessive.

This doesn't mean, however, that you shouldn't select for a sire a dog that has characteristics which are better than your female's poor characteristics, and vice versa, because only in that way can you help to assure that at least some of the puppies will be superior to the parents.

What is inbreeding? How does it differ from linebreeding?

Inbreeding is the breeding of mother with son, brother with sister, first cousin with first cousin, grandparent with grandchild. In linebreeding, related animals are also used for parent stock, but the relationship is much less close.

Don't you get better puppies through inbreeding or linebreeding?
In one respect, yes. You greatly improve your chances of producing puppies with the best characteristics of the parents, because both of the parents contain the same genes. But you also greatly improve your chances of producing puppies with the worst characteristics of the parents. In addition, by constant inbreeding you gradually reduce the size of litters and bring out so-called lethal genes which cause death or such serious deformities that the puppies will have to be put to death.

The dangers of inbreeding have been all too well demonstrated by people who breed dogs mainly for the show ring. They are so intent on producing winning dogs that they regularly inbreed for appearance without giving adequate thought to health and temperament. As a result, many of our finest breeds have been or are being turned into prize-winning animals with very little stability, bad health, etc. The spread of hip dysplasia, for instance, is in large part attributable to inbreeding. The fact that Saint Bernards seem recently to have developed a quite unnatural vicious streak is similarly attributable to constant inbreeding.

What is outbreeding?
Breeding two dogs with very few or no common relatives. It is the safest way to produce dogs which are superior in every way—not just in appearance but also in strength and intelligence. Furthermore, outbreeding sometimes results in unusually fine dogs with hybrid vigor.

What would be wrong with mating two dogs of two different breeds to produce a third breed I think might be better?
Nothing. After all, this is the way new dog breeds are developed. Read the breed descriptions in Section II; you will see that many of our accepted breeds were the result of deliberate mixed breeding. But before you follow suit, you ought to ask yourself some questions:

Do you honestly believe you should add another breed to the many we already have? Are you trying to achieve a worthy purpose or are you just trying to play God?

Do you think you can render an honest judgment of the dog you create? All puppies are beguiling. We become attached to them, and as they grow up we don't lose this attachment even though they are no longer beguiling. This sort of thing might happen to you, making it impossible for you to see that the new "breed" you have created is a dud rather than a winner.

Do you have the steely will to carry the project through to its conclusion? If you find the puppies are less than you expected, will you be able to put them to death or alter them so they don't perpetuate and perhaps compound your failure? Or, if you produce a few likely possibilities, will you be able to cull out and destroy the others?

Finally, do you realize that because the dogs are not purebred you cannot register them or any of their succeeding generations until you finally are able to convince the AKC or UKC or other registry that your crossbreed is worthy of ranking with today's accepted breeds?

How do you know if a pedigreed female is worth breeding?

You must make certain that she is a good representative of the breed. If you are not familiar with the most recent approved standards set by the breed club, go to the library and read the latest edition of the AKC's *Complete Dog Book.* If your dog meets these standards, consider whether she is good-tempered, intelligent, or well behaved. You may be her adoring owner and she may be the perfect example of the breed in appearance, but if she has serious psychological faults—for example, if she is vicious, nervous, unstable—she should not be bred.

Now consider her health and the possibility of any inherited defects. Start with a visit to your veterinarian and have her X-rayed to determine if she is free of hip dysplasia. She should also be tested for heartworm. Her eyes should be examined to assure that she has no abnormality that can be passed on to her puppies.

Now if you are satisfied that she is fine in every respect, start studying her pedigree and locate a stud.

Should a bitch be checked over by a veterinarian before she is bred?

She should definitely be checked for heartworm and other worms. Take a stool sample with you when you visit the vet. If worming is necessary, she should be treated at once so that if she needs a second worming, that treatment can also be completed before the breeding. It might be risky to worm her after breeding. This will not insure that the puppies won't have worms; but they are more likely to be free of heavy infestations.

A checkup on the bitch's general health may be advisable, because her pregnancy will be easier if she is neither too fat nor too thin and in good shape in all other respects.

Finally, be sure that she is up to date on all immunizations, including annual boosters against distemper, leptospirosis and hepatitis, and the biennial rabies vaccination.

How long can a female continue to bear puppies?

A female can bear puppies to the end of her days but she should not be allowed to.

The American Kennel Club will not register puppies from a dam over twelve years. However, you will be far wiser not to breed a female after she reaches the age of seven or eight. The proper care of a litter is very demanding and many older females lose the patience and energy necessary.

What is an average-sized litter?

The number varies widely, but the average is about nine. Setters may have as many as fifteen puppies. Giant breeds may go over twenty. Toy breeds on the other hand usually produce only two or three puppies.

How early can I breed my female?

At her second heat or when she is at least a year-and-a-half.

How do I choose a sire?

Get references from the breeder who sold you your female. Ask your veterinarian. Consult a stud book register for breeders in your vicinity. Have a chat with owners of other bitches of the same breed that have been bred.

After you've picked out the most likely prospects and determined the fees they command and whether they will be available when your bitch comes in season, go to see them. Compare their pedigrees with that of your female (this can be done on the telephone beforehand, but it's less confusing when you have both pedigrees in front of you). Study the dogs for appearance, behavior and temperament. Ask what possible defects they have been tested for and whether they passed. I have turned down many dogs that had not been checked for hip dysplasia by the Orthopedic Foundation for Animals.

Whether you decide on the first dog that passes muster is up to you. But if there are several good candidates, I prefer to take time after the initial screening to weigh one against the other to be certain to get the best possible match with my female.

Finally, when your bitch comes into heat, check with the owner of the dog you have selected to make sure the dog will be ready to perform and will be available when you need him.

What is a stud book?

Despite the name, it is a book in which all male and female dogs with newly registered litters are listed. It is useful to breeders who are trying to track down the owners of a particular dog or who are looking for a sire.

If the owner of a male simply says his dog is free of hip dysplasia and doesn't offer proof, what should I do?

If you're willing to accept his word, you can let it go at that. But it's always better to ask that he show you the certificate from the Hip Dysplasia Control Registry. If this is unavailable and time allows, you should ask that an X ray be taken. Or find another sire.

What is the age limit for a male to sire a litter?
AKC rules stipulate that puppies sired by a male over eleven years old cannot be accepted for registration. If AKC registration is not important to you, there is no age limit.

The sire chosen for breeding to my female is young and unproven. Will there be difficulties?
The sire should be at least one year old. Though unproven, he can turn out to be a successful stud dog if you are patient and understanding. It is wise to have an experienced breeder handle the mating.

What is the usual fee asked by the owner of the sire?
A straight fee is usually the average selling price of the top puppies in the litter. This is payable at the time of breeding. However, if the breeding doesn't result in a litter, the owner of the sire usually gives a second breeding, at the next heat, without further charge.

Some sire owners prefer to take the pick of the litter rather than a straight fee. The only disadvantage in this is that you cannot agree to sell a specific pup to a specific buyer until this choice has been made. I suggest, therefore, that you have an agreement with the sire's owner that he will make his selection before the puppies are eight weeks old.

The sire I want to use is a three-hour flight away. Is it wise to send a bitch such a distance?
If the use of such a sire is important, there is no reason why you should not ship your bitch to him. It's frequently done. Of course there can be delays; and if she's a maiden bitch, the whole experience can be so unnerving that the trip may all be in vain. Consult your veterinarian, and discuss shipping arrangements with the airline involved.

Should I have a written agreement with the owner of the sire at the time of breeding? What should it include?
You should have a written agreement that if no pups result

you will have a return breeding without charge. The agreement should also spell out how much the owner of the sire is to be paid and when.

Are dogs reproduced by artificial insemination?
On a very limited scale. The method works satisfactorily but there simply hasn't been too much need for it.

Puppies reproduced by artificial insemination can be registered with the AKC only if a veterinarian files a form with that organization stating that both male and female were present at the time he withdrew the semen from the male and injected it into the female. Puppies reproduced by frozen semen cannot be registered.

I have a fine male I would like to use for breeding. What's the best way to get business for him?
Advertise in the local papers. Ask your veterinarian to put a notice on his bulletin board.

What is the right day for breeding a female?
The period of heat, or estrum, is about three weeks. At about the midway point, the vulva will soften, the discharge may lessen in intensity and be pale in color, and your usually well-behaved female will act like a hussy. She will show great playfulness; and when males or even females appear by her pen, you will notice her standing firmly, legs outstretched and tail "flagged" to one side. With most females, some or all of these indications occur about the tenth day. But don't be ruled by the calendar date; be ruled by the female's behavior. Then, when she is ready, move fast. Breed her at once; wait twenty-four hours and breed her again. Success is almost certain.

Who supervises a dog breeding—the owner of the male, the owner of the female, or a veterinarian?
Usually the female is sent to the male and the breeding is supervised by the owner of the male. This is to safeguard the male, who could be injured by a difficult, unwilling female. Veterinarians are not generally able to take the time neces-

sary to supervise a breeding, but on occasion may do so; in which case both dogs are taken to him. However, if the owner of the female is experienced in breeding animals, there is no reason why the male could not be taken to the female. The person in charge is responsible for the safety of both dogs.

I have no experience in the mating of animals. Can a novice be successful? What is the procedure?
You will be successful if you are patient. Your male or female will be far easier to handle if you're in charge rather than a busy veterinarian. However, it may be well for you to have an assistant with you, at least until you have supervised one or two matings.

When the animals have been introduced and the female shows interest and seems receptive, take her out of her pen, on a leash, into the adjacent garage or some safely enclosed area. Keep her on the leash for the time being. Now bring in the male, also on a leash, and make certain all exits are firmly closed and locked. Release the female and let her frisk around. If she appears playful and amiable, release the male. He may attempt to mount at once or they may romp around for some time before he does. In any case, steady the female, talking calmly to her, because she may be frightened.

As soon as the male has effected a successful mount, he will shift his position by lifting his forelegs up and over the back of the female so the animals are standing, back to back, with all eight feet on the ground.

In a successful mount a "tie" resulting from the swelling of the glands in the penis is effected. This tie may last anywhere from fifteen to forty minutes. During this period, the female may become restless, whine and move around. Stay with her, talk encouragingly to her, calm her, and don't let her break away or fight off the male because he may be seriously injured. The dogs may be steadied but not hastened in any way.

When the male withdraws and the breeding is over, replace his leash and take him to his quarters. Return the female to her kennel. Have a second mating twenty-four to thirty-six hours later.

If a tie is not effected and the male is still interested, just wait and give them more time. A maiden bitch may be frightened and restless; some males get discouraged. But if there is still no progress, take the dogs back to their respective quarters and try again in six to ten hours. Unless there is some physical reason why mating cannot take place, the female will accept the male when she is ready.

What can be done if the bitch refuses to be bred?
Occasionally breeders have difficulties with a bitch who is so flighty or nervous she will not accept breeding. If yours is one of these, you will do well to give her up as a brood bitch because she probably won't make a good mother.

Is there any help for a male who shows no interest at all in a female to whom he is to be bred?
If he is an untried sire under four years of age, he simply needs encouragement. If he is over four, he may become infertile through inactivity.

If the dog is a proven sire, on the other hand, look for problems with the female. Is she being receptive or snappish? Is she racing around the mating area or is she being shy and lethargic? The male will lose interest. Try a second mating, and if that fails, you might ask your veterinarian to give him male hormones to sharpen his interest. This may help.

Who's responsible if a male is harmed during mating?
A male can be harmed if the tie is abruptly broken. He can also be bitten by an ill-tempered female. The male's owner and/or person in charge of the breeding is responsible.

Can a female be harmed during mating?
Generally not. But supervision prevents possible trouble.

How will I know if a breeding is successful and a litter will result?
You may notice about four weeks after breeding that your female looks a bit more rounded through her hips and lower

abdomen, but there are many females that do not show any change until as late as two weeks before the litter is due. Your veterinarian can detect the puppies' heartbeats; but lacking this check, you must just be alert to her appearance, and watch her appetite: it often increases radically. Some bitches are ravenous. About six weeks after breeding you will be able to detect definite lumps in her lower abdomen if the breeding was successful.

My female has been bred. What is the period of gestation?

Sixty to sixty-five days. Most litters arrive on the sixty-third day. A delay of a few days or so is not necessarily a sign of trouble if you can feel the puppies moving and the dam is eating well. A longer delay could mean trouble and you would be wise to seek veterinary advice.

Should I let my pregnant female exercise as usual?

There is no reason why not, but avoid any violent exercise. A daily walk is excellent, or just allow her her usual outdoor freedom. Avoid any rough tumbling, jumping, etc.

My female was bred four weeks ago and looks definitely pregnant. Should I increase her usual diet of meat and kibbled biscuit?

You must feed your female a highly nutritious diet to assure her puppies an ample supply of milk and to keep her from withering away, so to speak, after they arrive.

The amount of food she requires depends on her appetite. Do not feed her one or two large meals a day; give her several small meals instead. Increase the meat portion as needed, but do not greatly increase the daily amount of kibbled biscuit because you don't want her fat. Give her a good multiple vitamin supplement. Offer her skim milk as much as she wishes and always have water available.

My female is due to have her first litter in a few weeks and I find that her nipples are so inverted the litter will

be unable to nurse. Is there anything I can do?
You were wise to examine your female and discover this problem now. The litter should nurse as soon as they are whelped and a delay could be fatal.

Moisten the teats with a little baby oil and gently tug on each one. If you do this daily the problem should be corrected. You need not be concerned with the upper two because they are not very productive.

How can I tell when my bitch will whelp?
Her temperature drops two degrees or more several hours beforehand. Start checking her temperature daily during the last week of pregnancy to accustom her to having it taken and to give you a record of her usual normal range.

Is it advisable to have my children present when our dog has her litter?
This depends not only on how many children you have and what ages they are, but also on the disposition of your bitch. In very human fashion she prefers quiet and privacy, so a rollicking group of youngsters would upset her a good deal. It's far wiser to keep all children out until all puppies have safely arrived; then let them just look in quietly for the first few days. Even the most domesticated dog that is used to family living will pick up her puppies and hide them if they are subjected to too much activity and visiting.

Does the first-time mother need help in whelping her litter?
Instinct tells her exactly what to do, and in almost every case your assistance is not needed. However, many new mothers are nervous and are very grateful for your presence and your concern. And if a pup is slow to breathe or delayed in being whelped, your help may be needed. Toy breeds often have difficulties. Short-faced breeds need someone to cut the umbilical cord. Even a few members of the larger, calmer breeds can occasionally use assistance.

Should you be on hand when the experienced mother is about to whelp?

Definitely. Your actual assistance may not be needed, but your female will be comforted and encouraged.

Since you cannot be certain of the actual hour of whelping, do not go away for any length of time beforehand; and under no circumstances leave the dam outdoors while you are away. She may be quite content to whelp her litter in a deep hole, but you won't agree. Keep her inside.

What can be done if a bitch whelps her litter outdoors under a shrub?

If whelping is well underway, you probably will not be able to move her. Even if it is physically possible, it may upset her. But stay with her. Take each puppy as he is whelped, rub him dry, keep him warm in a basket, but keep the basket near the dam. The pups will cry because they're not nursing, but don't risk their becoming chilled. They will not die of hunger in a brief period but will surely die if chilled.

What actually happens during a normal whelping?

The physiological process is quite simple. Before birth, the puppies are nestled in the horns of their mother's uterus, which is shaped like the letter Y. When whelping starts, the pups come in rotation, first one from the right horn, then one from the left. They pass through the uterus and are expelled from the vulva.

The part of the whelping process which you see and participate in is not quite so formalized. On the day of whelping, the bitch's temperature drops several degrees and she becomes increasingly restless. She paces back and forth, gathers rugs and towels into nest-like heaps, demands to go outside where she digs frantically and then demands to come in again. She may not eat. You must stay with her whenever she is outdoors. Above all, be patient, because she's nervous and worried, and needs your affection. Encourage her to go into the room where the whelping box is ready. Sit by quietly and wait.

As labor progresses, the bitch's restlessness mounts and she pants steadily. Finally she lies down and arches her tail. A seepage of clear fluid appears. And suddenly there is a squirming pup wriggling in a mucous-like sac. The dam instantly twists into a half circle, bites off the sac, severs the connecting cord, and rolls the newborn pup over and over as she licks him dry.

You now have a responsibility to make certain that each pup is alive and is accompanied by the placenta. This is the deep purplish-red mass attached to the end of the cord. One must be expelled for each pup. Each placenta is then consumed by the dam.

As soon as the mother stops her violent cleaning of a new arrival, the pup starts crawling toward the nearest teat. If you want to help him now, you may. Pick him up carefully, look him over, rub him with a towel. Then place him by a nipple and watch him go to work. The instinct for survival in the healthy newborn pup never ceases to amaze me.

The arrival of the puppies follows no schedule. They may come in rapid succession or they may dawdle. Two or three pups may be born within fifteen minutes; and then you may wait an hour for the next. The entire process can take anywhere from about an hour for a very small litter to twelve hours for a large litter.

No clear signal marks the end of the process. Generally, if no puppies have arrived for an hour or so, and if the bitch is resting quietly, you may assume the end has been reached. Then, if you give the bitch a bowl of milk or broth and she takes it, you can be pretty sure her work is done. But as a final check, feel her lower abdomen. If you find any lumps, they're a pretty sure sign that more pups are on the way.

How do you know that whelping is not going well?
Generally, when a bitch starts to labor, a puppy is soon born. Sometimes, however, she will labor hard for a few minutes, then relax and perhaps even go to sleep. This merely means that an exceptionally large pup is on the way.

Trouble usually arises only when labor continues steadily

for about thirty minutes without results. This is an indication that, as one of the pups slipped down from the horns of the uterus, he slid into a sideways position blocking his own passage and that of those behind him. This requires an immediate call to your vet. Tell him exactly what has happened and follow his instructions to the letter.

If a newborn pup does not immediately start breathing, what can be done?

Free his mouth of mucus, and breathe slowly and gently into it while massaging his chest. Use a light touch, for this is a very fragile little being. He should jerk and start to breathe in a few seconds. If not, give his tail a quick jerk. His protesting yelp will open his minute lungs. You won't always succeed, but at least you will know you gave him a chance.

During whelping, if a puppy becomes stuck but is visible, what can be done to help him?

Don't be hasty. If you are certain the puppy is stuck, take a clean cloth, grasp him and pull him in cautious rhythm with the bitch's pushing. Do not attempt to turn him and under no circumstances reach into the vulva. If you are not successful, call the veterinarian.

Is it dangerous if a pup comes tail first rather than head first during whelping?

Puppies are frequently born tail first and generally there is no difficulty. But there are occasions when the small rump emerges easily but the larger head and shoulders are delayed. During this time the placenta may break off from the pup and he will suffocate if not whelped quickly. So be watchful and alert. If there is a long delay and he seems stuck, assist by grasping him with a piece of toweling and easing him out with the dam's contractions.

Should a dam consume all the placentas—even those of a large litter?

It is not necessary, but be guided by her actions. You must

make certain that a placenta is expelled for each puppy, and if you wish to dispose of some or all of them yourself there is no reason why you shouldn't. Consuming all the placentas of a large litter can result in diarrhea.

What should I do if I've counted fewer placentas than pups?

You may have miscounted, but don't take a chance that you have because if a dam retains a placenta it can cause infection. Call a vet; he will give an injection of pitruitrin that will expel any remaining residue in the uterus.

Is it all right to wash a bitch after she has whelped?

She needs it; but don't. There's a possibility that because the vulva is still partially open, you might bring about the onset of an infection. She will clean herself safely and well.

What special care does the dam require after whelping is over?

As soon as the entire litter is whelped, remove the soiled papers with as little upset to the dam as possible. Now pick up each pup gently, check him over, see that he is dry, warm and breathing easily. Put him against a nipple and make certain he is nursing. Offer the dam a bowl of milk or meat broth, holding it under her chin, for it will be some hours before she will move and disturb the litter. Keep a bowl of water always available, but not in the pen; a water bowl is as potentially dangerous for pups as a pool is to an adventurous child.

Call your veterinarian and tell him you believe whelping is over and complete. He may want to check the dam, and may give her an antibiotic against infection.

After the dam has rested several hours, encourage her to go outside. She will be opposed to leaving the litter but be firm; it is essential that she relieve herself and keep her bowels open at all times.

After whelping, the vaginal discharge will continue for about ten days after the pups are born. It may be slightly greenish at first, then bright red, then after a few days when the discharge decreases, brown. If there is ever any pus-colored material, call your vet at once.

Feed the dam whenever she indicates she's hungry. This may be as often as four times a day. Give her her usual nutritious diet fortified with the vitamins advised by the vet. This fortified diet should be continued until the litter is fully weaned.

If possible, don't shut the dam away from your family; let her come and go as she wishes. Although she is occupied with her litter, she will be more content if she can join you from time to time.

How is the dam fed while she is nursing a litter?

The nursing mother needs a very nutritious diet, and although she usually has one meal a day, she now wants three or four. A dam of about fifty pounds feeding a litter of nine pups eats one can of meat or a pound of fresh ground beef mixed with two cups of kibbled biscuit in the morning and again at night. For her midday meal, give her three to four cups of milk (powdered skim milk is fine) and a cup of cottage cheese. Continue her daily vitamin supplement.

Increase or decrease this diet for larger or smaller breeds. The dam herself is your best guide.

I have been told that pregnant and nursing bitches may suffer from eclampsia. What are the signs and how can I prevent it?

If you give your pregnant bitch supplementary vitamins rich in calcium and if she drinks milk daily, you need not worry.

Eclampsia sets in suddenly when the bitch has an insufficient amount of calcium. The growing unwhelped litter drains her resources; and nursing the litter depletes these even further.

The signs of eclampsia are clear: The bitch pants and shakes. Her temperature rises sharply. And she may go into convulsions. Get her to the vet quickly. The treatment is fast and usually recovery is rapid.

11
Raising Puppies

How much care does a litter of puppies require until they go to their new homes at six or eight weeks?

Raising a litter is not difficult, but a few hours of daily care is essential to their well-being; the more care they are given, the more easily they will accept training in their new homes. The hand-raised, home-reared pup is always more adaptable, more affectionate with people than the pup raised in a large kennel. Basic care of a litter is simple. They need a warm, secure place to live. The pen must be cleaned daily, otherwise it will build up odors; and the pups must be kept free of fleas

A comically lovable pair of Chinese fighting dog pups.

and other pests. The mother must be well nourished as she nurses the litter. When the pups are weaned, they should be fed three or four times daily. The litter must be wormed and given inoculations for distemper.

What special preparations should be made for a litter? Choose a small, ventilated but draft-free room that is easily accessible for you and the dam. It must afford safety against unwanted visitors. You should be able to maintain a temperature of 75 degrees for the first two weeks. Windows should be shaded against bright sunlight.

Build a whelping box of boards or plywood to accommodate the dam and litter comfortably. It should be twice the length of the dam to allow her to lie down. Three sides should be high enough to protect the litter from drafts, but one must be

Kept in a wire pen after progressing from a whelping box, these pups quickly learned to climb over the top.

lower to let the dam in and out. (In the box I always use, the fourth side is the same height as the others and has a small hinged door that can be let down part way for the dam to step over.) As a safeguard for the new puppies, run a bumper strip around all four sides of the pen; this is to prevent the dam from pushing back against the walls and crushing a puppy behind her. The strips are merely 1-by-2-inch wood strips mounted on the walls a few inches up from the floor. The bottom of the box should have a board floor that is either raised or insulated underneath to keep it warm. Line the box with layers of newspapers.

Have a good supply of newspapers and a container for the discarded, soiled papers. Collect some clean old towels to dry the newborn pups; the towels may also be used as bedding.

We had a June litter whelped in our basement, and in two days lost three pups. They had been husky and fine. What could have gone wrong?

The basement was probably too cool. Those three pups for some reason became chilled; and once chilled they were virtually doomed. Young litters must be kept at a temperature of at least 75 degrees for the first couple of weeks. Some breeders, in fact, start their puppies in a room that is kept at 85 to 90 degrees.

Is there any way to revive a little puppy that becomes chilled?

I'm sure it has been done, but I don't know how. When a puppy becomes chilled, he loses his vitality; then his mother rejects him, and he just doesn't seem to have a chance. I have cuddled them, tried to warm them by an open oven door, fed them whiskey, persuaded them to nurse a little—done just about everything I could think of. And I have still lost them.

Should I cull a litter?

Malformed puppies should be culled, or "put down," as soon as possible. Some breeders also cull an overlarge litter in the belief that a dam should not raise more than she can care for.

However, I have personally raised a superb litter of twelve retrievers without difficulty and others have raised even more. I would prefer to try to raise the entire litter than to destroy what might well be choice pups.

How do you put down newborn pups when the need arises?

You can have the vet give them a painless lethal injection or you can hold them in a bucket of warm water until all signs of life cease.

What is a cleft palate?

Puppies are sometimes whelped with a definite separation in the roof of the mouth. When they nurse, the milk dribbles from the nose. There is no cure. Put the puppies to sleep.

I was told a mother dog should not wear a flea collar when she is caring for a litter. Why?

Puppies will chew anything and the chemicals in the flea collar are lethal to small pups.

Is there anything wrong with a mother dog wearing a regular leather collar?

Probably not, but small wiggling pups in search of the best nipple have been known to get caught by a foot or neck in a loosely buckled collar. Leave it off for the first two days or so.

Why isn't the first pair of nipples—the ones at the front of the chest—useful in nursing puppies?

They're useful, but for some reason they don't contain much milk.

Can a bitch raise a litter of twelve puppies when she has just ten nipples?

She can, but you will have to make certain that each pup gets his full share. I raised a litter of twelve goldens and neither the dam nor I thought it too difficult, though I did give supplementary feedings.

Mealtime for a nursing litter.

Actually only eight of your bitch's ten nipples are very productive; but if she has an ample supply of milk, those eight will be sufficient and there is no need for you to rush in with bottles. Again, you must keep watch to see that each puppy has his full share. If one big fat fellow nurses too long at a full nipple while others seem dissatisfied, pull him away and put a smaller pup in his place. Then when the litter is two weeks old, start giving half of them a bottle at the early morning feeding when every pup is hungry at once. Give the other half a bottle the next morning. By alternating puppies in this way, all get enough food and all get the dam's milk, which is still far superior to any man-made formula.

What is mastitis?
An inflammation and swelling of the nursing dam's teats caused by an infection. Although puppies generally spurn these teats, any that do take milk become sick. The bitch

herself is in pain and may become seriously ill. Call your veterinarian.

What is colostrum?
This is the first secretion in the dam's nipples and most important to the infant pup. It is slightly laxative, rich in globulin and provides antibodies to those diseases to which the dam is immune. If the pup does not have colostrum, he must have an earlier immunization to distemper.

If supplementary feedings are needed what should be used?
You can use a prepared human baby formula available at drugstores and many supermarkets and add a vitamin-mineral supplement such as Pervinal. Or you can make your own formula:
- 4 ounces evaporated milk
- 4 ounces water
- 2 teaspoons Karo
- 2 drops cod-liver oil
- 4 drops Visorbin (available on prescription from your druggist)

All supplementary formulas must be warmed to just above body temperature.

How is a newborn pup given supplementary feedings?
The safest feeder to use is a rubber-tipped medicine dropper. Have the milk a bit warmer than body temperature. Push the rubber tip into the puppy's mouth and squeeze out a drop of milk. Then press the valve of the dropper at slow intervals, making certain the pup is swallowing. Do not overfeed; a 4-ounce pup can take only about 1 teaspoon every two hours. When his stomach begins to bulge a little, he's had enough. As soon as you're through feeding, put the pup back with his mother and help him to nurse at a full nipple with the rest of the litter.

Small animal bottles and stomach tubes, both available from veterinarians, are also used to feed puppies. The latter are advisable if a puppy will not suck on a medicine dropper or bottle. The tube is inserted down through the puppy's throat right into his stomach. Formula is fed in with a hypodermic.

Should I give supplementary feeding to a puppy that is slow to nurse?

Yes. If he isn't well nourished in the first few days you will lose him. Of course you must make every effort to help him to nurse for he must have the colostrum from his mother's milk. But he should also have booster feedings of formula three or four times daily, or as he requires it. He will cry when he is hungry; refuse the feeding when he is full.

Is there any need for supplementary feedings after a normal-sized litter is whelped?

Not unless you have one puppy who seems especially undersized or is not thriving. The majority of mother dogs have ample milk and great patience and they spend hours with their litters—feeding them, washing them and cuddling them. Their milk supply increases as the pups' needs increase, and not until you start weaning the litter at about three weeks need you worry about supplementary feedings.

How do you care for a newborn pup that is rejected by his mother?

You have three major problems if you hope to have such a puppy survive. He must be fed, kept warm, and his kidneys and bowels must be stimulated to encourage elimination.

Line a small shoe box with toweling and put it in a warm place. Most breeders start with a room temperature of 85 to 90 degrees for the first week, and then gradually lower the temperature to 70 or 75 by the end of the third week. (A lone puppy needs higher temperatures as he lacks the warmth of his mother.) This is vitally important because a chilled puppy is a dead puppy.

The puppy must be fed every two hours around the clock for the first three or four days; then if he is thriving, you can reduce feedings to every three or four hours. (See page 179 for formula and feeding directions.)

To stimulate kidney and bowel elimination, follow the mother dog's practice of rolling the pups over and over. This must be done after every feeding until natural functioning begins. Wrap a piece of wet cotton around your finger and massage the pup's lower stomach and rectum. Results are usually immediate.

Make regular attempts to have the dam accept her puppy, but watch her carefully when you put him to nurse. She may accept him, neglect him, or even destroy him.

If you lose the mother dog, how do you care for the orphaned pups?

If the pups are newborn, see the preceding question. But if they are more than a week old and natural elimination is now established, your main job is to keep them warm, nourished and clean.

All puppies must be kept in a warm place, but since orphans are deprived of the body warmth of the dam, supplementary heating must be provided for the first two weeks. An electric heating pad covered with toweling is a good substitute. Or direct an electric space heater at the pen from a safe distance.

Nourishment must be regular, warm and nutritious. Feed the pups every three or four hours around the clock until they are two weeks old; then every five or six hours until they are three weeks old. As they thrive and take more at each feeding, the feedings can be spaced further apart. Whatever formula you use, it must be rich in vitamins and calcium.

Clean the pen frequently and examine the pups regularly to make certain their bowels are functioning well.

Check with your veterinarian about inoculation for distemper. If the litter was orphaned early, they lack the immunity they would have had from the dam's milk; consequently unusually early immunization is required.

How do you keep a litter of pups neat and clean?

Wet, soiled papers have to be removed or covered over as

often as possible. During the first ten days the dam will eat all excrement. After that, regular attention is necessary to keep the pups clean. Once a day, put all the puppies in a nearby hamper, remove the soiled papers and mop the floor. Dry it well and cover the floor again with a layer of clean papers. It may be necessary now and then just to cover soiled papers with clean papers, but odors will build up this way. Store the soiled papers in a covered can and burn them daily.

What breeds must have their tails docked?

The following chart gives the tail length for all breeds that must be docked:

Breed	Length
Affenpinscher	Leave ⅓ inch
Airedale	Leave 1½ inches
Australian terrier	Leave ½ inch or ⅖ of length
Bouvier des Flandres	Leave ¾ inch
Boxer	Leave ¾ inch
Brittany spaniel	Leave 1 inch
Brussels griffon	Leave ⅓ inch
Cavalier King Charles spaniel	Optional, or remove ⅓
Clumber spaniel	Leave 1 inch
Cocker spaniel	Leave ¾ inch
Doberman pinscher	Leave ¾ inch
English toy spaniel	Leave ¾ inch
Fox terrier	Leave 1¼ inches
German short-haired pointer	Leave 1½ inches
German wirehaired pointer	Leave 1½ inches
Giant schnauzer	Leave ¾ inch
Irish terrier	Leave 1¼ inches
Jack Russell terrier	Leave ¼ inch
Lakeland terrier	Leave 1¼ inches
Miniature pinscher	Leave ⅓ inch
Miniature schnauzer	Leave ½ inch
Neapolitan mastiff	Leave ⅔ of length
Norwich terrier	Leave ½ inch
Old English sheepdog	Dock at first joint from rump

Breed	Length
Pembroke Welsh corgi	Dock at first joint from rump
Poodle (miniature)	Leave 1¼ inches
Poodle (standard)	Leave 1½ inches
Rottweiler	Dock at first joint from rump
Schipperke	Dock at first joint from rump
Sealyham terrier	Leave 1 inch
Silky terrier	Leave ½ inch
Soft-coated wheaten terrier	Leave ¾ inch
Spinone Italiano	Dock at first joint from rump
Springer spaniel	Leave 1 inch
Standard schnauzer	Leave 1 inch
Sussex spaniel	Leave 1½ inches
Toy fox terrier	Leave ½ inch
Toy poodle	Leave 1 inch
Vizsla	Leave 1½ inches
Weimaraner	Leave 1½ inches
Wirehaired pointed griffon	Cut to ⅔ of its length
Yorkshire terrier	Leave ½ inch

When should puppies' tails be docked?

The docking must be done when the pups are three to four days old. However, I know one good breeder of poodles who prefers to wait until they are a week old. It is simple surgery except for those breeds that have a pompon on the end of the tail. In these cases, the skin is sutured and pulled across the cut. Docking should be done by a veterinarian but some breeders handle the job themselves. (Be sure to check the standard for your breed for the proper length.) Watch the pups afterward, as occasionally there may be excessive bleeding. Keep an eye on the dam to prevent her from licking the small stumps, as this will prevent the blood from clotting.

What is "bloodless" tail docking?

This is an old method used by some breeders experienced in the technique. It is not for the amateur and never for the careless.

Two or three days after the litter is whelped, a rubber band is doubled tightly around the tail at the exact docking location. In less than a week the shriveled end drops off leaving a neat, bloodless stump. But it may also be gangrenous if you don't do the job correctly. Bloodless or not, I prefer a veterinarian.

Should puppies be kept in a darkened room when they are newly whelped?
It need not be dark, but the puppies should not be in bright light until about a week after their eyes have opened.

When do puppies' eyes open?
When the puppies are about a week old you will be able to see a shining slit. This gradually widens and by ten to fourteen days the eyes are fully open. Do not subject the pup to strong direct light for about another week. Never do anything to hasten the eye opening.

When do puppies' ears open?
Pups arrive without any visible ear opening but all the passages develop and open at about the same time the eyes do.

When do a dog's teeth develop?
Puppies start getting their needle-like baby teeth when they are three weeks old. These are fully developed at six to eight weeks. They start falling out at fourteen weeks (they are so small, you rarely find them; puppies swallow many of them).

By five months almost all the permanent teeth are in. There are forty-two of these.

How can you be certain young puppies can hear?
All breeders should test their pups because a deaf one should not be allowed to mature. Stand where the puppy cannot see you and make a sudden sharp noise by clapping your hands or whistling. If any pup fails to react, try again. If after several tries any pup appears unaware of the sudden sound, you will have to conclude he is deaf.

Should dewclaws be removed?
They have no value and may curl back into the dog's flesh or

may be caught in brush and torn off working dogs. But this doesn't mean they must be removed, and in the case of certain dogs, they definitely should not be. Briards and Great Pyrenees, for example, are disqualified from the show ring if they don't have dewclaws.

Removal should be done by a veterinarian shortly after a litter is whelped.

Should a young puppy's nails be cut? How do I do it?
A young pup's nails are needle-sharp and grow quickly. These will give the mother great discomfort when the puppies prod and push as they nurse. Cut their nails at least once a week.

Do not use adult dog nail clippers, just your own small clippers or scissors. Hold the pup firmly against your side in a good light and clip each nail carefully. Cut just the white edge, not the pale pink portion. If there is mild bleeding, apply pressure and it will stop in a minute. The puppy will be very unhappy about the whole process and will say so; but if you're gentle, he will soon find it is not so bad after all.

Is it safe for a mother dog to carry her pups in her mouth?
Yes, that's the way nature has taught her. She just grasps the scruff of the neck gently but firmly between her front teeth, lifts, and trots off.

What is the right way to pick up a small puppy?
No longer is it considered wise to pick up a pup by the loose skin at the back of his neck. He feels very insecure and rightfully so since you may lose your hold. Put one hand under his chest and the other under his rump and hold him firmly.

How much should people handle little puppies?
There is little harm in allowing puppies to be handled by knowing, watchful people. Puppies thrive on warmth and affection, and gentle handling will do nothing but make them more aware of humans. However, handling by young children needs much supervision and restriction.

Should young children handle little puppies?
They can and should, but under supervision. A small child is full of wonder at the sight of a tiny puppy and it will do no harm to let him share the joy of this miracle of life. Insist that he sit on the floor. Put a towel in his lap, place the puppy on the towel (the towel makes the puppy easier to hold) and guide the child's hand as he strokes the pup. Make sessions brief and be certain they do not upset the dam. Let her know that you are watching over the pup; but if she isn't convinced, give the idea up and wait until the pup is older.

Never let a child pick up a puppy because he may either hold it so lightly he will drop it or grasp it too firmly around the neck or stomach. The kennel area should not be so open that children can wander in and out. Even the most thoughtful youngsters might drop or step on a small puppy.

Is it wise to allow other adult dogs near the pups?
As a general rule, no. They may upset the dam or could bring infections or contagious diseases to the litter. However, if other dogs in the family are interested in these new developments, it will do little harm to let them come into the kennel area and take a look. They should not get close to the litter (and probably won't want to because they'll be fearful that the dam will take their heads off).

Will an old mother dog resent the litter of another female?
Not usually. The ones I know are quite certain that the new and younger mother has no idea how to care for a litter and are determined to take over all nursing care themselves.

While I was keeping three six-week-old pups last summer, our old lady, who had never seen the pups before, climbed into the pen several times to nurse them (though she had no milk and they had been weaned), cuddle them or just look at them.

The larger members of a litter often bully the smaller members. Shouldn't this be discouraged?
I put a stop to it if it goes on too long or too often. But rough-

housing comes second nature to puppies. Just as soon as they start walking, at about two weeks of age, they start playing—sometimes "ferociously"—and it's best not to intervene any more than you have to.

The puppy that's forever an underdog as an infant doesn't always grow up that way.

Should young puppies be brushed?
Their coats should be checked over often. Even if a pen area is kept clean, spilled food or excrement may be rubbed into them. Washing the area with a cloth wrung out in warm water will usually suffice. Brushing their coats removes dust, as well as alerting you to any sign of ticks or fleas.

How do I register a litter with the AKC?
Write to the American Kennel Club, 51 Madison Avenue, New York, New York 10010, and ask them to send you their litter registration application. You will receive an official form to fill out. As the owner of the dam, you must give the breed; date and place of whelping; the number of males and females

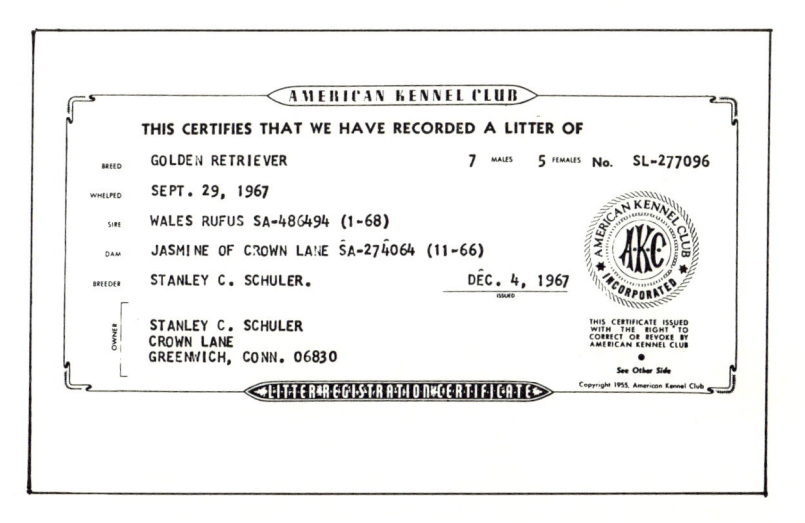

AKC litter registration.

living on the date of the application; and the registered names and numbers of the sire and dam. You must also check whether you did or did not witness the mating, and then sign the application.

The owner of the sire simply puts down the date and place of mating and then signs the application testifying that the mating actually took place.

Send the completed application to the AKC with your check for $7.00 (subject to change). In about four weeks you will receive the litter registration certificate and applications for registering each puppy. As each puppy is sold, fill out one of the application forms and give it to the new owner. This signifies that you have transferred title of ownership. The buyer then completes the application and mails it to the AKC.

How is a litter registered with the UKC?

The sire and dam must be registered with the UKC first. Then all you do is send for a litter registration application. Fill this out with the name of the breed you're registering; the birth date of the litter and the number of males and females to be registered; the names and registration numbers of the sire and dam; and the names and addresses of their owners.

On the back of the application you must name each puppy (in 22 letters or less) and give a brief description of its colors. Finally, you must fill out a "service certificate" certifying that the breeding of the parents of the litter took place on a specified date. This is signed by the owners of both dogs.

The fees for registering with the UKC are $4.00 for a litter of no more than four puppies under ninety days old; $6.00 for a larger litter of the same age. If the litter is over ninety days old, the fees are $5.00 and $7.00 respectively.

Upon receipt of the litter application, the UKC assigns a registration number and issues a puppy registration certificate for each of the named puppies. When the breeder sells a pup later, he signs the certificate, thus transferring ownership.

The transfer should be recorded with the UKC by the new owner, who returns the registration certificate to the UKC with a check for $4.00. If he wishes to change the puppy's name, he

UKC seven-generation pedigree.

THE PEDIGREE OF

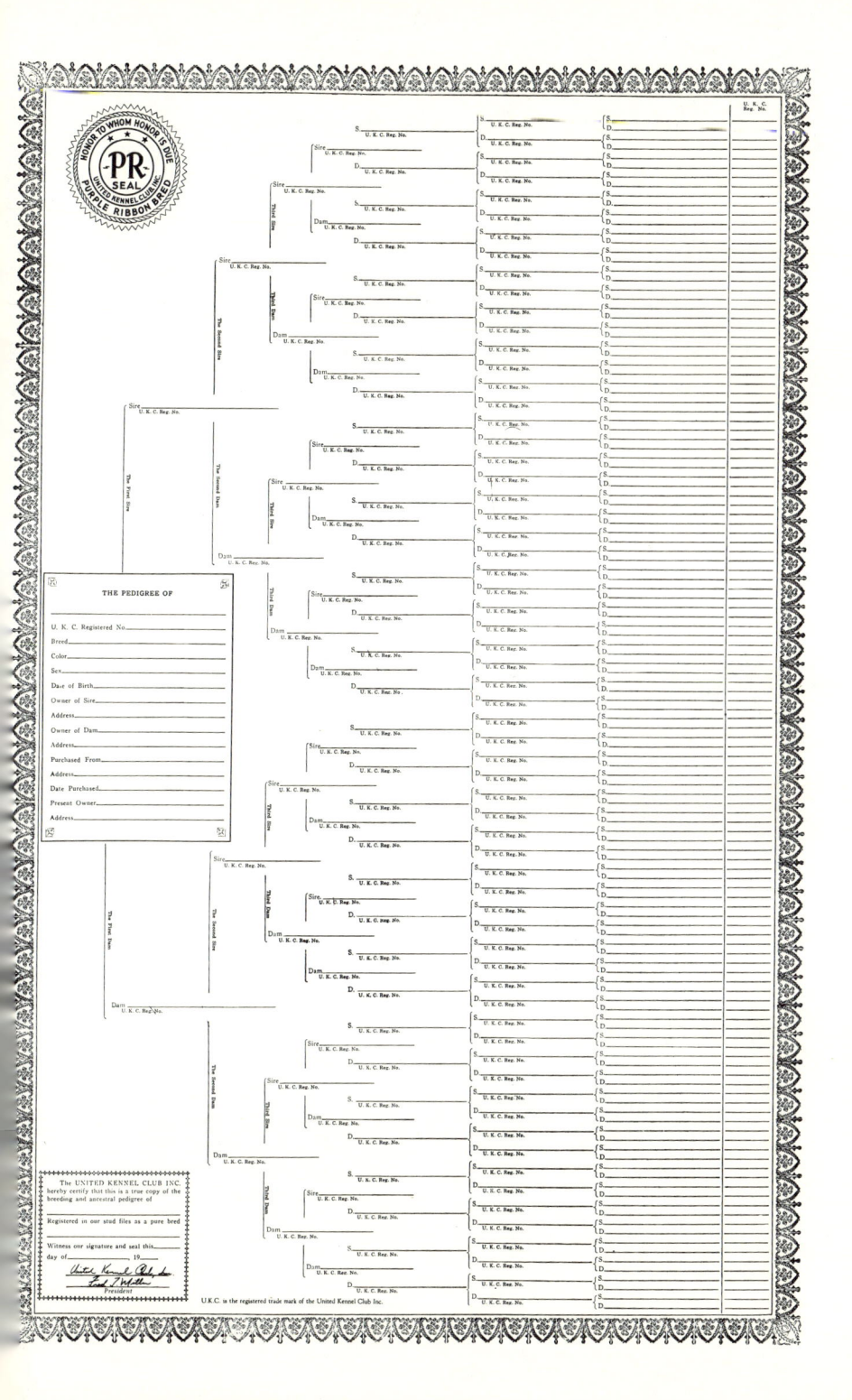

U. K. C. Registered No.
Breed
Color
Sex
Date of Birth
Owner of Sire
Address
Owner of Dam
Address
Purchased From
Address
Date Purchased
Present Owner
Address

The UNITED KENNEL CLUB INC. hereby certify that this is a true copy of the breeding and ancestral pedigree of _____ Registered in our stud files as a pure bred

Witness our signature and seal this _____ day of _____ 19__

President

U.K.C. is the registered trade mark of the United Kennel Club Inc.

HONOR TO WHOM HONOR IS DUE
-PR- SEAL
UNITED KENNEL CLUB
PURPLE RIBBON BRED

does so on the back of the certificate. In return, he receives a three-generation pedigree. If a puppy has three generations *registered with the UKC,* he is said to be Purple Ribbon Bred; and the owner may apply for a six- or seven-generation pedigree.

Is there any point in the breeder naming the pups in a new litter?

The UKC requires it. Some AKC breeders give every pup a registered name in order to perpetuate and advertise their kennel names (see page 57). But if you are talking about giving each puppy a pet name, there's no point in it.

My family used to do it simply because we thought it fun. But I daresay that only a third of our carefully thought-out names were adopted by the buyers of the pups. So we lost interest and wound up calling each pup by the name of the person who bought it: Mr. Colket, Mrs. McCall, Miss Hull, and so on.

Mother trying to outrace litter of six-week-olds who don't realize they are being weaned.

When should puppies be weaned?
This must be a gradual process, so don't wait until the dam becomes unhappy about nursing them. Start pan-feeding—one meal a day—at three weeks.

How do you wean a litter of pups?
When the litter is three weeks old, give them their first meal of formula before the dam starts nursing them. Use equal parts of warm water and evaporated milk with a teaspoon of corn syrup added to each cup of formula. For dishes, try small aluminum-foil loaf pans or pie pans. They're inexpensive, readily available, easy to clean and about the right height (use the loaf pans for big breeds and big pups; pie pans for small breeds and pups). Put one pup at a side of the first pan. Push his head down to the milk and let him taste it. He will wriggle, fuss and splutter, but in a moment will accept this new way of eating. Then put a second pup at the other side and start him

Pups eating out of throwaway aluminum bread pans.

lapping. Continue adding pans and pups to the row until you have the whole litter eating. Finally return them to the pen with their mother to nurse.

Continue this pan-feeding once a day, preferably at the same time of day, for a week. One-fourth cup of dehydrated baby cereal may be added to each cup of formula on the second day. As the pups take more from the pans, they are less hungry when you put them back with the dam; consequently her supply of milk begins to slow down.

At four weeks of age, start feeding them two meals a day. Introduce the pups to meat by giving each one a tiny meatball from your fingers. The strange new consistency will puzzle them but they will be wild with joy within seconds. Use good-quality ground fresh beef or a top-quality canned beef with at least twelve to fifteen percent protein. The next day, increase the amount of meat per pup and mix it with some of the baby cereal and enough warm water to make a soft but not runny mix. Continue to allow the puppies to nurse for brief periods after the pan-feeding, then remove the dam from the pen. As you increase the amount the puppies eat from pans, decrease the amount of time they spend nursing.

At five weeks, the puppies will be taking three meals a day from the pans—two of cereal and milk and one of cereal and meat. Now start giving them Purina Puppy Chow (or an equivalent puppy meal, but Purina is the best I've found) in place of the baby cereal at the noon meal. Soak this in a small amount of water until it is neither runny nor stiff. To prevent loose stools, mix cottage cheese with the meal at this feeding. Use about one-third cheese to two-thirds meal.

If the puppies adjust easily to the puppy chow, gradually substitute it for the baby cereal at the morning and night feedings, mixing it with the meat at those meals. At the same time, substitute water for the milk. Thus, when the puppies are six weeks old, they are eating puppy chow, meat and water, and cottage cheese. Add vitamins specified by your veterinarian.

The final step in this feeding process is to phase out the cottage cheese. This is done when there is no difficulty with loose stools. By the time the puppies start going to their new owners at eight weeks, there should be no more need for the cheese.

What causes the puppies to have loose stools? What can I do to stop this?

Puppies have loose stools if changes in their diet are made suddenly. Every new food must be introduced gradually.

To correct loose stools, give them cottage cheese or increase the amount you are already giving them. Change from evaporated milk to dry skim milk. Keep their food rather dry and crumbly—not wet. If the loose stools persist, ask your veterinarian for advice.

The dam of my four-week-old litter has brought a dead field mouse into the puppy pen every day for the last three. Why is she doing this?

She is just reverting to her natural instincts. The litter is being weaned and she is bringing them meat. Praise her for her thoughtfulness. But the puppies will do better if you substitute a balanced food for the mice.

Why does a mother dog go into the pen and spit up the food she has just eaten?

Startling as it may seem, this originally was the mother dog's method of giving her offspring solid food. In our more civilized world today, it is her way of showing you that the puppies need more than just nursing. It does no harm to let the pups eat the food. Having made the point, most bitches will gobble it up again anyway.

Our litter has been pan-feeding for three weeks but their dam still has a quantity of milk. What can I do to dry her up?

Cut down on her liquids somewhat. Give her meat as she wishes but no milk. Limit her time with the litter. If necessary, let a puppy or two draw off some of the milk; but if they are allowed to continue to nurse regularly, nature will continue to supply the needed amount.

How much should you feed a young puppy?
Be guided by the litter itself. They should eat with great enthusiasm, lick their pans completely clean and then be content until the next feeding. If they are restless and cry long before the next meal is due, you are not giving enough. However, if they do not lick the pans clean, you are giving more than you should.

Be very careful not to overfeed; a young puppy should look well filled out but not bloated; he should be lively but contented, never dull. The too-heavy, too-rapidly-growing pup has proved to have the highest incidence of hip dysplasia, so keep all your pups on the lean side.

When should a litter of puppies be wormed?
When the litter is about four weeks old take a stool sample to your veterinarian and have it checked. One sample from any of the pups is sufficient: if one has worms, they all do. If worms are present, you will be told what kind they are and will be given the correct medicine and dosage and the directions for administering it. Have a stool sample checked in another two or three weeks. When a puppy goes to his new home, all information about what worms he had and when he was wormed should be included. Urge the new owner to have the pup checked for worms on a regular basis every two months or so.

How do I worm a litter of pups?
When the veterinarian gives you the proper remedy for the type of worms that are present, he will give you exact directions for using it. Medicines vary and so do the methods of administering them. Some vets recommend a light feeding, then the pill. Others say do not feed at all. In any case, set a day aside for the job, read the instructions and follow them exactly. And do have someone with you to assist because it's quite a challenge to make sure each pup gets his pill, swallows it, keeps it down and does not get a second dose while a litter mate gets skipped.

I find it best to sit in a chair by the pen, pick up a pup, put the pill as far back in his throat as I can, hold his jaws shut and stroke his throat. He should swallow. But wait a minute or two to make sure the pill does not reappear. Now put that pup on the floor *outside* the pen to avoid dosing him a second time. Your assistant can watch him while you pick up the next puppy and give him his pill. Continue until each pup has been dosed and then stay with the pups for about half an hour to make certain no pill is vomited up.

When the medicine takes effect—the time will vary from pup to pup and also from medicine to medicine—remove the papers to a covered container and burn them all when the entire job is done. Then feed the pups as directed by your vet.

This is neither easy nor pleasant but far safer for young pups than taking them to an animal hospital.

What is the best protection against distemper for young puppies and when is it given?

Puppies can be vaccinated as early as two weeks and they must be vaccinated by six weeks. Human measles vaccine is now widely used, gives excellent protection against distemper, and is not affected by the antibodies the litter gains from the colostrum in the dam's milk.

When the puppies are fourteen weeks old, a permanent vaccine which will protect them against canine hepatitis, leptospirosis as well as distemper should be given. This vaccine must be given annually thereafter.

When do I start my litter of puppies on heartworm preventives?

Prevention can start as early as six weeks. Dosage will be based on weight. Discuss this with your veterinarian. Prevention is of utmost importance for a spring or summer litter and must be started as soon as possible.

Does a litter have a natural immunity to distemper, hepatitis and leptospirosis from their dam?

There is a natural immunity passed to the nursing litter but only to those diseases to which the dam is immune. This immunity wanes when the litter is weaned, or at about four weeks. Perfect safety is gained only through inoculation. Ask your veterinarian when inoculations should be started, as there are various methods.

What toys can I give a young litter?
By the time the litter is about four weeks old the pups are racing around, tearing up the papers on the pen floor, having mock battles with their litter mates, and are certainly ready for toys. One of the simplest and safest is knotted clothesline—not plastic and not hemp, but just sturdy cotton clothesline. A solid (not sponge) rubber ball far too large to be swallowed gives hours of fun. A solid rubber bone is great for small sharp teeth. One of the best toys on the market is a knotted or plaited piece of rawhide because it takes a lot of abuse, and does not have loose particles.

When can puppies be taken outdoors?
Puppies of any breed that normally lives outdoors at least part-time should be taken outdoors when they are between four and six weeks old. They will soon be leaving for their new homes and must start the transition from kennel life. At this point, you have been keeping them at an average 65-degree temperature or so, so a first outing even on a winter day will do no harm.

The day should be bright, mild, dry, and the outing brief. Open the kennel door and let the puppies have their first taste of freedom. They may flatten out in horror at the odd feel of grass, but soon will be chasing around with delight at all the new smells. On warm days it will do no harm to let them remain out for long periods during the middle of the day, but protect them from the hot sun as much as you would protect them from the cold.

What type of pen do I need for a litter that is outdoors for just part of the day?
The best pen I have found is sold through a mail-order house. It provides safety, is easy to erect, simple to store and reasonable in cost. It is available in panels of stout wire 3 feet high by 4 feet long. These panels are hooked together by long rods

that are pushed into the ground to hold it secure. You can buy as few as four panels for a small pen or as many as you like for a large pen. Place the pen in a shaded, wind-free place where the ground is dry. It may be moved easily to different areas but should always be in view of the house.

What breeds should have their ears cropped?

American (pit) bullterrier	optional
American Staffordshire terrier	optional
Boston terrier	
Bouvier des Flandres	
Boxer	
Brussels griffon	optional
Doberman pinscher	
Giant schnauzer	optional
Great Dane	
Manchester terrier	
Miniature schnauzer	optional
Standard schnauzer	optional

Note that ear cropping may be going out of style. Great Britain banned the practice in 1974. And there's less emphasis on it in the United States than there used to be.

When should puppies' ears be cropped?
At about six weeks of age. It will take about four weeks for the ears to heal.

Since cropping is minor surgery, it should be done only by a qualified veterinarian. It must, in addition, be done correctly; so locate a vet who knows your breed and is reputed to do an expert job.

How do I sell a litter of puppies?
Start your plans for selling when the litter is three weeks old. There may be a great deal of friendly interest already, but it takes time for a family actually to reach the point of buying a puppy. Place clear, informative ads in your local papers; give your telephone number but not your name or address since you do not want the casual public dropping in. When an

interested buyer calls, make a definite appointment for showing the puppies; have the kennel area as neat and clean as possible; take ample time to answer all questions; have pictures and all pedigree information available on the sire; and of course have the dam on hand.

Do not be so eager to make a sale that you make a poor one. Make certain that the buyer is willing to train the puppy properly and has the time to give real companionship and a home suitable for your particular breed.

When a sale is definite, ask for a deposit and make a record of the buyer, whether he wants a male or female and which choice he has—first, second, third, etc. Then after the owner of the sire has made his choice, you can mark and designate individual puppies for each buyer.

If a buyer chooses a particular pup of a nearly identical litter some weeks before I can let the pup leave the dam, how can I mark the puppy for clear identification?
The most foolproof way to mark a pup is to clip his coat in a certain way in a certain area: a clear V on the right shoulder of one pup; a reverse V on another pup in a different area; a small circle, or a one-inch straight line on another. Describe each mark and its location in your record book with the buyer's name and address.

If the hair grows quickly it is easy to recut the marking.

Can you make money raising puppies?
First, total up what it will cost you to produce the litter. This will include the cost of the dam amortized over the years when she can be bred, her food during pregnancy and while she is raising the litter, food for the litter, vet bills for the dam and the litter, boarding costs for the dam when she is in heat, stud fees, registration costs, advertising expenses. Then remember you must pay an income tax on your profits. Those are your expenses, not counting the hours you spend caring for the litter.

Your selling price for each puppy should be based on the average price asked in your area for that particular breed.

You should never panic and sell the pups for a much lower price just to insure a home. You do a breed a great injustice to undercut its value. And if you have started with a fine healthy sire and dam, raised the pups well, had them inoculated and wormed, you may be a novice breeder but there is no reason why you cannot charge a top price.

Whether you make money depends on how good your puppies are, how popular the breed, how much competition you have and whether the income exceeds your expenditures.

How early can a puppy be placed in a new home?

There are three factors to be considered: the breed, the home, and the buyer. Eight weeks is the average age for a puppy to go to a new home. By then he is ready for individual attention and companionship and is ready to learn. But you must make certain that his new family knows how to care for a young puppy and that the children in the family will be taught that the puppy cannot be played with steadily but must have rest, gentle treatment, and thoughtful care.

When the family takes the puppy, give them careful instructions on his care and training and offer to be available for advice. Your future success will depend a great deal on how well each puppy fits into his new home and the enthusiasm of his owners.

Can I safely bathe my eight-week-old puppies before they go to their new owners? If so, how?

For the very small, fragile toy breeds or during extremely cold weather you should use one of the many so-called dry shampoos that are sprayed on with an aerosol can, rubbed in and rubbed dry. These do a good job, but for the sturdier breeds you can bathe them in water if you don't let them become chilled.

About six hours or so before the puppy is to leave, fill a basin with warm—not hot—water in a warm room. Have a good supply of towels and use a mild puppy shampoo. Put the pup in the basin and support him with one hand under his chest. Drizzle some shampoo on his head, taking care not to get it in his eyes or ears, and rub it in well over his entire body. He may find this very distressing, but talk to him and make the whole process as swift and pleasant as possible. While you are rubbing in the soap, let the water drain out and refill with clean lukewarm rinse water. Rinse very thoroughly, for soap must not be left in his coat. Then lift him out, wrap him well in a towel and rub him dry. Take time to sit down and snuggle him in a second dry towel and keep rubbing him until no dampness remains. Don't be worried if he shivers violently: this is a reaction to his strange new experience. Finally put him on a blanket in a warm place, brush him well and let him go to sleep. He should not go outdoors for two or three hours.

When should a collar first be put on a puppy?
When he's six to eight weeks old. The idea is to start early and get him used to it. It should be not too snug and not too loose. Be sure there are no sharp points inside to hurt his neck. Buy an inexpensive one as he will outgrow it quickly.

When does a dog's coat change from a puppy coat to an adult coat?
You may see the change starting when he's only three to four months old, and by ten months or a year it is completed. Some dogs take as much as two years to change their coats.

How often are eight-week-old puppies fed?
Three times a day is sufficient for a husky, thriving pup. If a pup is puny or delicate, feed him four times a day.

When do pups change from puppy food to regular dog food?
At five months, but make the change very gradual. Sudden changes in diet can bring on loose stools.

How often should I feed a five-month-old pup?
Twice a day—morning and night. This schedule may be continued for the rest of his life, or you can switch to one meal every morning when he reaches one year.

12
Legal Problems

How can I judge whether a commercial kennel provides proper accommodation?

Commercial kennels in most states are governed by laws set by the state government. In Connecticut, for example, the following must be provided:

The facilities must be sound and in good condition.

Kennel floors and rest boards must be non-toxic and easily cleaned.

Inside and outside runs must be provided and shall be no less than 36 inches wide for a dog weighing up to 45 pounds; 48 inches for a dog weighing over 45 pounds.

Inside pens must have an area of 5 square feet for dogs up to 25 pounds; 9 square feet for dogs between 25 and 45 pounds; 16 square feet for dogs over 45 pounds.

Sunlight must be shaded during hot seasons.

Fresh air must be provided at all times and heat maintained at a reasonable level.

Debris must be removed from pens and runs daily and all areas must be washed down with disinfectants and hot water daily.

Clean fresh water and wholesome food must be provided; and containers must be kept clean and sanitary.

Lighting must be provided for a minimum of eight hours a day.

All dogs must have access to shelter which offers protection from inclement weather.

Ill dogs must be provided care and segregation from other dogs.

No two puppy litters may be housed together.

The dogs must appear eager and well fed without being fat. Eyes should be clear; coats, clean and healthy.

How can I judge whether a pet shop is well run or not?

A good pet shop conforms to state regulations governing kennels:

Enclosures must be carefully maintained so that the animals can remain dry and clean.

The dogs must be protected from direct rays of the sun.

Bedding, debris and excreta must be removed daily and must be sanitized weekly.

Adequate ventilation must be provided and the area must be sufficiently heated. The temperature in the area where puppies are kept must not fall below 50 degrees.

Heat, food and water must be provided at all times.

Any animal appearing unhealthy must be removed and taken to a veterinarian.

Enclosures must give sufficient space for the dogs to stand, move around or lie down comfortably. Wire or mesh floors that permit the feet to slip through are prohibited. Minimum requirements for dogs over three months are: for those weighing 5 to 15 pounds, 5 square feet; for those over 15 pounds, 9 square feet.

Are there zoning laws that prohibit the raising of dogs in residential areas?

Generally there are no restrictions against raising an occasional litter of dogs in a residential zone. But operation of a large kennel is another matter. You should check the zoning code in your own community.

Even if I don't breed dogs, is there any restriction against kenneling a number of dogs in a residential zone?

In some communities there is. Check your zoning code just in case: you don't want to go to the expense of building a kennel with runs only to have your neighbors take you before the zoning authorities or into court because you are in violation of the law.

What are leash laws?
They stipulate that all dogs must be confined to the owner's premises when by themselves. If they are taken off the property, they must be on a leash or in an automobile or truck. They are permitted to run loose off the property only when used for hunting, and in that case they must be under the control of a person.

The strictest leash law in the country is Ohio's. It states:

"It shall be unlawful for the owner, keeper or harborer of any female dog to permit such a dog to go beyond the premises of such owner or keeper at any time such a dog is in heat, unless such dog is properly in leash.

"The owner or keeper of *every* dog [the italics are mine] shall at all times keep such dog either confined upon the premises of the owner or firmly secured by means of a collar and chain or other device so that it cannot stray beyond the premises of the owner or keeper, or it shall be kept under reasonable control of some person, except when lawfully engaged in hunting, accompanied by an owner or handler."

Is there any law requiring that a bitch in heat be kept confined to the property of her owner?
Leash laws apply to bitches in heat as well as to all other dogs. Some communities may have laws applying specifically to bitches in heat.

At what age must dogs be licensed?
In Omaha, every dog must be licensed as soon as he is weaned. Salt Lake City pinpoints licensing age at two months. Other towns or states require licensing at three, four or six months. But generally you don't have to get a license until the dog is a year old.

Check the point yourself; don't make assumptions. What's true in one place isn't necessarily true in another.

> *If a dog that is considered dangerous or vicious but that has never bitten anyone bites a person, is he pardoned on the ground that "every dog is entitled to one bite"?*

No. There is a U.S. court ruling that "the dog is entitled to his first bite, provided he conceals his intention and makes no manifestation of his purpose in such a manner as to impart notice to his owner or keeper, but if the dog's vicious propensities be shown, or his inclinations to want to bite be manifested, then he is not permitted to carry out his designs before being recognized as a dangerous, vicious or ferocious animal."

> *If a dog bites a person who is teasing or hurting him, is he held guilty?*

Probably not, especially if he has never bitten anyone before.

> *How many bites does the law allow a dog?*

This varies from town to town. In some places, if he bites just one person, he is hauled off by the police and destroyed, even though not rabid. Elsewhere he's allowed several bites.

Whatever the law, a dog that bites must be reported to the health department and incarcerated until he is known not to be rabid.

> *Is the owner liable for damages if his dog bites a person on the owner's property?*

If the dog bites someone who has been invited to come onto the property or if the person is lawfully on that property to deliver mail, etc., the owner is liable. However, the owner is not liable if the dog was needlessly provoked into an attack or if there is a sign posted on the property clearly stating "Beware of the Dog."

> *When a person is bitten by a dog, shouldn't the owner of the dog pay all the expenses of the treatment?*

The owner of the dog is legally responsible for all expenses incurred. He may also be fined if there is a leash law in the area and the dog was running loose.

How does a person protect himself against a vicious dog?

He shouldn't make the initial mistake of approaching or trying to pet a dog he doesn't know. If he's minding his own business, the dog will probably mind his.

If a dog does attack, a strong person's best defense is to wrap his left hand and forearm in a coat and let the dog bite that. Meanwhile, he can choke or stab the dog with his right hand.

If a weak person is attacked, he should stand still with his hands at his sides, and speak quietly. If the dog actually attacks, he should cross his arms over his face. If the dog leaps at his face, he should drop to the ground, on his stomach, and protect his head with his arms.

Is the owner liable if his dog injures or kills another dog?

If the owner knows his dog is vicious and has not taken precautions to keep the animal chained or penned, he is definitely liable for any injuries caused by such a dog. However, if the dog is not known to be vicious, or if there were no witnesses to say how or why the attack occurred, the owner may not be judged liable.

Is a special insurance policy required to protect a dog's owner against paying damages if the dog bites a person or does a lot of damage to someone else's property?

The owner is protected against such eventualities by his home owner's policy or ordinary liability policy.

Can you cure a dog of killing livestock?

Once he's tasted the blood of a sheep or other animal, he's usually hooked and the only thing you can do is to keep him tied up. But you can probably cure him of killing chickens and other birds if you wire the dead bird tight to his collar, under his chin, where he can't chew it. Of course he will claw at it but that will just make him sick of dead poultry. Leave the bird tied to the dog until the stench is more than you can stand. By that time, the dog won't be able to stand it either.

Can a dog be destroyed because he kills livestock?
Yes, if the livestock is properly fenced in. If the livestock is wandering loose, the dog probably would be pardoned.

Can a dog that kills poultry also be killed?
Yes. But whereas he might be destroyed for killing only a single sheep or pig, he probably would have to kill a lot of ducks or chickens before he was ordered to meet the same end.

Is there a law against a dog running deer?
He won't get into too much, if any, trouble if he kills rabbits, woodchucks or other small game; but running deer is verboten and he can be killed for it.

Has anyone a right to kill a dog that wanders onto his property?
Only if the dog is attacking someone or killing livestock. And even then, some states require that the dog be destroyed by a dog warden or other peace officer, not by the property owner.

Is there any legal reason why a dog shouldn't bark or growl at people going by his house on the road?
None if he stays within the confines of his property; but if he ventures out on the road and annoys people going by, he may be violating your state or town laws. The thinking behind this is that roads are made for people, not for dogs.

Can a motorist be held liable for injuring or killing a dog on the highway?
In general, yes, but you will have to prove that the motorist was negligent. If he was speeding, operating a car with defective brakes or headlights, or driving without using proper control, you may be able to hold him liable.

In many states the law requires that a motorist who hits a dog must stop and give aid to him. This doesn't mean, however, that he is necessarily at fault.

Is excessive barking by dogs a punishable offense?
It is in some states. The owner can be fined; and if he doesn't succeed in quieting the dog, he can expect a stiffer penalty.

Are there laws about dognapping?
Absolutely. In addition to state laws, there's a federal law stipulating that dogs cannot be sold for research purposes (the reason most dogs are stolen) except by licensed dealers.

13
Dog Shows

What is the purpose of dog shows?
The basic purpose is to show the very best of each breed and to educate the public to the fine points of each breed. It also affords breeders an opportunity to win the title of "Champion" for their dogs and thus to command a higher price for the dog's puppies or stud fees.

Exactly what is a dog show?
A dog show offers an opportunity to see the majority of breeds. If the show is a benched show, you will have the opportunity to talk to the breeders and inspect the different breeds at close hand; at any show you will see breeds you have never known and will be able to judge their behavior, looks, and personality.

Is an obedience trial a kind of dog show?
Yes. You see certain breeds put through their paces in very definitive, demanding classes of obedience. You do not see a wide variety of breeds. (See Chapter 8 for a further description of obedience trials.)

Should I enter my dog in dog shows?
If you have a purebred dog who is a fine example of his breed, you may enjoy showing him in dog shows. Just as in any competition it will take time, effort, training and some expense, but it is very rewarding to win.

At a dog show owners get a chance to talk dogs, compare dogs, learn more about dogs. This is a young Great Dane.

What are the essential differences between dog shows? You must follow dog shows for some time before you can unravel the differences between them. Most people find them very confusing.

To begin with, dog shows, like swimming meets, are not the exclusive property of any group or organization. If you and some of your friends want to hold one, you can. But in the extremely insular world of dog owners, the American Kennel Club is the kingpin organization; and all the best-known dog shows held in this country have its approval and are run according to its rules and regulations.

In its booklet, *Rules Applying to Registration and Dog Shows,* the AKC describes four basic types of approved shows:

        Restricted-entry shows
        Limited-entry shows
        Specialty shows
        Sanctioned matches

These are discussed in questions following.

Other differences between AKC shows are denoted by specific words which are used either by the AKC or by dog-show-oriented people in casual conversation. For example, a "member show" is one held by a club or association which is a member of the AKC, whereas a "licensed show" is held by a club or association which is not a member of the AKC but which has been licensed by the AKC to hold the show.

A "point show" is any AKC-approved show in which a dog can win points toward becoming a champion.

A "benched show" is one in which the entries are displayed in individual stalls on benches. Each breed is grouped, and spectators can wander up and down the aisles between benches to observe the entrants at close hand. Owners and/or breeders are on hand to discuss the breeds they are showing.

The opposite of a benched show is an unbenched show.

An "all-breed" show is open to most (but not necessarily all) breeds; a "specialty show" is restricted to a single breed.

An "examined show" is one which a dog can enter only after he has been examined by one of the show's veterinarians. Such examinations are not required for most shows.

Are there other differences between dog shows?

Many. True, most of them are relatively minor. But having entered your dog in one show, you can't just assume that all other shows will be exactly like the first. To avoid surprises—perhaps unpleasant surprises—you should read the premium list for each show with utmost care (see page 212).

What is a restricted-entry show?

It is an AKC member or licensed show in which entries are restricted to specified dogs. In its booklet, *Rules Applying to Registration and Dog Shows*, the AKC describes two basic types of restricted-entry shows. In the first, entries are restricted to "puppies that are eligible for entry in the regular puppy class and dogs that have placed first, second or third in a regular class at a show at which championship points were awarded."

In the second, entries are restricted to "dogs that are champions on the records of the American Kennel Club and dogs that have been credited with one or more championship points."

Dogs entered in restricted-entry shows can win points toward their championship.

How does a limited-entry show differ from a restricted-entry show?

The total number of entries is limited but there may or may not be any restrictions on the kinds of dogs that are entered. Championship points may be awarded.

What is a specialty dog show?

A show run by a breed club formed for the improvement of a particular breed. Championship points may be awarded.

At an "American-bred specialty show" entries are restricted to dogs that were whelped in the United States.

Irish setters lined up for judging at a small show.

What is an AKC-sanctioned match?
This is an informal meeting sponsored by breed clubs or associations which may or may not be members of the AKC. It is run like a formal dog show according to AKC rules and regulations, and the judges are registered with the AKC. But no points are given dogs toward their championship.

Sanctioned matches are excellent training for new dog owners and their dogs who want to learn about show procedure.

Which are more common—benched or unbenched shows?
Most dog shows used to be benched, but today there is only a handful. Dog owners just do not want to keep their dogs confined on benches for the entire duration of the show.

What is meant by the premium list?
The premium list is the schedule for a dog show. It contains all show dates, names of all committee members, judges, veterinarians, classes, prizes, rules and regulations.

How do you enter a dog in an AKC dog show?
The list of scheduled dog shows at which championship points are awarded is published monthly in *Dog World, Popular Dogs,* and *Pure-Bred Dogs.* The list will give you the date and location of each show and the name of the superintendent. Write to him, and ask for the premium list and the entry blank. Fill out the blank carefully, enclose your entry fee and mail it back before the closing date. A week before the show, you will receive your dog's number, entry blank and the time schedule for the judging of each class.

To enter a dog in an AKC-sanctioned match, or match show as it is sometimes called, you must only fill out a form at the entrance just before the match begins.

Can any dog be entered in the Westminster Dog Show that is purebred and registered with the AKC?
No. A dog must have already won at least one point in a licensed AKC point show.

DOG SHOWS / 213

Saint Bernard waiting to be shown wears a bib to protect his handsome front.

Rules are set each year by the Westminster Kennel Club and are subject to change.

Do dog shows charge an entry fee?
At formal dog shows a fee is charged for each dog entered; and if a dog is entered in more than one competition, a fee is required for each entry. The amount of the fee varies with the size and importance of the show.

What's the earliest age at which a dog may be shown?
Six months.

What classes are shown in official AKC dog shows?
There are six regular classes:
 1. Puppy Class for dogs from six months to twelve months of age.
 2. Novice Class for dogs six months or over that have not won any points toward their championship, any first prizes in

the Bred-by-Exhibitor, American-Bred or Open Classes, or more than two first prizes in the Novice Class.

3. Bred-by-Exhibitor Class for dogs six months of age or over that are whelped in the U.S. or Canada, shown and handled by the owner-breeder or a member of the owner-breeder's family.

4. American-Bred Class for all dogs (except champions) six months or over that were bred and whelped in the U.S.

5. Open Class for any dog six months or over.

6. Winners' Class open only to undefeated dogs. (This class is omitted at sanctioned matches.)

All classes may be divided by sex.

What are the eligibility requirements a dog must meet to enter a dog show?

The AKC devotes more than five pages of small type to this subject, so this can be only a brief summary:

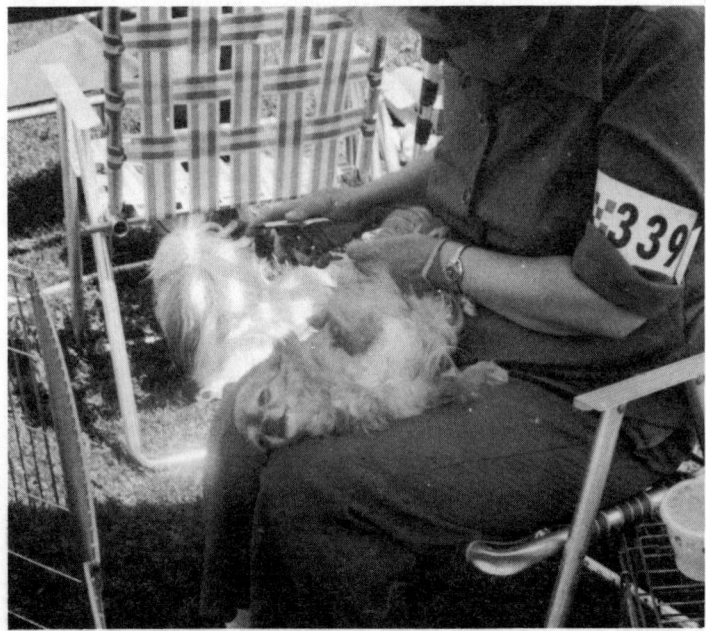

A Pomeranian gets his nails clipped before being shown.

1. If whelped in the U.S., the dog must be registered with the AKC. If whelped elsewhere, it must be registered in its country of birth with an organization approved by the AKC.

2. The dog must not be blind, deaf, castrated or spayed. A male must have two normal testicles.

3. The dog cannot be lame.

4. His color must be natural.

5. If his ears have been cropped, he cannot be shown in states with laws that prohibit cropping. On the other hand, dogs with docked tails and dewclaws removed can be shown anywhere.

6. The dog must be free of all communicable diseases and must not have been exposed to such diseases within the preceding thirty days.

What are the groups into which dogs are divided for show purposes?

Group 1	Sporting Dogs
Group 2	Hounds
Group 3	Working Dogs
Group 4	Terriers
Group 5	Toys
Group 6	Non-Sporting Dogs

For the breeds in each group, see pages 29–31.

Are dogs in the AKC's Miscellaneous Class allowed to compete in shows?

Yes, but only among themselves. In other words, they are not eligible to become Best in Show.

Not all shows have a Miscellaneous Class.

What is the Brace Class in dog shows?

The class in which two perfectly matched dogs of the same breed are shown together.

What is a team of dogs?

A foursome of the same breed. The more closely the dogs are matched, the better the team.

Teams are entered in a separate class at dog shows. But not every show offers a Team Class or a Brace Class.

Are there special classes for children to show their dogs at AKC shows?
At some shows and also at some obedience trials. There is no minimum age limit for the children; the maximum is eighteen.

Should I have a professional handler show my dog?
A dog will usually show to better advantage when handled by a professional. He is less inclined to play and more inclined to follow orders. However, if the owner handles his own dog with a firm, no-nonsense attitude and has learned proper show ring procedure, he has an equal chance to produce a winner.

What does a dog show judge look for when he goes over each dog?
Each breed has an official standard that gives in great detail the correct conformation, gait, coat, etc., for a perfect specimen. The judge weighs each dog against this. He also looks for all the musculature and structure under the skin that a casual observer cannot see. The gait is checked carefully and even the teeth and bite are examined.

A good judge is always looking for a completely perfect dog.

How is Best in Show chosen?
Simply by elimination. First a dog must be judged best in his own breed. Then he is chosen Best in Group (Sporting, Hound, Working, Terrier, Toy or Non-Sporting). Finally, the six group winners compete for Best in Show.

How does a dog become a champion?
Under AKC rules he must win 15 points during his lifetime. Of these 15 points, at least three must be won at a major show under one judge and another three must be won at a second major show under another judge. At least one of the remaining nine points must be awarded under a third judge.

The number of points which can be awarded at a show depends on the number of eligible dogs competing in the breed class at that show. The number of points is based also on a schedule of points established by the AKC's board of directors. This schedule changes from year to year, depending on how many dogs are registered in each breed. The most points any dog can win in a show are five.

Points are awarded only to winners of breed classes. Additional points are not given to Best of Breeds that go on in a show to win Best of Group or Best of Show. The only gain from winning Best of Group or Best of Show is the honor.

What is a "Champion of Record"?
A dog that has won enough championship points to be officially recorded as a champion by the AKC. He is thenceforth identified as "Ch. Omar of Khayyam" (or whatever his registered name may be).

The title of champion is awarded to dogs that compete either in shows or obedience trials. In the latter case, his title is Field Champion (Fld. Ch.). A dog that is a champion in both the show ring and obedience trials is called a Dual Champion (Dual Ch.).

A dog that becomes a champion in another country is so identified; for example, English Champion (Eng. Ch.).

How does a person become a dog show judge?
If he's in good standing with the AKC and feels he has the training, experience and knowledge to pass upon a breed or breeds, he applies to the AKC on a form supplied by that organization. If the directors of the AKC then vote in his favor he is issued a license and his name is placed on the AKC's list of eligible judges. Only persons licensed by the AKC are allowed to judge at an AKC member or licensed show.

Can a dog be disqualified from a dog show once he has been accepted for entry?
He can be disqualified on various grounds: for example, if his weight exceeds the standard for his breed; or if he has been

recently exposed to a communicable disease; or if his color has been changed.

What shows and competitions are held by the United Kennel Club?
Bench shows, field trials, night hunts for coonhounds and water races for coonhounds. The rules for these competitions, all of which are licensed by the UKC, are published every January in that organization's publication, *Bloodlines*.

The bench shows are generally similar to those held under the aegis of the AKC, but the dogs must be registered with the UKC and must be judged by people licensed as judges by the UKC. The shows are advertised in *Bloodlines* at least thirty days before they are held. The entry fee per dog is $8.00.

There are three classes:
1. Puppy Class for dogs less than one year old.
2. Junior Class for dogs between one and two years old.
3. Senior Class for all other dogs.

A special Champion Class may also be held. In this, UKC champions and grand champions compete against one another for the title "Champion of Show," but no points are awarded.

How does a dog become a champion under UKC rules?
Dogs may become Bench Show Champions, Field Champions, Nite (Night) Champions and/or Water Race Champions. The title is earned when a dog wins a minimum of 100 points as a result of competition in at least three different shows, or three different field trials, etc. In a bench show, 10 points are awarded a dog that is best in its class. The dog can then go on in the same show to win 15 additional points if he is judged Best of Breed and an additional 10 points if he is Best in Show. In other words, a dog can win as many as 35 points in one show.

Once a dog becomes a champion, he can become a grand champion or national champion, depending on the competitions in which he is entered. For example, a Grand Show Champion is a dog who wins top honors in champion classes in three different shows.

14 Guard Dogs, Hunting Dogs, Seeing Eye Dogs

Isn't a guard dog a lot more dangerous than an ordinary dog?

That depends on his training. For instance, dogs that patrol warehouses, etc., by themselves are usually extremely dangerous because they have been taught to corner anyone they encounter except their handler. I've heard several stories, which I'm sure are true, about guard dogs that have caused warehouse fires to spread. The dogs won't allow even the firemen to enter until their handlers are called.

But a dog that is properly trained to protect a family is usually less dangerous than an untrained dog.

Is it better, then, to have a guard dog trained professionally?

Yes. The experts can do the job faster and better—and without any of the emotion the owner almost surely puts into the work.

They also train *you* to work with the dog. That's just as important as training the dog himself.

Isn't a guard dog a one-man dog and doesn't that negate his value somewhat in the home?

Guard dogs are usually trained to work with one person because a close rapport between dog and handler is essential; so when a dog is brought into a home, he is fully responsive and effective only when his master is present. But if the other members of the family are trained to work with him, and vice versa, this shortcoming can be corrected.

It can't be said too often: The key to a good guard dog is training. He should be trained to work with every member of a family. And each member should be trained to work with him.

What is the best age to train a guard dog?
Between one and two years.

How long does it take to train a guard dog and what does the training consist of?
One of the country's most respected trainers emphasizes that producing a good guard dog is no "pushbutton job." The K-9 Operation for the Baltimore Police Department, for example, takes fourteen weeks to train a dog; but of course the dog is expected to do more jobs than to guard a home. Furthermore, unlike a family dog he must be trained to deal with crowds of people and meet many unusual emergencies.

For a family guard dog, six weeks of *intensive* training under an experienced trainer is about enough. His owner should continue training with him for a couple of months. After that, the dog may require some retraining.

The training program always starts with work in basic and advanced obedience. Then it progresses to attack work.

Can I train my own guard dog?
You probably can, but it's doubtful whether you should unless you've had considerable experience in attack work. But you certainly can give your dog all the obedience training required for a good guard dog; reputable trainers generally feel that, for protection, the average family needs no more than a good obedience-trained dog.

Which breeds make the best guard dogs?
The German shepherd is far and away the favorite, although some trainers prefer Dobermans. Other breeds which are used include Rottweilers, Labradors, Chesapeakes, Dalmatians,

giant schnauzers, German short-haired pointers, and collies. After all, it's the dog—not the breed—that matters.

Whatever the breed, the dog must be sound physically and mentally. Even so, he may not make the grade. Only about one in four does.

Are guard dogs effective?
The overwhelming consensus of those who have had them is that they are. Of course, there are opinions and actual incidents to the contrary. But these are rare.

The effectiveness of guard dogs depends to some extent on how they are used. But in the end it all boils down to the fact that most people are wary of a large dog; and when they see or hear one, they think twice about doing anything which might bring the dog down on them.

Do many private individuals own guard dogs?
There are no statistics on which to base an answer. Obviously some families own guard dogs. But the big dog trainers I have talked to—the men who specialize in training dogs for protection—indicate the number is pretty small. Most guard dogs are used by the police, industry, stores, schools, museums, racetracks, zoos—even churches.

Is a guard dog the same as an attack dog?
The phrase "attack dog" is unpopular in the United States, so trainers or users of such dogs rarely employ it any more. Instead, all dogs trained for protection work are called "guard dogs," and one dog is the same as another, although it's easy enough to point out differences if you want to split hairs.

Are all guard dogs trained to attack?
Most responsible trainers are afraid of putting attack-trained dogs in the hands of some people. As one of them told me, "An ordinary dog will protect its owner instinctively and pretty well. An obedience-trained dog is just that much better. But to put an attack dog in the average person's hands is like giving a kid a loaded pistol."

As this comment suggests, some so-called guard dogs are trained only for obedience, not for attack work.

Of those that actually are trained to attack, some attack only on command; some attack either on command or automatically when their owners are threatened. There are also dogs used in empty factories, warehouses, etc., that are trained to attack anyone who moves.

> *I live in a high-crime-rate area. My own apartment has been robbed several times. Would you advise that I get a guard dog?*

Anyone thinking about owning a guard dog should ask himself a few pointed questions:

Does a guard dog offer the best protection at a reasonable price?

Have my family and I enjoyed other dogs we've owned?

Am I temperamentally equipped to live with a guard dog and handle him?

The last question is the hardest, but in some ways it's the most important because a guard dog is, in the final analysis, a dangerous weapon and you must treat him accordingly. You must know how to use him, be prepared to use him, and not be afraid of him. And of course you must not abuse him. I recently heard of a guard dog that turned neurotic and nasty because his owner bought him not so much for protection as to show off. He made a habit of boasting, "Make a pass at me and see what the dog does."

If you don't know yourself whether you're equipped to live with a guard dog, the trainer you go to can probably answer your question. No responsible trainer will sell or train a dog until he has carefully sized up the person who wants it.

> *How should I go about buying a fully trained guard dog?*

There are three essential steps:

1. Check the trainer out thoroughly to make sure he's been in business a long time and has always turned out good dogs.

2. Demand a full demonstration of the dog he wants to sell.

3. Insist on being trained with the dog until you are completely comfortable with each other.

How can I tell a good from a bad dog trainer?
That's pretty hard; and unfortunately, the demand for guard dogs has grown so in recent years that every Tom, Dick and Harry has set himself up as an expert in the business, whether he has the credentials or not.

Don't put too much stock in the people who advertise in the yellow pages. Make inquiries first of individuals or companies who own guard dogs. City and state police departments are probably your best sources. Ask for the officers in charge of the K-9 department. I've found them very willing to steer you to the best trainers.

What basic obedience must all gun dogs be taught?
To walk at heel, sit and stay.

Which breeds are used for pointing game?
Pointer, setter, Brittany spaniel, German short-haired pointer, weimaraner and wirehaired pointing griffon.

How does a good pointing dog work?
He is attracted by and follows the body scent of the bird. He should not follow foot scent.

What does a hunter mean when he says, "the dog came to a perfect point"?
A "point" is the motionless position of a hunting dog when he has located game. He makes no attempt to seek the game but points the direction for the hunter.

Is a hunting dog always trained to a whistle?
As a rule, because the sound carries farther than your voice. Send him out with two short, sharp blasts; bring him back to you with a prolonged blast. Use a single short blast and a wave of the arm to direct him while he is working the field ahead of you.

A German wirehaired pointer does his job in the field.

I have a six-month-old setter I hope to use for hunting, but on the first day out I found she is terrified by a gunshot. Is there any hope of correcting this fault?

It will take time. Get a simple cap pistol, fire it off now and then at a distance. Fire it off when you put out her dish of food, or when you have just said you would take her for a walk. Do not overdo it; let her associate the sound with something pleasant and usual and she will gradually lose her fear of it.

How is a hunting dog trained?

The long process of training hunting dogs is beyond the scope of this book. Briefly, however, the following steps should be taken:

1. While the dog is still young, let him run and hunt pretty much as he pleases to stimulate his interest and to assure yourself that he has good hunting dog instincts.

2. Get rid of any tendency to gun shyness by taking him out into the field and firing your gun when he is working at

some distance from you. Never fire while he is close to you or unless he is after game.

3. Teach him to respond to your whistled commands.

4. Teach him to hold a point steadily, or "staunchly," not simply to flash-point and then rush on after the game. This takes patience and luck. If you can catch up with him while he is holding a point, pat him proudly and tell him what a fine fellow he is; and hold him steady. Then put your hand on his rump and push him gently toward the game. His natural reaction, instead of rushing forward, is to resist the pressure; and this teaches him to stand firm.

5. Teach him to hold steady when the birds take wing. To do this, tie a long, strong cord to his collar and hold the other end. When the birds are flushed, just as the dog darts after them, command him to "whoa." This may stop him, but probably not. Just before he reaches the end of the cord, call "whoa" again, and brace yourself. When he hits the end of the cord he will be jerked off his feet. After this happens several times, he will learn what "whoa" means.

What is a blinker?
This word is ascribed to a hunting dog that fails to hold his point on finding a bird.

What is a babbler?
A hunting dog that barks when not on the trail of game.

What are spaniels used for in hunting?
The Brittany is a pointer. All others are used to flush birds within gunshot, which is about 30 yards. In other words, they work back and forth immediately ahead of the hunter.

Spaniels are trained much like pointing dogs. The main difference is that when they flush or "spring" game, they should be taught to sit (some are taught to drop flat). The command for this is "hup."

How are dogs taught to retrieve?
Many retrieve naturally; but even they are put through a long

training program so that they will perform quickly and perfectly in the field. The two commands they work to are "fetch" and "give." Start by teaching the dog to fetch, using some small object such as a corncob; progress to a dead game bird; and finally turn him loose on birds in the field.

Important points in the training are to teach the dog to carry the retrieved objects or birds with a "soft mouth," to be watchful so he can mark where a bird falls, and to ferret out birds that come down with his nose.

What is meant by a non-slip retriever?
A perfectly trained dog that stays in the heel position, and although alert to the shooting of game, will not retrieve until a command is given.

What are field trials? Where are they held?
Field trials are competitions between dogs under actual field conditions. They are held in all parts of the country for bird dogs, retrievers and beagles. Dogs are not judged by established rules and to a set scale of points but simply on how well the judges think they perform. Winners in the large stakes are awarded substantial cash prizes.

In all field trials, except water tests for retrievers, dogs work in braces determined by a drawing. In water tests, the dogs work singly.

What kind of a field competition is a night hunt?
This is a three-hour competition held at night for registered coonhounds. No more than three or four hounds with their handlers hunt through woods for raccoons. Dogs are scored on how well they perform. These events, known as "Nite Hunts," are licensed by the UKC and held under that organization's rules.

How many Seeing Eye dogs are now in service?
Roughly 7,000, but not all are produced by the Seeing Eye organization.

Are dogs other than German shepherds used in guiding the blind?
Yes, but they're a fairly small proportion. Next to shepherds, the breeds most used are Labradors and golden retrievers. Boxers, collies, Dobermans and Chesapeakes are also used.

Are only females used for guide work?
No, both males and females. All of them are altered.

What are the essential qualities for a good guide dog?
He must be large (but not a giant breed), strong, healthy, and have a coat that can be cleaned easily. He must, of course, be stable. He must have low body sensitivity in order to shoulder his way through a crowd of people. And he must be intelligent, though in a somewhat unusual way, since he must know when to disobey commands that could lead his master into danger, and he must be able to substitute a safe course of action for one he sees is unsafe.

How long does it take to train a guide dog?
About four months. First he is taught obedience; then how to guide; and finally how to take the safe course of action. Once a dog is trained, he is turned over to a blind person and the two are trained together for about another month.

At what age is a dog trained for guide work?
When he is between about 12 and 30 months of age.

Where can one secure a guide dog?
1. Eye Dog Foundation, Los Angeles, California
2. Guide Dogs for the Blind, Inc., San Rafael, California
3. Guiding Eyes for the Blind, Inc., Yorktown Heights, New York
4. Leader Dogs for the Blind, Rochester, Michigan
5. Pilot Dogs, Inc., Columbus, Ohio
6. Second Sight Guide Dog Foundation, Forest Hills, New York
7. Seeing Eye, Morristown, New Jersey

15 / The Old Dog

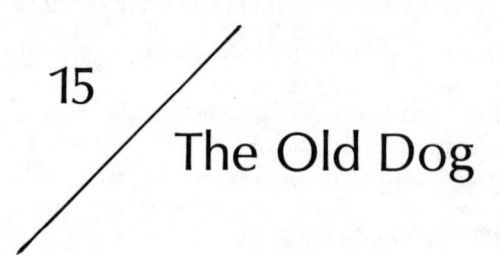

How long does a dog live?
One expert has figured that, counting every single dog that's born, the average life expectancy of dogs is only five years. If you start, say, with an eight-week-old puppy, however, you can expect him to live about twice as long as this.

Breeds with nasal problems tend to die at about nine to ten years of age. Others live to be about twelve to fifteen. A few have even lived to twenty years.

Do dogs turn white as they age?
A great many do. They first turn white around the muzzle, and gradually white hairs appear further back on the head.

Can you insure a dog's life?
Yes. Several companies offer life insurance for animals. The cost is about $12.00 for each $100 valuation. A dog cannot be insured before he's six months old or after he's six years old.

I have a very old dog. Should he continue to eat the same diet he always has or should I make any change in it?
The aging dog will do better if he has two small meals a day rather than one large one. If he has any tooth trouble, give him a softer, more liquid diet. If you prefer, there are special

canned prescription diets that are carefully planned for the older dog. These can be purchased from your veterinarian.

My eight-year-old dog is suddenly terribly thirsty. What is the reason for this?

He may be suffering from nephritis, a common kidney ailment, especially among older dogs. Acute nephritis calls for immediate treatment and a special diet. Avoid too salty foods and any unnecessary exertion. Chronic nephritis may result in uremia and must not be neglected either. The dog will appear listless, lose weight, may vomit, is continually thirsty, and has a generally unhealthy look. See your veterinarian as soon as possible for treatment. A special diet will be ordered. He must not have meat, but needs a diet high in protein, cooked oatmeal, and dairy products. He also needs small amounts of liquid frequently.

My male dog is twelve years old and lately has developed a dribbling problem. Is there anything that will help this?

This is probably a result of aging. The sphincter muscle has weakened and nothing can correct it. Take him out more frequently, put papers near his sleeping area, and do not scold. He knows he is making a mistake; he cannot help it.

When an old dog has frequent constipation, what should be done for him?

Add some roughage to his diet—shredded wheat or bran—and give him two meals daily rather than one large one. A dose of milk of magnesia, a teaspoonful for each ten pounds of body weight, may be helpful. His system is sluggish due to age and less exercise. If the condition persists, take him to the vet.

Our retriever is now nine years old. He seems to be in good health, but is there any special care we should give him?

As your pet ages you are wise to be alert for possible problems.

Have him checked over by your vet once or twice a year. Keep his coat scrupulously clean and free of parasites. See that his diet is nourishing but cut down on the calories. Provide a warm, comfortable bed for him in the winter months and a cool, quiet place in hot, humid weather. Check him for worms regularly. Be sure he is not troubled by constipation.

Take him for walks, but don't expect him to enjoy vigorous exercise; don't be overdemanding. Above all, do not fail to make him know that even if he cannot be as active as he was, he is still your beloved companion.

> *We have a dog we adore who is becoming so feeble we know the time is coming when we will lose him. Would it be wrong to get a new puppy now?*

There is no easy answer. It depends a great deal on the personality of your older dog. If he has always been your special pampered pet and is jealous when you pet a neighbor's dog, he will be totally shattered if you bring home a new pup now.

On the other hand, if he has often romped with other dogs

A new puppy will ease the ache when your beloved old pet is gone.

in the neighborhood and shown no sign of jealousy, he might find the addition of a new pup very pleasant. Don't allow the puppy to tease him, nibble his feet, pull his ears or eat from his dish. Don't lavish affection on the puppy and ignore the old fellow. You must make certain that the older dog knows his importance to the family. If he finds the youngster has not usurped his rightful place, not upset his comfort and peace, he may well enjoy a romp now and then and take pride in showing the youngster around and teaching him.

We have to move to another city and I am concerned for our fourteen-year-old poodle who is totally blind. Can she adjust to a new house and surroundings?
If she has managed her blindness in your present house, she has a good chance of being able to adjust to a new place. Her other senses must be quite perceptive; and with your help she should be all right. For at least the first few weeks keep her confined to a small area, and when she seems secure there, give her a bit more freedom. Always take her outside on a leash and keep her well away from busy sidewalk areas. Other people will expect her to get out of their way and she could risk injury from bikes, running children, etc. Talk to her and make her aware that she is not alone. In a few weeks she will be as independent as she was in your former home.

My old dog is now totally deaf. Will she be able to adjust to this or should we put her to sleep?
There is no easy answer. If her senses of sight and smell are sharp, she can probably overcome the loss of hearing. I would limit her freedom to a small area when she is outdoors and be certain she is well away from busy roads. Keep her in the house as much as possible and she may manage with little problem. If not, you will have to consider putting her to sleep.

What is the meaning of "to put down"?
An old dog with incurable ailments or a malformed puppy is "put down," or put to sleep.

Our dog is having so many old-age problems that cannot be remedied we feel we must put him away. What is done and will it be painful?

It will assuredly be painful to you; but your pet will not suffer. A major dose of Sodium Pentothal will be injected directly into a vein and death is immediate and painless. You may ask permission to stay with him when the injection is administered and you will be convinced that this is the most merciful thing you can do for a beloved pet.

What is usually done with the body when a dog dies?

Usually disposal of the body is left to the animal hospital, where it will be cremated. However, there are an increasing number of pet cemeteries in many states offering every type of service from simple burial to very costly, elaborate funerals. They frequently offer perpetual care at a high cost. If you wish to bury your pet on your property, you will be wise to check the laws in your community.

We have just lost the dog we loved for thirteen years. Would it help to get a new puppy?

If you loved the dog so deeply, you are going to be very miserable—that is obvious. No new gamboling pup is going to take his place, but he will ease the ache. The affection and playfulness of a pup are irresistible; and caring for him and enjoying him will be a comfort. He may never in your eyes be as fine a dog as his predecessor, but in time you will find yourself saying, "Aren't we lucky to have had two dogs that gave us such pleasure."

I well remember when our youngest daughter's golden retriever died. He was the light of her life; and when he suddenly became ill just before she went off to college, she was terribly upset. We didn't tell her when he died (of a rare parasitic disease) a few days later. We just scoured the countryside for a replacement and finally found one we liked. On Parents' Day, about a week later, we took the pup to see her.

Of course, the instant she saw the little fellow she knew her beloved dog was dead. Her eyes overflowed with tears; but she fell on her knees, scooped the pup into her arms and her hurt soon melted away.

SECTION TWO

Breeds

Dogs are listed alphabetically by their official AKC breed names. For example, corgis will be found under Cardigan Welsh Corgi and Pembroke Welsh Corgi.

Affenpinscher

Forefather of the Brussels griffon, the affenpinscher was well known on the European continent in the seventeenth century. Often called the monkey dog, he is recognized by his monkeyish facial expression, bushy eyebrows and striking black eyes. His wire coat leads to the belief that there is some terrier blood in his background.

The affenpinscher is snobbish, smart and very demanding. If not cared for by a stern master, he will try to get away with everything. He can be quite a little tyrant. As with other toy breeds, his health must be watched carefully.

HEIGHT: Male—9–10¼ inches   Female—8–9 inches
WEIGHT: Male—8 pounds   Female—7 pounds
COLOR: Black; tan and black; red; or gray
COAT: Short, dense, wiry, shaggy in parts
Registered with the AKC (toy group)

Afghan Hound

This oddly noble hound with the "monkey face" has changed little since he was immortalized in Egyptian carvings. Remaining purebred for countless years, the Afghan prospered as a pet of the pharaohs and later became established in Afghanistan. There he was highly valued for his easy speed, incredible flying leaps and ability to hunt in mountainous areas. Hunting by sight alone, he is a favorite for going after leopard and gazelle. The rugged winters and torrid summers of Afghanistan have developed in him a fine ability to withstand all kinds of weather.

The Afghan's popularity in the U.S. has risen slowly, but people now not only accept his unusual appearance but also value his noble handsomeness. He is an excellent house dog, does not need great space or exercise, is devoted to his family, and is loved for the happy, affectionate clown he is. Inclined to be quiet, even aloof and reserved with outsiders, he barks rarely and is never bad-tempered. But his stubbornness makes him one of the hardest dogs to train and you can make little headway with him until he is a half-year old.

    HEIGHT: Male—26–28 inches   Female—25–27 inches
    WEIGHT: Male—58–64 pounds   Female—48–52 pounds
    COLOR: All colors and hues
    COAT: Very lush, long and silky
    Registered with the AKC (hound group)

Airedale Terrier

Records of the origin of the Airedale terrier are sketchy prior to 1850, but it is known that he goes back centuries to the old English, or broken-haired, terrier. In the early nineteenth century, he was crossed with the rough-coated otter hound, who had a sharp nose and great ability in water. Often referred to as the "king of the terriers," he has been used in a variety of ways: as game hunter, police dog and war-dispatch bearer.

The Airedale is the largest of the terrier family. He is bold and aggressive but rarely high-strung. A courageous hunter, he is one of the few dogs that will hunt grizzly bears and mountain lions. He also retrieves ducks and is an outstanding ratter. He is easy to train; faithful; has a rather happy-go-lucky personality; and is a good family dog, kind with children. He needs a fair amount of exercise to work off his energy. His wiry coat requires little grooming.

>HEIGHT: Male—23 inches   Female—22 inches
WEIGHT: Male—45–50 pounds Female—40–45 pounds
COLOR: Rich tan with black or grizzle markings
COAT: Wiry, hard, dense, lying straight and close

Registered with the AKC (terrier group) and UKC

Akita

This large, handsome Japanese dog has had his ups and downs, and even today breeders in Japan and the United States cannot agree on how big he should be. Developed as a big-game hunting dog, he was later turned into a pit fighter, was almost starved out of existence during World War II, then was taken up by American servicemen in the occupation forces, and today has won an astonishingly high place (though not officially accepted until 1973) in the breeding totals.

The Akita suggests a heavy-set German shepherd with a massive head. He carries his tail over his back or against a flank. He is alert, courageous and aggressive, but dignified, faithful and loyal.

> HEIGHT: Male—26–28 inches   Female—24–26 inches
> WEIGHT: Male—75–85 pounds   Female—60–70 pounds
> COLOR: Any color; brindle; or white with big color patches
> COAT: Straight, hard outercoat; soft, dense undercoat

Registered with the AKC (working group)

Alaskan Malamute

The Alaskan malamute was named for the Eskimo tribe, called Mahlemuts, that settled in upper western Alaska. He is one of the oldest Arctic sled dogs. The Mahlemuts were skilled hunters and fishermen and they learned early that it was necessary for their dogs to pull their sleds when they traveled. Never without the dogs, they relied on their power and endurance. When sled racing became a popular sport in the early part of this century, the Alaskan malamutes achieved a fine racing record.

The malamute is courageous, strong and loyal. He is devoted to his master and usually friendly with others, and can be quite playful with people but a tough, aggressive fighter with other dogs. Because he grew up in the wilds, he needs careful and complete training by a firm master. He is basically a sled dog and a protector of his family.

HEIGHT: Male—23–25 inches   Female—20–23 inches
WEIGHT: Male—75–85 pounds   Female—50–75 pounds
COLOR: Wolf-gray or black and white
COAT: Thick, coarse, never soft, and long

Registered with the AKC (working group) and UKC

American Eskimo

If you're old enough, you remember the thick-coated, white dog called the spitz. The American Eskimo is the same animal. Descended from the larger Alaskan Eskimo dog and very much larger Greenland Eskimo, he came to the U.S. by way of Germany many years ago and was subsequently recognized by the UKC.

Because the American Eskimo has been bred down to a small dog, he can no longer herd reindeer and pull sleds, but he's a good hunter of small game, a satisfactory watchdog and a fine pet. He thrives in cold weather and lives to a considerable age. For show purposes only, the breed is divided into two classes—miniature and standard.

HEIGHT: Male—13–20 inches   Female—12–18 inches
WEIGHT: Male—12–30 pounds   Female—10–25 pounds
COLOR: Pure white preferred; white with cream permissible
COAT: Thick, short, soft undercoat with long,

straight, harsh hair growing through to form outer coat
Registered with the UKC

American Foxhound

In the diary of one of de Soto's men there is mention of the foxhound, used then to hunt Indians rather than fox and hares. Later, in 1650, a pack of hounds were brought to America, and it became the stock from which many of this widespread breed is descended. The foxhound has been, in fact, so popular with hunters across the country for such a long time that it is hardly surprising that numerous varietal offshoots have been produced. By determined efforts, however, fanciers have succeeded in developing this more or less standard type.

Here is a versatile dog as excellent in the home as in the field. Easily trained to trail any ground game, he excels in courage, stamina and speed. He is also affectionate and stable.

    HEIGHT: Male—22–25 inches   Female—21–24 inches
    WEIGHT: Male—65–70 pounds   Female—60–65 pounds
    COLOR: Any hound color but usually black, tan and white
    COAT: Close, hard

Registered with the AKC (hound group)

AMERICAN STAFFORDSHIRE TERRIER or AMERICAN (PIT) BULLTERRIER

This terrier has experienced a number of name changes. In the 1800's he was called the bull-and-terrier dog, half-and-half, pit bullterrier, American bullterrier and Yankee terrier. Today he is known by the AKC as the American Staffordshire terrier; by the UKC as the American (pit) bullterrier. He is the result of a cross between the English bulldog (selected for tenacity) and the old English terrier (selected for agility).

The fact that the Staffordshire or bullterrier is a fighter cannot be concealed. When he has tasted blood, he'll fight an enemy to the death; but when loved and patiently trained, he is docile and obedient. He is a great guardian. If sold to another person, he quickly accepts the new master. This is a dog for one who knows the breed and is willing to spend plenty of time teaching him.

HEIGHT: Male—18–19 inches   Female—17–18 inches
WEIGHT: Male—40–50 pounds   Female—35–45 pounds
COLOR: Any color either solid or patched; avoid white or about eighty percent white
COAT: Close, short, stiff to the touch, glossy

Registered with the AKC (terrier group) and UKC

American Water Spaniel

The American water spaniel developed in the Middle West but his exact origin is unknown. From the appearance of his solid liver or dark chocolate coloring, his closely curled coat and his sturdily constructed body, we are led to believe his ancestors were the Irish water spaniel and curly-coated retriever.

The American water spaniel is a top-notch retriever. He works well on any terrain and is especially good in water, where his tail works as a rudder. He springs for his game. Alert and stable, active and muscular, he does well with rabbit, quail, pheasant, grouse and duck. He is sensitive and thrives on praise, but sometimes sulks when reprimanded. If you're unkind, he doesn't forget. He is good with children and fits well into family life.

HEIGHT: Male—16½–18 inches Female—15–17 inches
WEIGHT: Male—28–45 pounds Female—25–40 pounds

COLOR: Rich liver or dark chocolate
COAT: Closely curled and dense
Registered with the AKC (sporting group) and UKC

ANATOLIAN SHEPHERD DOG

Also called Turkish guard dogs, this ancient breed from Asia Minor was introduced to the U.S. in 1968. The dogs were utilized for centuries as war dogs and hunting dogs, and were valued for their wolf-fighting ability as they guarded flocks in every extreme of weather. They are now used as guard and working dogs. They show similarities to the Great Pyrenees, mastiff and kuvasz, but are leaner and tougher, and more nimble and alert.

There are now upwards of thirty-five Anatolian shepherds in this country and their owners have found them quick to learn, reliable with children, possessive toward the home and property, sensitive to any reproof, and grateful for affection. But any person considering an Anatolian should know this is not a gentle, friendly neighborhood dog. He must be kept in a fenced yard.

HEIGHT: Male—28–30 inches   Female—26–28 inches
WEIGHT: Male—100–150 pounds   Female—90–130 pounds
COLOR: Buff or white; often with black ears and muzzle
COAT: Straight, harsh, thick

Australian Cattle Dog

The Australian, or blue, cattle dog is a worker who has been a mainstay of Australian ranchers for many years. He is also used as a guardian of suburban properties. Whether going after steers or humans, he has the unique habit of always attacking the heels.

Descended from the collie, kelpie and wild dingo, he is sharp and cunning, free-moving and lithe. His endurance is so great that he can work stock in open ranges that would normally wear out other breeds.

- HEIGHT: Male—17–19 inches Female—16–18 inches
- WEIGHT: Male—40–50 pounds Female—35–45 pounds
- COLOR: Blue-mottled with or without black and/or tan markings; or red-speckled with dark red markings on head
- COAT: Straight, moderately short, medium harsh

Accepted in AKC Miscellaneous Class

Australian Kelpie

Known only since about 1870, the kelpie has proved to be an invaluable sheepherder down under. Ranchers accustomed to top trained sheepdogs are impressed by his speed and enthusiasm and his instantaneous response to hand signals and whistles even from a distance.

Similar to the Border collie and the dingo, from whom he is probably descended, the kelpie is a handsome foxlike dog, vigorous and agile, with a bright, alert expression.

HEIGHT: Male—18–20 inches   Female—17–19 inches
WEIGHT: Male—25–30 pounds   Female—20–25 pounds
COLOR: Black; black and tan; red; red and tan; fawn; deep brown or bluish-gray
COAT: Crisp, thick, short, straight

Accepted in AKC Miscellaneous Class

Australian Shepherd

Stemming from Australian and New Zealand stockdogs, the Australian shepherd accompanied his sheepherding owners to California in the mid-1800's. He has been working the range —driving and penning farm animals—ever since. Sturdy and fairly low to the ground, he is so fast that if a cow or horse lashes out at him with a hoof, it almost invariably kicks where the dog *was*.

Generally a silent worker, the sturdy, medium-sized Aussie speaks when necessary in a half-bark, half-howl. His tail is bobbed; his eyes, frequently blue. As a family dog, he is loyal, warm, alert and playful. Dogs under 21 inches are preferred for work, since they present a smaller target for animal hooves.

HEIGHT: Male—18–23 inches   Female—17–21 inches
WEIGHT: Male—30–45 pounds   Female—27–40 pounds
COLOR: Merle, black or red—solid or with tan markings
COAT: Medium-long, harsh, weather-resistant

Australian Terrier

The Australian terrier is rather a newcomer, first exhibited in Australia in 1885. He comes from a cross of the scottie and the broken-haired, or rough-coated, terrier who resembled the scottie. Other breeds contributing to his makeup were the cairn, Dandie Dinmont, Irish terrier and Yorkshire. The Australian terrier quickly gained popularity as a hunter in the bushland, a guard of mines and a tender of sheep.

Although one of the smallest working terriers, the Australian is among the toughest and most courageous. He is full of personality, rarely tires, and can withstand any climate. He is affectionate and not too demanding, and is suitable for a single person or couple who enjoy a little, high-spirited companion.

HEIGHT: Male—10 inches   Female—9–10 inches
WEIGHT: Male—13–14 pounds   Female—12–13 pounds
COLOR: Blue-black or silver-black with tan markings on head and legs
COAT: Straight and harsh, about 2½ inches long over entire body

Registered with the AKC (terrier group)

Basenji

This very ancient breed from Egypt reached the U.S. by way of England. Many of the first specimens were lost to distemper, but finally in 1941 a pair brought to this country was bred and a litter survived. Their influence was strong, for in just five years the Basenji Club was formed and in the following year the breed was accepted by the AKC.

This quick popularity is due to several things: the basenji is intelligent; keeps himself beautifully clean, washing all over like a cat; and doesn't bark but has a sort of yodel when he's happy. He is adaptable to either activity or peaceful relaxation. But he has a sizable stubborn streak and a reputation for meanness.

HEIGHT: Male—17 inches   Female—16 inches
WEIGHT: Male—24 pounds   Female—22 pounds
COLOR: Black and tan, deep red, or pure black. White marks on chest, feet and tip of tail
COAT: Very fine and silky

Registered with the AKC (hound group)

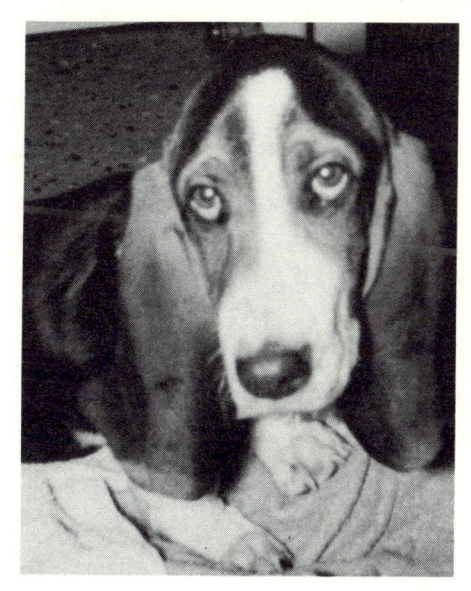

Basset Hound

The low-slung, laughable-looking basset—an offshoot of the French bloodhound and Saint Hubert hound—was known for centuries in France and Belgium, where he was bred for the royal hunts. His excellent scenting ability and extremely short legs made him invaluable for hunting pheasants, rabbits and foxes in dense undergrowth.

A quiet, gentle dog, the basset can be a fine and loyal family pet if well trained and kindly raised. There are many, however, who have found the basset hard to housebreak; but when that problem is finally conquered, they have a most satisfactory companion.

HEIGHT: Male—14–15 inches Female—12–14 inches
WEIGHT: Male—35–45 pounds Female—25–35 pounds
COLOR: Any hound color—tan, black and white in any combination
COAT: Firm, dense, short

Registered with the AKC (hound group) and UKC

Beagle

Although the origin of the beagle is uncertain, there is no doubt that it is one of the oldest breeds. In the United States, the National Beagle Club was formed in 1888 and interest in field trials has steadily increased since then. But quite aside from his inherent talent for hunting, the beagle has earned great popularity as a family pet.

He requires little but companionship and affection. His coat needs no grooming, and he can adapt to almost any environment, but tends to become overweight if not exercised. He is affectionate, excellent with children and good-natured to a fault. On the other hand, he's very stubborn and if you try too much force, he may turn mean and aggressive. Careful, patient training is necessary to prevent this eventuality. For show purposes there are two classes based on height.

HEIGHT: Male and female—13–15 inches in one class; under 13 inches in second class

WEIGHT: Male and female—13–15-inch class: 30 pounds under-13-inch class: 18 pounds

COLOR: Any hound color, black and white or tan in any combination
COAT: Close, firm
Registered with the AKC (hound group)

Bearded Collie

Gainsborough and Reynolds portraits of the Duke and Duchess of Buccleigh provide our earliest glimpse of the bearded collie. But it was not royalty or city dog fanciers who made the breed what it is. Credit for that goes to the shepherds and drovers of southern Scotland who bred and valued the dog for his working ability, adeptness in rough country and adaptability to a cold, wet climate.

The bearded collie resembles, not the ever popular standard collie, but the komondor and puli and other shaggy-haired continentals with whom he shares ancestry. His free and surprisingly lithe movement is in keeping with his alert, lively and confident expression.

> HEIGHT: Male—21–22 inches   Female—20–21 inches
> WEIGHT: Male—40–50 pounds   Female—35–45 pounds
> COLOR: Shades of gray, brown or black with or without white markings
> COAT: Topcoat long, harsh and flat; undercoat soft and furry
> Accepted in AKC Miscellaneous Class

Bedlington Terrier

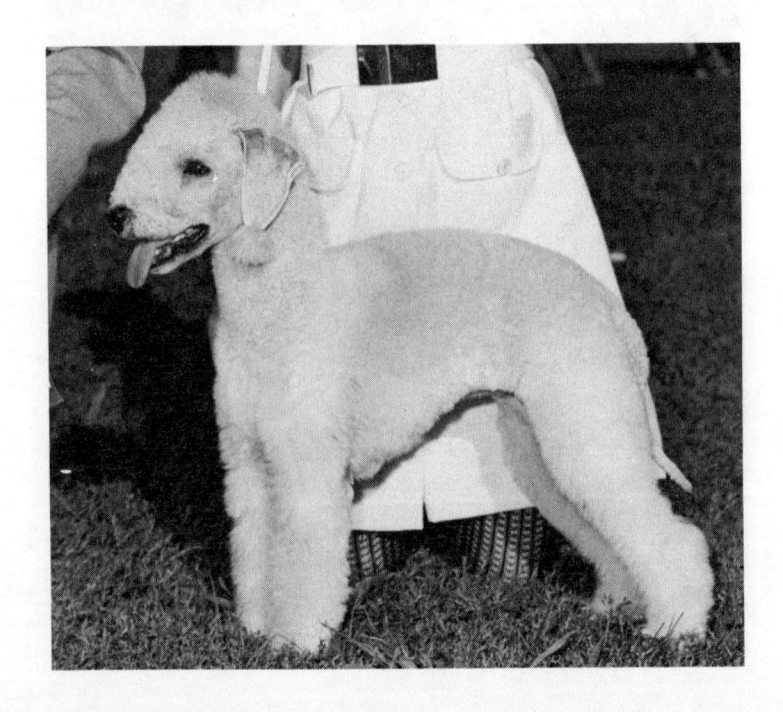

The Bedlington terrier received his name from the mining district of Bedlingshire in Northumberland, England. His ancestors were probably the old Border sleuthhound and the rough-coated terrier, and he is undoubtedly related to the Dandie Dinmont because, unlike other terriers, both have long ears and topknots. He won recognition in his homeland for his ability to catch vermin or draw out a badger.

The lamblike appearance of the Bedlington is misleading. He is quarrelsome and jealous of other household pets, with whom he will gladly fight. However, he is fond of his master, polite and hardy. He adapts to any weather. Known for his endurance, he can gallop at high speed and needs room to exercise.

HEIGHT: Male—18 inches   Female—15 inches
WEIGHT: Male—23–24 pounds Female—22–23 pounds
COLOR: Blue; blue and tan; liver; liver and tan; sandy or sandy and tan
COAT: A mixture of hard and soft hairs standing out from the body

Registered with the AKC (terrier group)

Belgian Malinois

The Belgian Malinois was not accepted for registration by the AKC until 1959, but he was first identified as a distinct strain of the old Groenendael breed just before the turn of the century. He is identical in conformation and behavior to the Belgian sheepdog and Belgian Tervuren, his first cousins. Chief differences: his dense coat is short, particularly on the head and ears, and brown with a black overlay.

    HEIGHT: Male—24–26 inches   Female—22–24 inches
    WEIGHT: Male—55–60 pounds   Female—50–55 pounds
    COLOR: Rich fawn to mahogany with black overlay
    COAT: Short, straight, dense
    Registered with the AKC (working group)

Belgian Sheepdog

After years of widespread, indiscriminate breeding, early in the twentieth century the Belgian sheepdog we know today was finally standardized. Although his coat was fixed as black and long-haired (instead of several colors and textures), the dog remained the strong, sturdy, alert animal he had always been through years of sheepherding on Belgian farms.

Trained for special police and messenger work in World War I, this handsome, well-muscled, alert dog was valued for his fearless courage; but many are known for their obvious terror of small children. It is essential that he have an owner who will give careful, experienced training, for he can be a fierce fighter. He adapts to any climate.

HEIGHT: Male—24–26 inches Female—22–24 inches
WEIGHT: Male—55–60 pounds Female—50–55 pounds
COLOR: Black
COAT: Slightly crisp, long, straight guard hairs; very dense undercoat

Registered with the AKC (working group)

Belgian Tervuren

Another shepherd dog, the Belgian Tervuren is registered in France and Belgium as the Chien de Berger Belge. He has the same ancestors as the Belgian sheepdog. All the Belgian shepherd dogs were bred together with little definite plan. The herdsmen basically wanted a dog that would take care of sheep, and put little thought into the dogs' colors and coats. The Tervuren's coat is light fawn until around eighteen months; then changes gradually to a warm mahogany. In character, the Tervuren is like the Belgian sheepdog.

    HEIGHT: Male—24–26 inches   Female—22–24 inches
    WEIGHT: Male—55–60 pounds   Female—50–55 pounds
    COLOR: Rich fawn to mahogany with black overlay
    COAT: Strong, dense, straight, not silky or wiry

Registered with the AKC (working group)

BERNESE MOUNTAIN DOG

One of four varieties of Swiss mountain dog, the Bernese stems from the dogs that accompanied the Roman invaders into Switzerland over 2,000 years ago. In later times, they were used to pull small wagons loaded with weavers' wares to the market. Then they dropped out of sight until 1892, when a Swiss attempted to find good specimens to breed. Soon the breed became popular with wealthy Swiss.

The Bernese mountain dog is very tough and can withstand

extremely cold weather. He is not happy in a warm climate. Not terribly outgoing, he prefers to love only one person, to whom he is very faithful. He needs room to move and is not made for apartment life.

HEIGHT: Male—23–27½ inches   Female—21–26 inches
WEIGHT: Male—60–70 pounds   Female—50–65 pounds
COLOR: Jet black with russet-brown or deep tan markings on all legs
COAT: Soft, silky, with natural sheen; long and slightly wavy; should not curl

Registered with the AKC (working group)

Bichon Frise

The Bichon Frise didn't get his name until 1933, but he has been well known in the Mediterranean region for several hundred years. During that period he has been off and on a friend of the common people, then the aristocracy, and then the common people again. One look at him explains why. He is a ball of white fluff with black eyes and nose, alert, appealing.

HEIGHT: Male—9-12 inches   Female—8–11 inches
WEIGHT: Male—8–12 pounds   Female—7–10 pounds
COLOR: White or white with cream; apricot or gray on ears and/or body
COAT: Profuse, silky, loosely curled

Registered with the AKC (non-sporting group)

Black-and-Tan Coonhound

The black-and-tan coonhound was recognized first by the UKC, then by the AKC. His history goes back to the eleventh century. Known then in England as the Talbot hound, he was crossed with the bloodhound and then with the fox-hound.

The black-and-tan is a great hunter of opossums and raccoons as well as larger game such as lion and bear. Like the bloodhound, he trails with nose to the ground, "barking up" the moment his quarry is treed. Fundamentally a working dog, he can withstand the coldest winters and warmest summers. He is agile, powerful and alert; also extremely even-tempered and affectionate. He is good with children; best suited to country life. He is a good watchdog.

HEIGHT: Male—25–26 inches   Female—22–25 inches
WEIGHT: Male—50–75 pounds   Female—40–65 pounds
COLOR: Black with tan markings above eyes, on sides of muzzle, chest and legs
COAT: Short, dense, glossy

Registered with the AKC (hound group) and UKC

BLOODHOUND

Always known for his peculiarly strong ability to follow even the faintest scent, the bloodhound was in existence in Egypt, Greece and Italy years before Christ. In the twelfth century, when used in the hunt, he got his modern name. This was given, not because of his trailing ability, but because he was owned by so many members of the aristocracy.

The bloodhound is an extremely docile dog, and although he successfully follows any trail, he does not harm his captive. He is affectionate and as fatherly with other dogs as with children. He is devoted to his master and sensitive to any correction by him. Because of his hunting instinct, he needs exercise and is not happy in a small home and small yard.

HEIGHT: Male—25–27 inches   Female—23–25 inches
WEIGHT: Male—90–110 pounds Female—80–100 pounds
COLOR: Black and tan; red and tan; or tawny
COAT: Thin to touch

Registered with the AKC (hound group) and UKC

Bluetick Coonhound

Also called the bluetick English hound because he's descended from several strains of English foxhound, this rather large, swift dog with fine treeing instinct is used to hunt fox and cougar, but his main quarry is the raccoon. Because he starts trailing on his own at an early age, he is very easy to train for field work.

Stories that the bluetick coonhound cannot be both a good hunter and a good house dog are not borne out by many owners. He's gentle with everyone, including children, but sounds an alarm when strangers come to his owner's home.

    HEIGHT: Male—22–27 inches   Female—20–25 inches
    WEIGHT: Male—55–80 pounds   Female—45–65 pounds
    COLOR: Dark blue thickly mottled; body spotted with black. Black predominant on head; dark red ticking on feet and lower legs
    COAT: Medium-coarse, but appearing smooth and glossy

Registered with the UKC

Border Collie

This hard-working sheepdog is descended primarily from the Scandinavian reindeer shepherd which was brought to Scotland during the Viking invasions; but he also traces his lineage to the sheep and cattle dogs that accompanied the Romans into Britain about 100 B.C., and to the Valée shepherd. He derives his name from his work with Colley sheep, an ancient Scottish breed, and also from the fact that he was developed in the borderland between Scotland and England.

The Border collie is not a pet or show dog. He was bred for work and should be used only for that purpose—for one reason, because if he has nothing to do, he gets into trouble out of boredom. He is durable, untemperamental, intelligent; tireless and agile; willing and adept. Born with a unique trait known as the "eye," he creeps up on a flock with trance-like attention and forces them to move without stampeding. He is easy to train, but the job must be done carefully because he is highly sensitive and thrives on praise. There are two varieties: rough-coated and short-coated.

HEIGHT: Male—17–20 inches   Female—16–18 inches
WEIGHT: Male—30–50 pounds   Female—30–40 pounds
COLOR: Black and white; black, white and tan; solid black
COAT: Rough-coated—abundant, straight, harsh, about 3 inches long
Short-coated—similar to rough-coated, but about 1 inch long

Border Terrier

Popular in the Scottish borderland, the Border terrier is probably the oldest and rarest working terrier. Farmers and shepherds used him to hunt the powerful hill foxes, kill badgers and vermin, and follow a horse. He is ideally built for these jobs.

Sharing ancestors with the Lakeland, Bedlington and Dandie Dinmont, the Border terrier is strictly a working dog, and is totally courageous and full of energy. His coat is weather-resistant. At home he is obedient, good-natured and easily trained, but in the field he is as tough as nails and bent on getting the job done.

HEIGHT: Male—12–13 inches   Female—11–12 inches
WEIGHT: Male—13–15½ pounds Female—11½–14 pounds
COLOR: Red, grizzle and tan; blue and tan; wheaten with some white on chest
COAT: Very wiry and somewhat broken

Registered with the AKC (terrier group)

Borzoi

Known prior to 1936 as the Russian wolfhound, the graceful, aristocratic borzoi has been used for coursing and hunting hare and other game since the early seventeenth century. He is the result of breeding the gazelle hound, a speedy runner with a thin coat, with a heavy-coated, powerful Russian breed similar to the collie.

The borzoi is generally docile and aloof. He is a satisfactory dog for older people, but can be nervous around children and reacts suddenly if upset. He is happiest in frigid weather; lethargic in warm weather. Developing slowly, he needs much sleep during puppyhood.

    HEIGHT: Male—28–31 inches   Female—26–29 inches
    WEIGHT: Male—75–105 pounds   Female—60–90 pounds
    COLOR: Any color or combination of colors but with white usually predominating
    COAT: Long, silky, either flat or wavy

Registered with the AKC (hound group)

Boston Terrier

The Boston terrier is one of the very few native American dogs. Resulting from a cross between the English bulldog and white English terrier, he is clean-cut and wiry.

The Boston terrier is generally kind and obedient, stubbornly adaptable, and a good watchdog. He has no body odor, does not shed and is very suitable for an apartment. On the other hand, being a short-nosed breed, he slobbers and snores, and often vomits. The breed also has trouble during whelping because the puppy has a large head and the dam a rather small pelvis.

HEIGHT: Male—15–17 inches Female—14–16 inches
WEIGHT: Male—20–25 pounds Female—13–19 pounds
COLOR: Brindle or black with white markings
COAT: Short, smooth, fine-textured
Registered with the AKC (non-sporting group)

Bouvier des Flandres

The Bouvier des Flandres has been known for several hundred years in southwest Flanders and the French northern hills. Originally owned by farmers, he was impressive as a cattle-driver. The name Bouvier means cowherder or ox-driver. During World War I he served as a messenger and ambulance dog. Many were killed. But because of his working ability, he was not allowed to die out. Today in Belgium a Bouvier cannot win the champion's title on looks alone; he must also win a prize in work competition.

This is a high-spirited dog mainly for farmers and cattlemen. He definitely should not be confined to an apartment. His rough coat is a good protection in bad weather; and he is rugged and strong. He is fine with children, and with people he cares about, he is loyal, kind and devoted.

HEIGHT: Male—23½–27½ inches   Female—22¾–27 inches
WEIGHT: Male—65–70 pounds   Female—60–65 pounds
COLOR: Pepper and salt; black; gray; brindle
COAT: Unkempt, thick and rough. Topcoat harsh; undercoat soft

Registered with the AKC (working group)

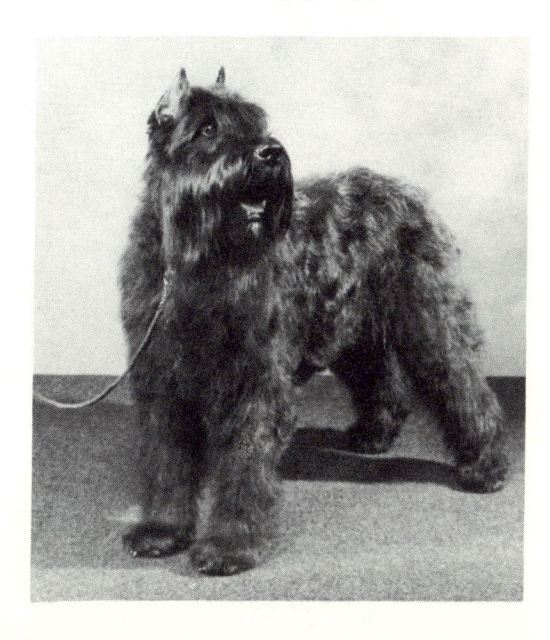

Boxer

Although the boxer has won greatest recognition in Germany in the past 100 years, it is quite certain that he originated in other lands at a much earlier time. His direct ancestors are unknown, but his kinship to all recognized bulldog breeds is accepted. One theory is that he is the result of a cross between a Great Dane and an English bulldog, and was developed for dog fighting and bull-baiting. His name, like his origin, is a matter of controversy. Some say "boxer" comes from a German word, *beisser,* or "biter." Others say he earned his name from the way he fights with his front paws. He has been used in Germany for police work.

The boxer is fearless, agile, animated and strong. Generally even-tempered, at his worst he ranges from nervous to aggressive. He is an excellent pet, loves his master and family. His short hair requires little attention, but he has other personal problems that do. He salivates a great deal and will leave wet spots on rugs or furniture. He snores and snorts like other short-nosed dogs. He sometimes has digestive problems, including congenital colitis, and vomits often. He also is subject to tumors on the gums when he is about seven years old. These can be removed, but if he chews on them, they bleed.

HEIGHT: Male—22–24 inches   Female—21–23 inches
WEIGHT: Male—70–75 pounds   Female—60–70 pounds
COLOR: Fawn or brindle usually marked with white
COAT: Short, smooth, shiny, tight to body
Registered with the AKC (working group)

Boykin Spaniel

Stories have it that this hunting dog wandered into a church one Sunday about forty years ago, found a friend and took off from there. Part cocker spaniel, he was bred with a cocker bitch; the result—the Boykin spaniel—is similar to American water spaniels. He is very quick, a strong swimmer and an excellent duck and dove retriever. He needs little training. A distinctive feature is his yellow eyes, which suggests that a Chesapeake retriever is mixed up in his heritage.

HEIGHT: Male—15–17 inches   Female—14–16 inches
WEIGHT: Male—30–38 pounds   Female—25–32 pounds
COLOR: Deep mahogany or liver
COAT: Wavy or curly

Briard

The briard, or Chien Berger de Brie, is today seen all over France herding sheep. He is perhaps the oldest sheepdog in that country, and is depicted on French tapestries of the fifteenth and sixteenth centuries. At one time he was widely used for defense against wolves and thieves. He has also served as a police dog.

The briard is strong and substantially built. He is protected by a long, wavy "goat's coat" which allows him to withstand almost any climate. He is generally placid but if provoked, will fight to the death. A one-man dog, he needs training but is a quick learner. He will usually stay close to home.

HEIGHT: Male—23–27 inches   Female—22–25½ inches
WEIGHT: Male—75–80 pounds   Female—70–75 pounds
COLOR: Any solid color except white—usually black, gray or tawny
COAT: Long, stiff, sturdy, slightly wavy

Registered with the AKC (working group)

Brittany Spaniel

More a setter than a spaniel, the Brittany is a French breed that has been known to European hunters for hundreds of years. It is generally agreed that the basic stock of all spaniels, setters and pointers originally came from Spain. The Brittany's ancestors were the Spanish pointer and spaniel. About 100 years ago the Brittany had become almost extinct as a result of excessive inbreeding, but a French sportsman took an interest in him because of his all-round working qualities, and by 1907 the breed was rehabilitated.

The Brittany is easily trained as a retriever. He is a fine water dog, aggressive and courageous. He is devoted to his master only, and is known sometimes to be very mean with strangers. He is a good watchdog and takes the job seriously. Raise him as a pet if you wish, but he is happiest as a sporting dog.

HEIGHT: Male—18½–20½ inches Female—17½–19½ inches
WEIGHT: Male—35–40 pounds Female—30–35 pounds
COLOR: Dark orange and white or liver and white; some ticking desirable
COAT: Dense, flat or wavy; not curly or silky

Registered with the AKC (sporting group)

Brussels Griffon

Loved more for his personality than his looks, the Brussels griffon stemmed originally from the German affenpinscher and the Belgian sheepdog. At some later date, the smooth-coated pug and ruby spaniel had a part in his development. Like other breeds, he won popularity in the nineteenth century when he was a favorite of the Queen of Belgium.

The griffon is full of bounce and energy and is a good companion to take along on outdoor adventures. But he is equally suited to an apartment. He requires early, firm training because he is willful and may become defiant otherwise. Having a terrier coat, he needs regular grooming. One variety has a rough coat; the other, a smooth coat.

HEIGHT: Male—7–8 inches   Female—7–8 inches
WEIGHT: Male—10–12 pounds   Female—5–9 pounds
COLOR: Reddish-brown; black and reddish-brown with black mask and whiskers; or black with uniform reddish-brown markings; solid black allowed in rough-coated variety
COAT: Rough-coated—wiry, dense, the harder the better
Smooth-coated—smooth, like the Boston terrier

Registered with the AKC (toy group)

Bulldog

Originating in the British Isles some time in the early thirteenth century, the bulldog was trained in the sport of bull-baiting. Bred from a long line of fighting ancestors, he was courageous and vicious. But when bull-baiting was declared illegal some 140 years ago, the bulldog seemed bound for extinction. Fortunately, he was saved by a relative handful of admirers, who set out to eliminate his fearsome qualities for battling.

The result is a superlative house pet. Despite his terrifying mien, the bulldog is now kind, affectionate, faithful and companionable. Since he is not very active, he adapts nicely to any kind of home—especially one with children. He does not shed, but he does snore thunderously, slobbers, and is a messy eater. Because of his pushed-in nose, he has some trouble breathing and has a short life span. He is also prone to heart attacks when subjected to sudden heat.

HEIGHT: Male—14½–15 inches   Female—13½–14½ inches
WEIGHT: Male—45–50 pounds   Female—38–42 pounds
COLOR: Brindle, white, fawn or red
COAT: Straight, close, short, smooth and glossy

Registered with the AKC (non-sporting group)

Bullmastiff

The bullmastiff was developed in England in 1860 by crossing the bulldog with the mastiff. The aim was to combine the aggressiveness of the former with the strength of the latter to produce a guard for large estates and game preserves.

The bullmastiff is still basically a police and guard dog. He has excellent night vision and sharp hearing. If confronted with a trespasser, he will keep him pinned to the ground for hours if necessary. He is tremendously strong, alert and fearless. Although pretty much a one-man dog, he will eventually accept his master's family.

HEIGHT: Male—25–27 inches Female—24–26 inches
WEIGHT: Male—110–130 pounds Female—100–120 pounds
COLOR: Any shade of brindle or fawn
COAT: Short and dense

Registered with the AKC (working group)

Bullterrier

The bullterrier is the result of a crossing of the English bulldog and now-extinct white English terrier. The breed dates to about 1835, and was developed specifically for fighting, bullbaiting and ratting. The original dogs were black or brown; but in 1860, dog fanciers in England came up with a solid white. In the pit he was known as the "white cavalier," taught to defend himself and his master but not seek a fight.

The sturdy bullterrier requires lots of exercise and should be walked daily. He also is a voracious eater and needs more food than other dogs his size. He is an excellent watchdog. Although he will not start a fight, when provoked he gives furious battle and is able to kill bigger dogs. For those who are familiar with dogs and able to take much time to train them, the bullterrier is a suitable pet. The female is often preferred because she is gentler and easier to housebreak. For show purposes there are two classes: white and colored. (For information about the miniature bullterrier, see p. 344.)

HEIGHT: Male—21–22 inches   Female—19–21 inches
WEIGHT: Male—45–60 pounds   Female—30–50 pounds
COLOR: White or other solid color with or without white markings
COAT: Short, flat, harsh, glossy

Registered with the AKC (terrier group)

Cairn Terrier

From various accounts written in the 1800's, we have an accurate description of the cairn, the smallest of the working terriers. Originating on the Isle of Skye, he has always been favored by the Scots for his vermin-killing ability and sporting instincts. He can rout badgers, otters and foxes from their hideouts among rocks and cliffs. His small size is a great attribute in these forays.

The cairn is a fine house dog. He doesn't require much exercise, is totally devoted to his owner, full of spirit, healthy and strong. His hard, water-resistant coat allows him to adapt to any climate, and it does not shed to any great extent.

    HEIGHT: Male—10 inches   Female—9–10 inches
    WEIGHT: Male—14 pounds   Female—13–14 pounds
    COLOR: Any color except white—usually wheaten, tan or grizzle
    COAT: Hard, profuse outer coat; soft, dense undercoat

Registered with the AKC (terrier group)

Canaan Dog

Known in Israel for possibly three millennia, the Canaan dog is thought to be that mentioned in the Bible. The breed served in those days as stalwart guardians of flocks and herds and the camps of the Hebrews. But as wars and famines swept the land, the dogs became wild and were on their way to extinction until several were captured before World War II. Then they were domesticated and trained for sentry work, mine detection and searching out the wounded. Today the dog is the symbol for the Israel Kennel Club's lapel pin.

Canaan dogs were imported to the U.S. in 1965. They are very hardy, adaptable to any weather conditions, devoted to their homes and families, and very wary of strangers. Their eyesight is unusually keen; hearing and scent excellent.

HEIGHT: Male—19–24 inches Female—18–22 inches
WEIGHT: Male—40–55 pounds Female—35–50 pounds
COLOR: All shades of brown; sandy to reddish; black; white with black, brown or red markings
COAT: Crisp, short, close-lying

Cardigan Welsh Corgi

The Cardigan Welsh corgi is one of the oldest breeds in the British Isles. It is thought that he came to Wales with the Celts from central Europe about 1200 B.C. He was used to drive cattle by nipping at their heels. He also was an important guard and companion. In later years he was bred with native herding dogs and dachshunds to produce the dog we know.

The low-set, sturdy, powerful Cardigan Welsh corgi is one of the best small working dogs. He works well with horses, sheep and cattle; and will also kill any vermin that come in sight. He is very fast in spite of his short legs and out-turned feet, can adapt to any temperature, and usually lives a long life. He is not friendly with strangers or stray animals, and is mainly a one-man dog.

HEIGHT: Male—11½–12 inches   Female—11–11½ inches
WEIGHT: Male—20–25 pounds   Female—15–20 pounds
COLOR: Red; brindle; black and tan; black and white; or merle
COAT: Short, thick, hard, weather-resistant

Registered with the AKC (working group)

Catahoula Leopard Dog

Developed by the early settlers of Louisiana, the Catahoula leopard dog owes his name to the fact that he was particularly popular in Catahoula Parish and has a spotted or splotched coat like a leopard. He is used today, as he was originally, for working cattle and hogs. A trained dog will round up animals that have strayed over forty or more acres. Even in untrained dogs, the herding instinct is strong.

The Catahoula is also a good squirrel and raccoon hunting dog, a devoted pet, and an aggressive watchdog. He is a ready learner. The eyes of some dogs of this breed are almost turquoise blue and are highly prized.

HEIGHT: Male—22–25 inches   Female—20–23 inches
WEIGHT: Male—60–80 pounds   Female—50–70 pounds
COLOR: Usually blue-gray with black spots or splotches; or solid red, yellow or black
COAT: Thick, dense, short

Cavalier King Charles Spaniel

It may be surprising to know that, in addition to the AKC-recognized King Charles spaniel (listed as a variety of the English toy spaniel), there is a Cavalier King Charles spaniel not as yet recognized by the AKC. They are not two breeds but two varieties of the same breed with the same root stock. The main difference is that the Cavalier looks like the original flat-skulled, long-nosed King Charles spaniel depicted in paintings of the fifteenth, sixteenth and seventeenth centuries.

To quote an owner and breeder of Cavaliers: "They are easy to train because they are most anxious to please. I have never had to strike one for training or disciplinary purposes, as they are sufficiently intimidated by a tone of voice. Cavaliers are very gay, happy, outgoing and adaptable little dogs, hardy enough to be kenneled outdoors, but do best as housedwellers because of their nature as people dogs."

HEIGHT: Male—12–13 inches   Female—11–12 inches
WEIGHT: Male—13–18 pounds   Female—11–16 pounds
COLOR: Chestnut on white with red ears; black on white with tan markings; red; black and tan
COAT: Long, silky, slightly wavy

Accepted in the AKC Miscellaneous Class

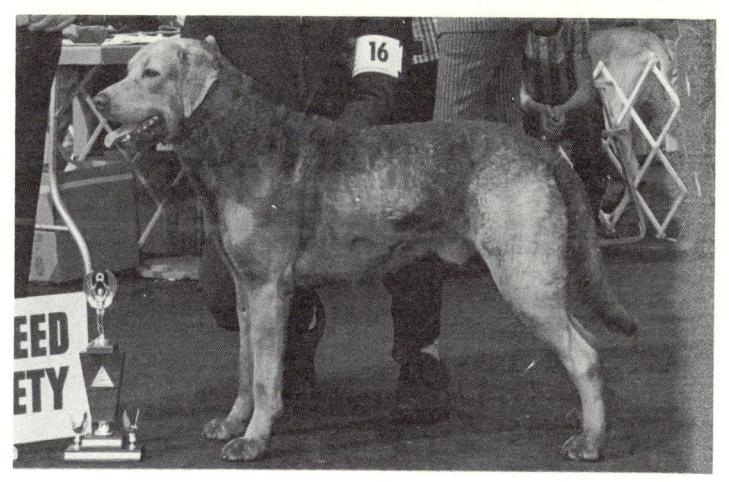

Chesapeake Bay Retriever

A native American, the Chesapeake Bay retriever traces his antecedents to a pair of Newfoundland puppies that were shipwrecked off the coast of Maryland in 1807. The Newfoundlands were crossed with yellow and tan coonhounds and the result was the powerful chestnut or sedge-colored dog that hundreds of duck hunters rely on today.

Although the Chesapeake lags far behind the Labrador in field trial wins, he is an outstanding retriever on land as well as in the water. His strength and power are well nigh incredible; and sometimes this combination of virtues leads him into trouble when he picks a fight (which he often does). He is hardly a gentle dog and he doesn't always disguise the fact when he meets strangers. His yellow eyes can be baleful. But with his owner he is steady, loyal and determined to please.

HEIGHT: Male—23–26 inches   Female—21–24 inches
WEIGHT: Male—65–75 pounds   Female—55–65 pounds
COLOR: Solid dark brown to faded tan
COAT: Thick and short with a dense, fine, woolly undercoat

Registered with the AKC (sporting group)

Chihuahua

Probably the smallest dog known, the Chihuahua's history is established in Central America. As early as the ninth century in what is now Mexico there was a small dog called the Techichi. He was the progenitor of the Chihuahua. The present-day Chihuahua probably developed from a crossing of the Techichi with an even smaller hairless dog from the Orient. He was named for the State of Chihuahua.

This alert, smart, diminutive dog appeals especially to older people living alone. He eats very little, needs practically no outdoor exercise and detests cold weather—perhaps because he is susceptible to rheumatism (as well as pyorrhea). He likes having the run of the house, and particularly enjoys the full attention of his owner. But he is slow to make friends, can be moody, and is not sociable with other dogs. There are two varieties: smooth-coated (more common) and long-coated.

HEIGHT: Male—5 inches   Female—5 inches
WEIGHT: Male—1–6 pounds   Female—1–6 pounds
COLOR: Any color; solid, marked or splashed
COAT: Smooth-coated variety—close, glossy and soft
Long-coated variety—long, soft, flat or slightly curly

Registered with the AKC (toy group) and UKC

Chinese Crested Dog

The Chinese crested breed probably originated in Africa and dates back into prehistory with many of the breeds found in Asia, South America and India. First shown in the U.S. in 1926, they were recognized then as a provisional breed by the AKC but were later dropped because of their extreme rarity. At present their number is growing.

Two varieties are raised: the hairless and the powderpuff. Both are small and graceful—gazelle-like in appearance. The hairless has hair only on his feet, head and tail, and he also lacks his pre-molars. The powderpuff, on the other hand, is fully coated and possesses a full set of teeth. Geneticists feel that the powderpuff, who occurs once in every litter whether the parents are hairless or powderpuffs, is so planned by nature to keep his hairless litter-mates warm. Both varieties are gay, smart and dignified. They are never "yappy" or aggressive.

HEIGHT: Male—11–13 inches Female—9–12 inches
WEIGHT: Male—Not over 10 pounds Female—Not over 10 pounds
COLOR: Any color; plain or spotted
COAT: See above

Chinese Fighting Dog

Very little is known about the Chinese fighting dog, or Shar-Pei, except that he seems to have originated many years ago in southern China, where dog fighting was a popular "sport." He may have been related to the chow chow, although the only visible link between them is their blue-black tongues.

A sad-looking fellow with loose, rippling skin that resembles a popular form of zoysia grass grown in California, he is strong, compact and very swift of movement. He gets along amicably with other dogs in the same household and makes a willing pillow for children who lie on the floor.

In addition to the profusely wrinkled skin (which makes

puppies especially look like old-fashioned washboards), the fighting dog's other unusual features are his small, cramped ears and highly carried, almost ring-formed tail. All are related to his fighting background: the loose skin permits him to twist around and retaliate when grabbed by an opponent; the little ears are hard to grip; and the tail just can't admit defeat.

HEIGHT: Male—18–20 inches Female—16–18 inches
WEIGHT: Male—45–55 pounds Female—35–45 pounds
COLOR: Fawn; cream; red or black
COAT: Short, ranging from mohair to harsh

Chinese Imperial Ch'in

This very rare little aristocrat originated long ago in China and until this century was owned only by the Chinese royalty. The last empress of China is said to have kept 50 of them in the throne room, and when she entered, they would line up from the door to the throne, stand on their hind legs (which they can do for long periods) and bow until she was seated.

The Imperial is closely related to the Chinese Temple dog and Japanese spaniel, both of which are classified as Ch'ins; and is also related to the Pekingese and chow chow.

A woman who owns several types of Ch'ins reports that the Imperial (called the duck-footed Ch'in because of his peculiarly shaped front feet) is "the most regal, most sensitive, most intelligent, most demanding. He moves very slowly and languidly; spends a lot of time 'pondering.'" Coming from Peking, he withstands cold.

288 / THE DOG LOVER'S ANSWER BOOK

Like other types of Ch'ins, the Imperial comes in four sizes: giant, classic (the average size), miniature and sleeve dog. The Japanese call the last the Stirrup Cup Dog because he's small enough to fit in a stirrup cup.

HEIGHT: Male and female: Giant—9–10 inches
Classic—4–6 inches
Miniature—4 inches
Sleeve dog—3 inches

WEIGHT: Male and female: Giant—15 pounds
Classic—4–5 pounds
Miniature—3–4 pounds
Sleeve dog—1½–2 pounds

COLOR: Usually black and white; also solid black and sometimes solid red

COAT: Extremely long, profuse and cottony

Chinese Temple Dog

A member of the Ch'in family (see Chinese Imperial Ch'in), the Temple dog is an ancient Chinese breed which was used to guard the temples. Though bred for gentleness, they do a good job of sounding the alarm when strangers approach.

Rather massive for its size, the Temple dog has a very large

head, and often has double rows of teeth. Though he looks ferocious (a fact which was exaggerated in ancient stone carvings), he is quiet, loyal, and seems to have a sense of humor. He often holds long, earnest "conversations" in rounded tones with his master.

The dog can withstand very cold temperatures; and in warm weather, sheds almost all his undercoat and is left only with his lustrous 6- to 10-inch topcoat. There are four sizes of dog: giant, classic (average size), miniature and sleeve dog.

HEIGHT: Male and female: Giant—12–14 inches
Classic—10–11 inches
Miniature—4–5 inches
Sleeve dog—3 inches

WEIGHT: Male and female: Giant—20 pounds
Classic—10–15 pounds
Miniature—4 pounds
Sleeve dog—1½–2 pounds

COLOR: Usually black and white
COAT: Extremely long and silky

Chow Chow

The chow chow can definitely be traced to about 150 B.C. as an unusually gifted hunting dog of China. Some authorities believe he originated from a crossing of the old mastiff of Tibet and the Samoyed of Siberia. Others say he is descended from the elkhound, Keeshond and Pomeranian. Whatever the truth, he acquired from somewhere a blue-black tongue.

Because of his very thick coat and mane, the chow chow appears more massive than he actually is. His expression is heavily sober and he is, in fact, aloof and very aggressive. A one-man dog, he is rather suspicious of or indifferent to strangers; and he's not recommended for a family with children. He requires much grooming and is unsuited to hot climates.

HEIGHT: Male—19–20 inches Female—18–19 inches
WEIGHT: Male—55–60 pounds Female—50–55 pounds
COLOR: Red, fawn, black, blue
COAT: Abundant, dense, straight and coarse
Registered with the AKC (non-sporting group)

Clumber Spaniel

The Clumber spaniel differs greatly from other spaniels; consequently his origin probably will always be in doubt. Because of his long, low, heavy body and massive head, it is presumed that he originated from crosses of the basset hound and early Alpine spaniel. The Clumber got his name from Clumber Park, the home of the Duke of Newcastle in Nottingham. The duke took great interest in the breed and made it popular in England in the mid-nineteenth century.

The Clumber is a slow worker but, when trained, an excellent retriever. He is strong and able in the field, and extremely faithful to one master. He does have a rather sullen disposition and is cautious with strangers. His face resembles that of a Saint Bernard, and he has an unusually attractive lemon-and-white coloring.

    HEIGHT: Male—16–18 inches   Female—14–16 inches
    WEIGHT: Male—55–65 pounds   Female—35–50 pounds
    COLOR: Lemon and white or orange and white
    COAT: Silky, dense, straight, not very long
    Registered with the AKC (sporting group)

Cocker Spaniel

Originally, all spaniels were known simply as spaniels. Gradually their owners began to sort them out by size and function, and in 1892 the cocker spaniel—or spaniel used to hunt woodcock—was finally given official recognition. This was the progenitor of today's cocker, though he was a considerably larger, stronger and more stable dog.

The cocker spaniel is an unhappy success story. Always popular for his beauty, alertness and good hunting ability, he rose to the top of the dog world in the '30s and promptly won so many hearts that the big breeders put him on the production line, and pretty soon the old cocker was no more. To be sure, many thousands of people still find him very appealing. But he is full of psychological problems: temperamental, timid, sometimes aggressive and addle-pated. He is prone to indigestion because he swallows anything in sight. He also has a tendency to have a discharge from the eyes and to develop cataracts; has problems with his ears; and suffers from ailments related to rheumatism.

For show purposes, cockers are segregated into three varieties: solid black; any other solid color including black and tan; parti-color.

  HEIGHT: Male—15 inches   Female—14 inches
  WEIGHT: Male—24–28 pounds Female—22–26 pounds
  COLOR: Black, white, tan, liver, parti-colored
  COAT: Slightly wavy or flat, never curly; silky and of medium length

Registered with the AKC (sporting group)

Collie

The collie goes back several centuries to his Scottish homeland. He was used to herd sheep and keep watch over them. He gained recognition after the start of the nineteenth century, and the first organized dog show for collies was held in England in 1859. Queen Victoria liked the breed and because of her interest it became popular.

There are two varieties of collie: the rough, who is very well known; and the smooth, who is quite rare. Both got their name from the Colley sheep, with which they worked. It was one of the first purebred dogs brought to the United States.

The collie is affectionate and faithful, and fine with children. He is a protector and makes a good watchdog. He tends to be distrustful and timid with those he doesn't know. Training must be started early. The rough-coated variety loves the outdoors and needs plenty of exercise and regular grooming. He is subject to skin problems. Other problems with the breed are: they often seem nervous and bark at almost anything; many specimens are susceptible to progressive retinal atrophy and an equally serious ailment known as "collie eye."

HEIGHT: Male—24–26 inches   Female—22–24 inches
WEIGHT: Male—60–75 pounds   Female—50–65 pounds
COLOR: Sable and white; merle; white; black with tan and white
COAT: Abundant, straight, harsh to the touch

Registered with the AKC (working group)

Coton de Tulear

This delightful small dog arrived in the U.S. in 1971 but has been known for several decades in Tuléar in southern Madagascar. Dogs resembling it date to the eleventh century.

The Coton de Tulear has an unusual coat. The long hair resembles heavy cotton, hence the name. He is devoted and affectionate and as one owner says, "prefers a caress to something to eat." Most satisfied outdoors, he will follow a rider many miles, or swim happily. But at day's end he is content to cuddle up beside you.

    HEIGHT: Male—12¼ inches   Female—11 inches
    WEIGHT: Male—8¾ pounds   Female—7¾ pounds
    COLOR: White with slight yellow markings on ears
    COAT: Cotton-like and long

Curly-coated Retriever

Probably one of the oldest retrievers, the curly-coated's origin is still unsettled. Most authorities believe he is descended from the sixteenth-century Irish water spaniel and the retrieving setter. Then, to obtain the breed, a small Newfoundland was used along with a water spaniel or poodle. Strangely enough, all these crosses were tried but no one knows which resulted in the curly-coated retriever we know today. Several were brought to America in 1907. Here they were trained as working gun dogs and also for show.

The curly-coated retriever loves water. He needs room to swim, hunt and run about. Aggressive and smart, he is devoted to his master and family. His woolly coat requires much care and he needs close supervision as a puppy, otherwise he may become distrustful and snappish.

>   HEIGHT: Male—23–24 inches   Female—22–23 inches
>   WEIGHT: Male—65–70 pounds   Female—55–65 pounds
>   COLOR: Liver or black
>   COAT: Crisp curls over entire body
>   Registered with the AKC (sporting group)

DACHSHUND

In German, *dachshund* means "badger dog," and from early in the seventeenth century, this comical-looking, jaunty little fellow has been used to go after badgers as well as boars, foxes and wounded deer. He has the stamina, courage and tracking ability to satisfy even the most demanding hunter.

Today, however, he is primarily a pet—and a wonderful one. He adapts to any environment, and is exceptionally clean (he never sheds), affectionate, responsive and playful. It should be noted, however, that because of too much inbreeding, the breed is susceptible to spinal disk trouble; and when this occurs, a dog may become paralyzed and die. The female is also susceptible to false pregnancy. Both males and females are difficult to housebreak.

There are three varieties: the short-haired, or smooth, and long-haired date to the breed's early days. The wirehaired won official recognition in 1890.

HEIGHT: Male—5–9 inches   Female—5–9 inches
WEIGHT: Male—5–20 pounds   Female—5–20 pounds
COLOR: Solid red of varying shades; black and tan; chocolate and tan
COAT: Short-haired—thick, smooth, glossy
Long-haired—soft, sleek, often wavy, glistening
Wirehaired—uniformly tight, short, thick and rough

Registered with the AKC (hound group) and UKC

Dalmatian

Even though the Dalmatian's origin remains a mystery, we know no other breed that has played so many roles: warrior, shepherd, firehouse mascot, hunter, retriever, stable dog and follower of carriages.

The Dalmatian is clean-cut, strong-bodied, even-tempered and very much a gentleman albeit a very stubborn one. He is an all-round pet that loves the family he lives with and is a good playmate for children. He is rarely quarrelsome or noisy, but is a good watchdog. He prefers much freedom and exercise. He sheds considerably but is otherwise clean and healthy. However, the breed has an inherited tendency to deafness, so the puppies' hearing should be tested carefully before they are sold or bought. You should also beware of the overly aggressive pup, because he might turn nasty.

    HEIGHT: Male—21–23 inches   Female—19–21 inches
    WEIGHT: Male—45–50 pounds Female—35–45 pounds
    COLOR: Pure white marked with small, distinct black or dark brown spots varying in size from a dime to a half-dollar
    COAT: Short, dense, hard, glossy

Registered with the AKC (non-sporting group)

Dandie Dinmont Terrier

Named after a character in Sir Walter Scott's *Guy Mannering*, the Dandie Dinmont is thought to have been bred from selected pups of the Scottish rough-coated terrier. He became a distinct breed in 1700.

Originally used for hunting, the Dandie Dinmont is today known mainly as an excellent house dog. He is hardy, intelligent and friendly; extremely loyal to his family and good around children. He can be stubborn and should be trained early, otherwise he's difficult to control. His crisp coat requires regular care. Frequent plucking helps the texture and color.

He is subject to skin ailments such as non-specific dermatitis and summer itch. He should not be kept in an overly warm room. He usually lives to a ripe age.

HEIGHT: Male—10–11 inches Female—8–10 inches
WEIGHT: Male—21–24 pounds Female—18–22 pounds
COLOR: Pepper-colored varying from dark blue-black to silver-gray; or mustard ranging from reddish-brown to pale fawn
COAT: About 2 inches long; crisp, but not wiry

Registered with the AKC (terrier group)

DOBERMAN PINSCHER

The Doberman pinscher originated in Apolda, Germany, around 1890. Named for Louis Dobermann, who developed the breed, he is a mixture of the black-and-tan terrier, Rottweiler, and smooth-haired German pinscher. Through careful breeding, the Doberman seems to have inherited all the best qualities of these other breeds. He has been used as a guard, police and war dog. Since he has a good sense of smell, he is also well adapted to hunting.

The Doberman is an extremely intelligent dog and can be trained for nearly anything. He has great muscular power and needs a good hour of exercise daily. He adapts to any climate. At times he can be temperamental, easily provoked or vicious, so he is best kept away from children. Basically, however, he is companionable and fond of his family, but will have little or nothing to do with outsiders. (For information about the miniature pinscher, see p. 345.)

    HEIGHT: Male—26–28 inches   Female—24–26 inches
    WEIGHT: Male—65–75 pounds   Female—60–70 pounds
    COLOR: Black, red, blue, fawn
    COAT: Smooth, short, hard, thick, close-lying
    Registered with the AKC (working group)

ENGLISH COCKER SPANIEL

If mention of cocker spaniels brings to your mind a picture of a husky little dog dashing through the fields, you're probably thinking of the English cocker—not the ordinary cocker sometimes called the American cocker. The two have the same history, dating to the fourteenth century, but the English cocker has always been the bigger and stronger—more of a sporting dog and less of a toy. He wasn't recognized by the AKC as a breed separate from the American cocker until 1946.

In addition to the physical differences, the English cocker is what you might call a more "solid" dog than the American.

He's less temperamental, less snappy, less timid. Yet he still has that spark that has always attracted people to cocker spaniels.

HEIGHT: Male—16–17 inches   Female—15–16 inches
WEIGHT: Male—28–34 pounds   Female—26–32 pounds
COLOR: Various colors, although no one should predominate
COAT: Flat or somewhat wavy and silky

Registered with the AKC (sporting group)

English Coonhound

Records dating back to 1200 refer to the English coonhound, but the dog bred today in the U.S. has been considerably changed since he was introduced in about 1860. The present strain is derived from the Henry, Birdsong, Walker, Trigg, July, Galloway and Bluetick hounds. This is a deep-chested, heavily muscled dog with strong feet and tough, thick, heavily covered pads that can withstand the punishment of a long chase through rough country. Although primarily a determined and spirited hunter, he is, like other coonhounds, even-tempered and affectionate.

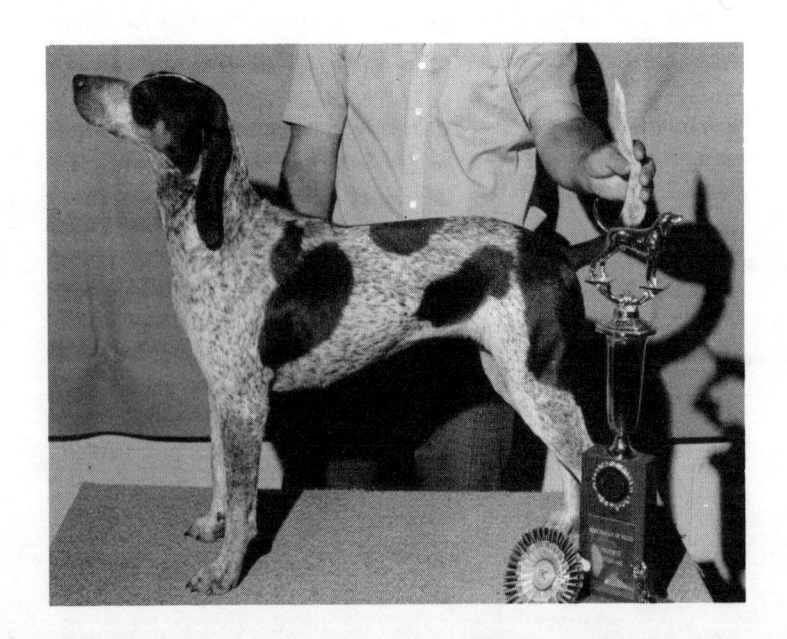

HEIGHT: Male—22–25 inches   Female—21–24 inches
WEIGHT: Male—55–70 pounds   Female—45–55 pounds
COLOR: Any hound color—in ticks or tricolor, or with a black saddle
COAT: Hard, dense, medium-long
Registered with the UKC

English Foxhound

The English foxhound has been bred along careful lines for over 170 years, and the breeders have kept such good records of what they did that the ancestors of each foxhound can be traced as far back as 1800. The breed was brought to the U.S. around 1738, and was used, as in England, for fox hunting.

The English foxhound is somewhat sturdier and tougher than the American foxhound. Though reserved with others, he is affectionate and loyal to his master.

HEIGHT: Male—22–25 inches   Female—21–24 inches
WEIGHT: Male—65–70 pounds   Female—60–65 pounds
COLOR: Any hound color—usually black, tan and white
COAT: Short, hard, glossy
Registered with the AKC (hound group)

English Setter

From writings in 1582 we find definite evidence that the English setter was a trained bird dog in England even then. His ancestors can be traced back to some of the land spaniels of Spain. He sometimes was referred to as a spaniel in spite of the fact that the spaniels' tails were docked and the setters' were not. The setter was derived from breedings with the Spanish pointer, springer spaniel and large water spaniel. Final development took place about 1825.

The lovable English setter is friendly with everyone. He is beautiful and smart and is high on popularity lists with hunters as well as families. He does very well in obedience classes. His hunting prowess is not spoiled when he becomes a family pet. But it takes a lot of work to train him (and to housebreak him) because he has a strong will and often resists orders.

> HEIGHT: Male—23–25 inches Female—23–24 inches
> WEIGHT: Male—60–70 pounds Female—50–60 pounds
> COLOR: Black, white and tan; black and white; blue, lemon and white; orange and white; liver and white; solid white
> COAT: Of good length and flat
> Registered with the AKC (sporting group)

ENGLISH SHEPHERD

This is a fine all-purpose dog—a pet for the children, a watchful guardian and companion for everyone, and a hard-working dog for the farm. Known for his affectionate, obedient nature and calm, dignified manner, he can corral the stubbornest cattle with stamina and fearlessness. He is also a hunting dog and will kill animals far larger than himself.

HEIGHT: Male—18–22 inches   Female—16–20 inches
WEIGHT: Male—40–50 pounds   Female—35–45 pounds
COLOR: Black and white; black and tan; white and tan
COAT: Heavy, glossy, straight or curly
Registered with the UKC

English Springer Spaniel

The English springer spaniel got his name because of his ability to spring at game. Most authorities are certain that he descended from the original spaniel, perhaps dating back thousands of years. In 1387, a French nobleman wrote about the spaniel we now know in a famous hunting book. In 1902, the Kennel Club of England recognized the English springer as a distinct breed.

The English springer spaniel is trained chiefly to hunt game. He has adapted beautifully to family life, however, and is determined to please, quick to learn and willing to obey. With children he is patient; willing to roughhouse as much as they like. He makes a good watchdog. His rugged coat allows him to withstand extremely cold weather, but causes him to suffer on very warm days. He may also be afflicted by skin ailments. He sheds regularly and eats moderately.

HEIGHT: Male—18–20 inches   Female—17–19 inches
WEIGHT: Male—47–55 pounds   Female—35–45 pounds
COLOR: Black or liver with white markings; liver and white or black and white with tan markings; blue or liver roan; predominantly white with tan, black or liver markings

COAT: Wavy or flat, of medium length, reasonably dense and fine

Registered with the AKC (sporting group)

English Toy Spaniel

Surprisingly, the English toy spaniel's history goes back to the Japan of 2000 B.C., and perhaps to China of an even earlier age. Somehow he made his way to England, and in the sixteenth century gained public attention as a favorite of Mary Queen of Scots. Her spaniel accompanied her to the scaffold.

For a long time the toy spaniel was bred without any reference to color. There were a black and tan variety, white and chestnut, chestnut-red, and white, black and tan. Now the varieties have been set apart from one another and are bred by firm rules.

Having been a favorite of royalty, the English toy spaniel still is inclined toward the finer things in life. He likes to be indulged. But he's lovable, friendly, affectionate with adults and children. He needs little exercise.

HEIGHT: Male—10 inches Female—9 inches
WEIGHT: Male—10½–12 pounds Female—9–11 pounds

COLOR: King Charles variety—black and tan
Prince Charles variety—white, tan and black
Blenheim—red and white
Ruby—red
COAT: Long, silky, wavy but not curly
Registered with the AKC (toy group)

Field Spaniel

The field spaniel was developed by repeated crosses of the Welsh cocker and the Sussex spaniel. As a sporting dog, he is not outstanding because he's slow and doesn't retrieve well, but he makes up for this with his perseverance. He is best as a companion—calm, stable, smart and loving.

HEIGHT: Male—18 inches   Female—17 inches
WEIGHT: Male—45–50 pounds Female—35–45 pounds
COLOR: Usually black; sometimes liver, golden liver or deep red
COAT: Flat or slightly wavy
Registered with the AKC (sporting group)

Finnish Spitz

This is another member of the ancient breed of spitz dogs that has been saved from near extinction. Located in northern Finland by a group of sportsmen, the first Finnish spitz were brought to England in 1927, and though the breed is not very prolific and breeding fell off during World War II, a number are now found in the U.S.

This brilliantly colored reddish-gold dog is one of the handsomest of the spitz group. He is clean, free of "doggy" odor, hardy and immune to most canine ailments. A devoted companion, he adores children. Though never aggressive, he stands ready to protect his owner and home. One of his more charming characteristics is his happy crooning or yodeling when greeting his family. But he is quite sensitive and can be stubborn, so he must be trained early with firmness and affection.

HEIGHT: Male—16–19 inches   Female—15–17 inches
WEIGHT: Male—30 pounds   Female—25 pounds
COLOR: Various shades of golden red
COAT: Dense, soft

Flat-coated Retriever

Developed in England, the flat-coated retriever resulted from a cross of the St. John's Newfoundland and Labrador; then pointer and setter blood was introduced. Although the flat-coated was introduced in the United States many years ago, the breed is not plentiful even in hunting areas.

This is a fine dog for the person who enjoys upland hunting and duck shooting, and also wants a good field companion with an even disposition. He loves water and is an efficient retriever of fowl in any temperature. Easy-going and gentle, he gets along beautifully with children. He should be exercised daily.

HEIGHT: Male—23 inches Female—22 inches
WEIGHT: Male—65–70 pounds Female—60–65 pounds
COLOR: Black or liver
COAT: Dense, fine-textured, flat

Registered with the AKC (sporting group)

Fox Terrier

This well-known dog comes in two varieties: the smooth and the wire. It is quite possible that they trace to completely different sources.

The smooth fox terrier was developed in the mid-nineteenth century. His ancestors are the beagle, bullterrier, greyhound and smooth-coated black-and-tan terrier. The wire fox terrier goes back to the mid-eighteenth century, and his ancestor is the rough-coated black-and-tan working terrier of Wales, Derbyshire and Durham. In earlier days, both varieties were often interbred. They are still used in England to force foxes out of holes, but in the U.S. they are almost entirely pets.

The fox terriers like to play, and if they had their way, they would do so all day. They are high-spirited, energetic and nervy. They have so much energy and bark so much that they need a strong restraining hand. They adapt readily to any environment. (For toy fox terriers, see page 391.)

HEIGHT: Male—15½ inches Female—14½ inches
WEIGHT: Male—16–19 pounds Female—15–18 pounds
COLOR: Mostly white with markings of black or black and tan
COAT: Wire variety—hard and wiry, the more so, the better
Smooth variety—smooth, flat, dense, abundant

Registered with the AKC (terrier group)

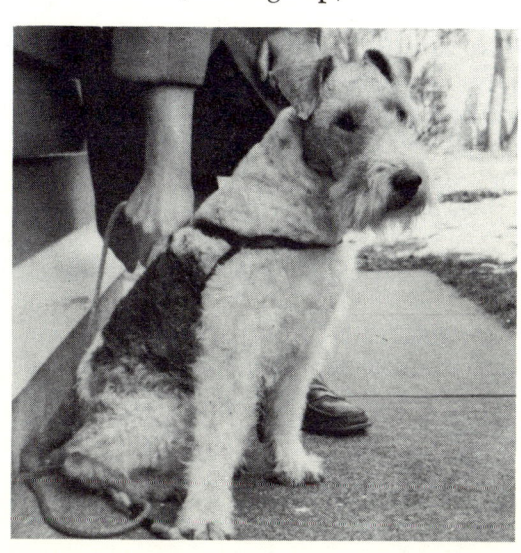

French Bulldog

Although this small bulldog originated in England, he was not popular there, and around 1860 he was sent to France in considerable numbers. French breeders crossed him with several native dogs until they finally developed the Boule-Dog Français. His two distinctive features were—and are—his erect, bat-like ears and domed skull.

Although bred principally as a pet and companion, the French bulldog is a good watchdog. He is alert, playful, sweet-tempered and dependable. Like other short-nosed breeds, he vomits often and has a constant, quiet wheezing.

        HEIGHT: Male—11½–12 inches   Female—11–12 inches
        WEIGHT: Male—21–28 pounds   Female—19–22 pounds
        COLOR: Fawn; brindle; white; brindle and white
        COAT: Fine, short, smooth
Registered with the AKC (non-sporting group)

German Shepherd

The German shepherd owes his ancestry to the old herding and farm dogs of Germany. He is basically a shepherd dog that has been carefully bred into an extremely intelligent animal able to assimilate instructions and train quickly. Known all over the world as a protector and companion, the shepherd can be found in a variety of roles. He is a working dog, a herder of sheep, a police dog, a Seeing Eye dog, a watchdog and a family pet.

It is a tribute to this dog that, despite years of exploitation and inbreeding, he is still essentially the bright, trainable, strong, stable, loyal friend and guardian of his early days in the films. But no one should assume that all shepherds share these traits equally. Far too many modern shepherds are nervous, temperamental, untrustworthy and sometimes vicious without provocation. And an extremely high percentage have hip dysplasia. So before you buy a shepherd, study him well and take plenty of time to find out how his parents and grandparents, uncles and aunts have turned out. Beware especially of overly large dogs and those with white coats.

HEIGHT: Male—25 inches   Female—23 inches
WEIGHT: Male—75–85 pounds Female—60–70 pounds
COLOR: Black and tan; gray; or black
COAT: Straight, harsh, thick
Registered with the AKC (working group) and UKC

German Short-haired Pointer

The origin of the German short-haired pointer cannot be pinpointed. The German hunting fraternity spent years trying to develop a truly all-purpose dog, which the short-haired pointer has come to be known as. He stems from the Spanish pointer, which was brought to Germany in the seventeenth century; assorted German hounds; the bloodhound, who contributed sturdy bones and trailing instinct; the foxhound, used for speed; and the English pointer, who added pointing ability.

The resulting dog is handsome and versatile. He is a natural retriever; a hardy swimmer who doesn't mind the coldest water; a keen trailer. He is more rugged and determined than fast, and needs lots of room for exercise. Basically a one-man dog, he shows loyalty and affection to his owner; but with others is reserved and doesn't make friends. He is rarely moody but very strong-willed and high-strung.

HEIGHT: Male—23–25 inches Female—21–23 inches
HEIGHT: Male—55–70 pounds Female—45–60 pounds
COLOR: Solid liver or liver and white
COAT: Short, thick, tough to the touch

Registered with the AKC (sporting group)

German Wirehaired Pointer

Most of the early German wirehaired pointers were a combination of griffon, German short-haired pointer and Pudelpointer (a cross between a poodle and English pointer). The Germans demanded much from their sporting dogs. They preferred an extremely rugged hunter able to work on any terrain. This is what they found in the wirehaired pointer, which was developed in the middle of the nineteenth century.

The wirehaired pointer has great stamina, can handle himself in any climate and over any ground. He is even-tempered, courageous, affectionate toward his master and aloof with strangers. Basically a field dog, he should be kept as that.

HEIGHT: Male—24–26 inches   Female—22–24 inches
WEIGHT: Male—60–70 pounds   Female—50–60 pounds
COLOR: Liver and white
COAT: Straight, harsh, wire, flat-lying, as much as 2 inches long

Registered with the AKC (sporting group)

Giant Schnauzer

For history, origin and characteristics, see Standard Schnauzer.

HEIGHT: Male—23–25½ inches   Female—21½–24 inches
WEIGHT: Male—73–78 pounds   Female—65–75 pounds
COLOR: Black or pepper-and-salt
COAT: Close, hard, wiry
Registered with the AKC (working group)

Glen of Imaal Terrier

This tough little terrier made his official entry into the dog world at the Irish Kennel Club Championship Show in 1933. A game fighter, he enjoyed a good bit of popularity in Ireland; and he was also valued for his skill in hunting fox and badger. He was not brought to the U.S. until 1968.

The Glen of Imaal resembles the Welsh corgi, but his coat is hard and crisp and, as one owner says, "he is notoriously pugnacious with dogs, chases cats and is rough on rats." His gaily carried tail, bright dark-brown eyes, and deceptively appealing face belie his fighting Irish spirit.

HEIGHT: Male—14 inches   Female—13 inches
WEIGHT: Male—30–35 pounds   Female—30 pounds
COLOR: Wheaten or soft blue-gray
COAT: Hard and crisp

Golden Retriever

Theories about the origin of the golden retriever vary. One has it that he comes from a cross between the bloodhound and a Russian circus dog called the Russian tracker. Others believe he originated from a cross between a Gordon setter and the St. John's Newfoundland. The offspring of this cross were then bred with a hardy retriever known as the Tweed water spaniel.

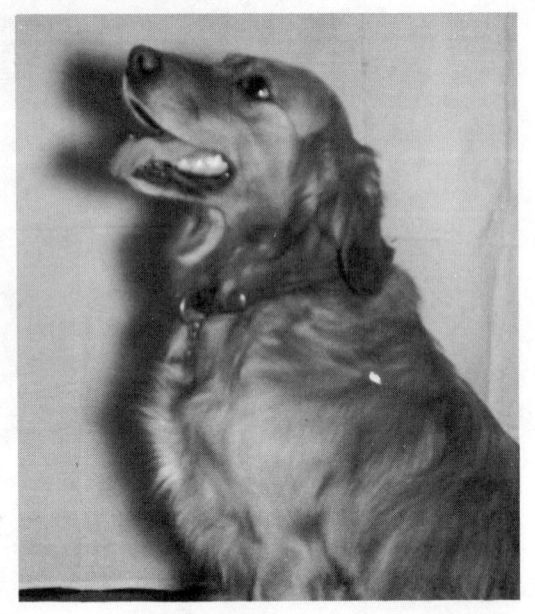

A superlative field dog, the golden is gentle and so very friendly that even garbage collectors like him. He definitely is not a watchdog, although if he manages to keep his tail from wagging, he can scare off some people by his size alone. He can also be stubborn if it pleases him. But I forgive him all these faults. Of the many breeds my husband and I have owned, we have never found one to rival the golden. His happy, gentle way with even the smallest children is reason enough to love him—and it is only one. Just be sure to buy a pup who comes from parents certified to be free of hip dysplasia, which plagues the breed.

HEIGHT: Male—23–24 inches   Female—21½–22½ inches
WEIGHT: Male—65–75 pounds   Female—60–70 pounds
COLOR: Rich gold of varying shades
COAT: Long, straight or wavy, moderately silky, water-repellent

Registered with the AKC (sporting group)

Gordon Setter

A methodical and dependable bird-finder, the Gordon setter dates to the 1600's in Scotland. He was named after the Duke of Gordon, and became known to hunters for his keen nose and excellent staying power. He has been used by American sportsmen for over 130 years.

This black-and-tan setter is sturdily built and able to do a full day's work. Though not known for speed, he's a good one-man shooting dog. He is devoted to family and children but is not particularly friendly with strangers. He is quiet, stubborn and stable—much more so than the Irish setter. A breed such as this should not be kept in a kennel with many other dogs for long periods. Give him freedom to exercise. He adjusts poorly to city life.

HEIGHT: Male—24–27 inches   Female—23–26 inches
WEIGHT: Male—55–75 pounds   Female—45–65 pounds
COLOR: Coal black with tan markings
COAT: Shining and soft, slightly waved but not curly
Registered with the AKC (sporting group)

Great Dane

The Germans are responsible for today's Great Dane, and developed him for the purpose of chasing boars. There are varying opinions as to the breed's exact beginnings. Some claim that the dog is depicted on Egyptian tombs dating to 3000 B.C.; others believe there is a written description of the dog in Chinese literature of 1121 B.C. Still others hold that he is a descendant of the Molossian dog of Greco-Roman times. Many students today believe he is the result of a crossing of the Irish wolfhound and English mastiff. Development of the modern Dane began in the late nineteenth century.

The Great Dane is spirited and courageous, quick and intelligent, and possesses a good sense of smell. His appetite is enormous. He needs plenty of exercise and should not be confined. He is good with children but needs to be watched because he can accidentally knock them over. He gives the appearance of great strength and elegance—never clumsy in spite of his size. Occasionally he shows a temper, and if kept around other animals he has been known to take this out on them. He is subject to heart attacks and kidney troubles, which shorten his life to roughly eight to ten years. As a puppy, he may also develop problems in the joints of his forelegs, so be on the alert for the lame pup and don't let any dog under about a year romp around too much.

HEIGHT: Male—31–34 inches Female—28–31 inches
WEIGHT: Male—135–150 pounds Female—120–135 pounds
COLOR: Brindle, fawn, blue, black, harlequin
COAT: Short, thick, glossy

Registered with the AKC (working group)

Greater Swiss Mountain Dog

In 1968 the first imports of this centuries-old breed reached the United States from Switzerland, where it is a common, sturdy working dog. The Swissy's appearance is striking: He has a shiny black or bronze coat; rust-red markings on all four legs and cheeks; white blaze on chest, feet and tail tip. Powerful in appearance, alert and obedient, he is gentle with children, friendly with other animals, and an enthusiastic worker. Although not naturally combative, he can be trained to be a dependable watchdog.

HEIGHT:	Male—25½–28½ inches	Female—23½–27 inches
WEIGHT:	Male—130–150 pounds	Female—115–135 pounds
COLOR:	See above	
COAT:	Short, smooth, crisp	

Great Pyrenees

It is generally accepted that the Great Pyrenees came from central Asia and dates to around 1800 B.C. He is a member of the mastiff, or giant-dog, family. Once in Europe, he settled around the high mountain area of the Spanish Pyrenees and stayed there until medieval times. He was the official guard dog of the flocks and, armed with a collar of spikes, could fight off wolves and bears. In 1675, Louis XIV chose him as the royal dog of France, and with that honor, he became known pretty much throughout Europe.

A beautiful dog, the Great Pyrenees is extremely lovable. He is gentle, untemperamental, affectionate with children and adults and rarely has an enemy among other animals. He has keen sight and smell and loves the outdoors. His long, heavy coat is weather-protecting and needs combing about three times a week. In spite of his size, he is not an enormous eater. He is a good watchdog.

> HEIGHT: Male—27–32 inches Female—25–29 inches
> WEIGHT: Male—100–125 pounds Female—90–115 pounds
> COLOR: White or white marked with gray, tan or badger
> COAT: Long, heavy, flat, coarse, straight or slightly waved
> Registered with the AKC (working group)

Greyhound

In the Tomb of Amten in the Valley of the Nile, carvings have been found showing a dog resembling the greyhound. These date to the years between 2900 and 2751 B.C. A complete written description from Ovid leaves little doubt that the dog of ancient times is nearly the same as that of today. The greyhound was a symbol of the aristocracy, and ownership was restricted to the ruling classes. Throughout the ages he was used to hunt practically all kinds of small game, but he instinctively prefers to go after hares. It is only in comparatively recent years that he has become a racer.

The greyhound is the fastest dog on earth and probably the most graceful. But he is reserved, cautious, high-strung and extremely nervous—not a very good family dog. He is one of the few purebreds that is not tainted by hip dysplasia.

    HEIGHT: Male—26–27 inches   Female—25–26 inches
    WEIGHT: Male—65–70 pounds   Female—60–65 pounds
    COLOR: Gray and white or pale fawn and white
    COAT: Short, smooth, firm in texture
Registered with the AKC (hound group)

Harrier

The most widely held theory about the origin of the harrier is that his ancestors were brought to England by the Normans for hunting. He was a favorite of all hunters of small game, especially because he could be easily followed on foot.

The harrier of today is merely a smaller edition of the English foxhound. Similar also to the black-and-tan coonhound and beagle, he is durable and will adapt to nearly any weather and terrain. He is stable and patient. Though basically a field dog, he makes a good house pet.

    HEIGHT: Male—20–21 inches   Female—19–20 inches
    WEIGHT: Male—45–50 pounds   Female—40–45 pounds
    COLOR: Black, tan and white in combination
    COAT: Short, hard, dense and glossy
Registered with the AKC (hound group)

Ibizan Hound

Here's a mystery: Are the dogs depicted in ancient Egyptian carvings greyhounds or Ibizan hounds? Or are they both?

Whatever the answer, the Ibizan is a tall, extremely lean, greyhound-like dog. Hunting and coursing are second nature to him, so it's easy to understand why he hates being kenneled. On the other hand, he is well behaved in a house and highly protective of it. He is playful and friendly with humans and other dogs; healthy, clean and sheds very little. One of his amusing characteristics is his odd way of clicking his teeth as an invitation to romp. He rarely barks.

HEIGHT: Male—25–29 inches   Female—24–27 inches
WEIGHT: Male—45–50 pounds   Female—42–47 pounds
COLOR: White and red; white and tawny; solid white; red or tawny
COAT: Short-haired variety—short, thick, coarse
Rough-haired variety—1 to 3 inches long, coarse and thick

Accepted in AKC Miscellaneous Class

Iceland Dog

The Iceland dog is derived from the dogs which accompanied the settlers of this north Atlantic island in the ninth century. The breed was almost wiped out by an epidemic of distemper a thousand years later and was also almost bred out of existence by mixed breeding. But thanks mainly to the work of one woman in southern Iceland and to a small group in England, it is now being bred true once more.

Belonging to the large spitz family, the dog is a member of every Icelandic farm household and is used for sheepherding, rounding up ponies and guarding the home. He is also a fine family dog—bright, affectionate and active. A Connecticut man who owns a pair reports they are ideal hiking companions since they don't go off on private hunting expeditions and are surefooted and fearless climbers.

The dog seems to require close contact with humans to mature (at the rather late age of eighteen months). He often has double dewclaws on his hind feet.

HEIGHT: Male—13–16 inches Female—12–15 inches
WEIGHT: Male—25–30 pounds Female—20–25 pounds
COLOR: Brown, fawn, gray, dirty white or black with white markings; sometimes all black
COAT: Medium-long, dense, close to body

Irish Setter

The boisterous, beautiful Irish setter won popularity in the early eighteenth century throughout the British Isles as a bird dog. Then the dog was red and white, with white sometimes predominating. The solid mahogany-red setter we know today didn't make his appearance in Ireland until the beginning of the nineteenth century. Though opinions differ, most believe the Irish setter developed from a combination of English setter, spaniel, pointer and Gordon setter. Brought to the U.S. in 1860 as a bird dog, it has more often been bred for show.

This is a grand dog if you can find one from a strain that hasn't been inbred too much. He's tough and active, can search out birds in rough country like no other; and when not at work, he is a joy to have around—happy, devoted and loyal. Training is slow; but once you're over the hump, you have something to be proud of. But, unfortunately, Irish setters of this sort are rather uncommon today. A high percentage are taut, nervous, very stubborn and temperamental—not at all easy to handle. And they may be afflicted with progressive retinal atrophy.

HEIGHT: Male—24–26 inches   Female—23–25 inches
WEIGHT: Male—55–60 pounds   Female—50–55 pounds
COLOR: Rich mahogany or golden-chestnut red
COAT: Flat, silky and of moderate length
Registered with the AKC (sporting group) and UKC

Irish Terrier

The oldest of the terrier breeds, the Irish terrier bears a marked resemblance to the Irish wolfhound, though he's smaller. The terrier is quite the sportsman, and is excellent for chasing rabbits and vermin. He is also a natural water dog and does well as a retriever. In World War I, he served as a messenger and general utility dog. Fearless and energetic, he has often been referred to as a daredevil.

The Irish terrier is a high-spirited dog. He is a great pal to those he loves, full of spunk and adaptable to any living situation. He loves to join in children's play and will serve as a guard. Although devoted to his family, he is sometimes belligerent toward people he doesn't know and may have to be watched when dealing with them.

HEIGHT: Male—17–18 inches   Female—16½–17½ inches
WEIGHT: Male—27 pounds   Female—25 pounds
COLOR: Bright red, golden red or wheaten
COAT: So dense and wiry that when the hair is parted the skin hardly shows

Registered with the AKC (terrier group)

Irish Water Spaniel

Speak of the Irish water spaniel and those who know the dog usually think instantly of his skill in the water and his rather unusual appearance. Solid liver in color, his coat is composed of tight ringlets and there is a peak of curly hair between the eyes. As for his affinity to water, he needs no urging to go for a swim and likes nothing better than retrieving ducks. His dense coat not only protects him from frigid temperatures but also sheds water like a raincoat. He is strong and fast, and has a keen nose.

The Irish water spaniel's history is thought to date to about 4000 B.C. in Persia, but is known to be centered in Ireland in more recent times. Like the good Irishman he is, he is fond of his family but reserved with strangers.

HEIGHT: Male—22–24 inches   Female—21–23 inches
WEIGHT: Male—55–60 pounds   Female—45–55 pounds
COLOR: Solid liver
COAT: Dense with thick, crisp ringlets
Registered with the AKC (sporting group)

Irish Wolfhound

Of great size and commanding appearance, the Irish wolfhound is the heroic dog of Ireland often depicted in paintings and stories. The earliest mention of these dogs was made in the second century, when it was said that they were brought to Greece during the invasion by the Celts. Later, in A.D. 391, a Roman consul wrote of the dogs' fighting ability in the circus. Always valued hunting dogs, Irish wolfhounds made pleasing gifts to royalty. They were used to hunt the Irish wolf as well as the gigantic Irish elk. But with the disappearance of wolves and elk, and excessive exportation, the wolfhound became almost extinct; and it was only through the efforts of a Scottish officer in the middle 1800's that he was saved.

The Irish wolfhound is a courageous, fierce fighter, but does not seek trouble. Even-tempered, he makes a wonderful companion for both adults and children, and enjoys a permanent home situation. He is best suited to country life.

HEIGHT: Male—32–33 inches   Female—30–31 inches
WEIGHT: Male—120–140 pounds   Female—105–115 pounds
COLOR: Gray, brindle, red, black, white or fawn
COAT: Rough and wiry
Registered with the AKC (hound group)

Italian Greyhound

The Italian greyhound is a miniature version of his large coursing cousin. He was loved by the ancient Egyptian, Greek and Roman nobility, but reached his popularity in the Victorian era. Although from Italy, he flourished in England and Scotland. Charles I, Frederick the Great and Queen Victoria were among his supporters.

The Italian greyhound prefers warm weather, for he is frail and susceptible to chills. He is affectionate, gentle and kind, and rarely flies off the handle. He wants very much to please and can be trained readily. In short, he makes a fine little companion.

HEIGHT: Male—8–10 inches   Female—6–7 inches
WEIGHT: Male—9–10 pounds   Female—7–9 pounds
COLOR: Fawn, red, blue, cream, white or gray
COAT: Thin and glossy; the skin is fine and supple

Registered with the AKC (toy group)

Jack Russell Terrier

The Jack Russell terrier was developed by the Devonshire fox-hunting parson, the Reverend John Russell, in the early 1800's. A larger dog than today, he ran with the foxhounds and was used to go to ground after foxes. He is still used for the same purpose but is carried along following the hunt until his services are called for.

Produced for keen hunting sense, fearlessness and stamina, the little terrier is hardy, healthy, alert, lively and affectionate. He is a good guard dog and death to rodents.

HEIGHT:	Male—9 inches Female—9 inches
WEIGHT:	Male—10 pounds Female—9 pounds
COLOR:	White with brown, tan, yellow, black or brindle spots
COAT:	Ranging from thick, firm and smooth to wire-haired

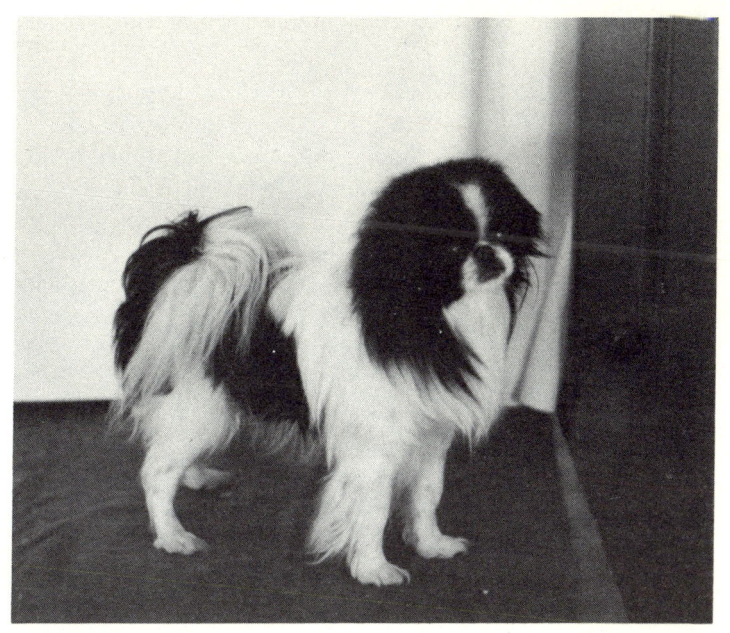

JAPANESE SPANIEL

The Japanese spaniel, or Japanese Ch'in, is a very old toy breed depicted on Chinese temples, pottery and embroideries dating back nearly two millennia. He was treasured by the nobility and often presented as a diplomatic gift. In 1853, Commodore Perry gave some of the dogs to Queen Victoria, and in time they became known in the United States.

The Japanese spaniel looks quite Oriental: proud, astute, yet vivacious. He makes an excellent companion and will adapt to his owner's moods. Typical of other toy breeds, he is quite delicate and doesn't do well in extreme temperatures; sheds considerably; and is best suited to apartment living.

  HEIGHT: Male—9 inches Female—8–9 inches
  WEIGHT: Male—7 pounds Female—6–7 pounds
  COLOR: Black and white or red and white
  COAT: Profuse, long, straight, silky
  Registered with the AKC (toy group)

Keeshond

A dog of the people, the Keeshond became the national dog of Holland in the mid-eighteenth century. He was named after Kees de Gyselaer, the leader of the lower and upper middle classes at that time. The Keeshond's heritage is the same as that of the Samoyed, Norwegian elkhound, Finnish spitz and Pomeranian. Authorities believe he is most closely related to the Pomeranian. Although he was kept primarily as a pet and watchdog, he was known as the "barge dog" because he traveled throughout the Netherlands on the barges that moved up and down the rivers.

Tough and healthy, the Keeshond adapts to any weather conditions. He is truly a one-man dog, devoted to his master and a bit standoffish with strangers. He is a superior watchdog. But if not trained properly, he can be spoiled, high-strung, super-sensitive and stubborn.

HEIGHT: Male—18 inches   Female—17 inches
WEIGHT: Male—35–40 pounds   Female—32–36 pounds
COLOR: Gray and black mixture
COAT: Long, straight, harsh hair standing straight out from the undercoat

Registered with the AKC (non-sporting group)

Kerry Blue Terrier

The Kerry blue terrier comes from the rugged mountain region of County Kerry in Ireland. He has been purebred for nearly 135 years. An all-round dog, he has been used as a working and utility terrier—a hunter of birds and small game, a retriever on land and in the water, and a herder of sheep and cattle. At times he was used in England for police work.

The Kerry blue is very long-lived, provided that he has love, proper food and exercise. He does not hide his feelings and can be extremely stubborn, furious, humorous or affectionate. He is sometimes fickle and is not above biting. His dense coat shrugs off cold weather; but like other terriers, he suffers from eczema during the summer. He loves dog fights.

HEIGHT: Male—18–19½ inches   Female—17½–19 inches
WEIGHT: Male—33–40 pounds   Female—29–34 pounds
COLOR: Deep slate to light blue-gray
COAT: Soft, wavy and dense

Registered with the AKC (terrier group)

Komondor

Originating in Tibet about 2000 B.C., the Komondor is a direct descendant of the Aftscharka, a huge Russian dog of the herdsmen. For the past ten centuries, the breed has been kept pure by the Hungarians. He was a protector of the herds.

The Komondor can live in the open all year long. He is an outstanding guardian of cattle and sheep, and can fight off coyotes, wolves, foxes and bears. A powerful, courageous dog, his one purpose, which he takes seriously, is to give protection. He is devoted to his family, always on the lookout, and will attack anyone who tries to endanger them; but he is otherwise calm, even-tempered and playful. His long, heavy, white coat is a mat of unkempt cords unless it is carefully controlled—as it should be—by dividing the hairs into cords and then by trimming. The coat must never be brushed or combed.

The plural of Komondor is Komondorok.

HEIGHT: Male—27–32 inches   Female—25–29 inches
WEIGHT: Male—100–125 pounds   Female—90–115 pounds
COLOR: White or white marked with gray, tan or badger
COAT: Long, thick, coarse hair developing into rope-like cords

Registered with the AKC (working group)

Kuvasz

Although the Kuvasz is essentially a Hungarian dog, he derives his name from the Turkish word *kawasz* meaning "armed guard of the nobility." He has existed in his present form for over 1,000 years. Hungary is responsible for the development of the breed. King Matthias I of Hungary, fearing assassination, relied more on his Kuvasz than on his human bodyguards. He also was a great admirer of the dog's hunting ability. Later the dogs were found suitable for herding sheep and cattle.

A remarkable farm dog and guard, the Kuvasz seems to know immediately who is friend or foe. He is intelligent and fearless, and you cannot help being impressed by his strength and activity. He is a one-man dog.

HEIGHT: Male—25–26 inches   Female—24–25 inches
WEIGHT: Male—65–70 pounds   Female—60–65 pounds
COLOR: Pure white
COAT: Long and slightly wavy

Registered with the AKC (working group)

Labrador Retriever

As you would not expect, the Labrador retriever comes from Newfoundland. He was brought to England by fishermen in the 1800's and soon was famed for his strength, hunting and retrieving ability, and quickness. In the U.S. he has far outshone all competition in field trials.

The Labrador is an ideal shooting companion, water retriever and family pet. Of powerful build, he is handsome, bright and—most of all—even-tempered. He is also calm and polite, reserved with outsiders and completely faithful to his owner. He should have about two hours of exercise daily. An unfortunate habit is his tendency to swallow rocks.

HEIGHT: Male—22½–24½ inches Female—21½–23½ inches
WEIGHT: Male—60–75 pounds Female—55–70 pounds
COLOR: Black, dark chocolate or yellow
COAT: Short, very dense, hard to the touch, straight

Registered with the AKC (sporting group)

Lakeland Terrier

The Lakeland terrier, known years ago as the Patterdale terrier, is one of the oldest working terriers. Cumberland, a beautiful lake-dotted part of England, is his birthplace. Stemming from the same family as the Bedlington and Dandie Dinmont, he was bred by mountain farmers for courage and toughness, and was used to destroy foxes which raided the sheepfolds. It is said that the Lakeland terrier can follow an otter underground for tremendous distances. Some were known to have been locked underground for ten or twelve days, and still to have come out alive.

The Lakeland is a small, workman-like dog that is intended for a hard life. He has great strength and determination, but is not particularly boisterous. Since he is principally a working dog, he needs plenty of exercise. He is even-tempered, devoted to his master and good with children.

HEIGHT: Male—14 inches   Female—13–13½ inches
WEIGHT: Male—16–17 pounds   Female—15–16 pounds
COLOR: Blue and tan; blue; black; black and tan; red, mustard; yellow and gray
COAT: Dense, hard, wiry

Registered with the AKC (terrier group)

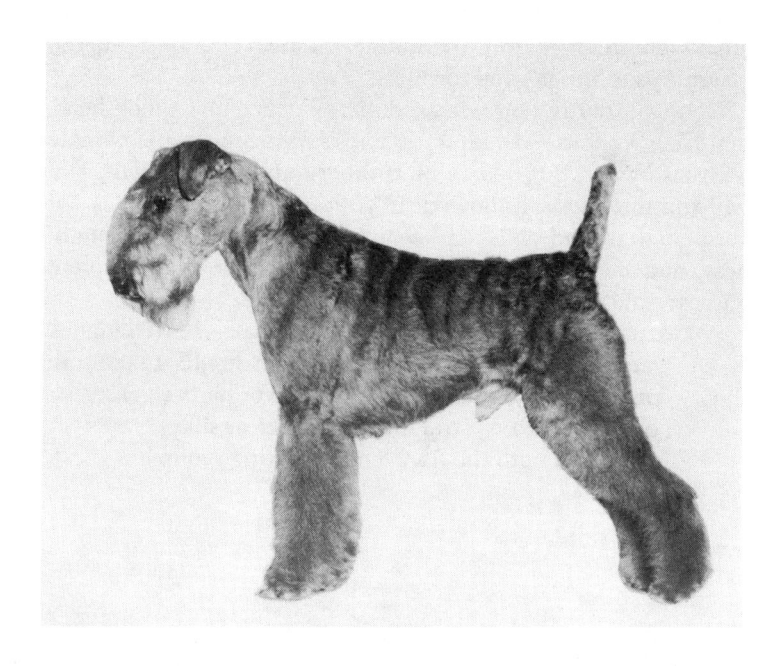

Lhasa Apsos

The Lhasa Apsos comes from Tibet, where he was kept mainly as a guard inside dwellings. Known in that land as Abso Seng Kye, the "Bark Lion Sentinel Dog," this little fellow has been in existence for over eight centuries. He was often presented as a gift to the imperial families of China and to other important world dignitaries. Many believe that the Lhasa Apsos brings good fortune.

Here is a hardy dog with keen intelligence and quick hearing. He is responsive to kindness and is particularly affectionate with his owner. But he can be stubborn and independent, and will run the house if allowed. Like other small dogs, he is not very good around children because he doesn't tolerate roughness, and may turn mean. His heavy coat requires frequent and careful grooming. He needs little exercise.

HEIGHT: Male—10½–11 inches   Female—10–10½ inches
WEIGHT: Male—14–15 pounds   Female—13–14 pounds
COLOR: Gold, black, white, brown or parti-colored
COAT: Heavy, straight, not woolly or silky
Registered with the AKC (non-sporting group)

Little Lion Dog

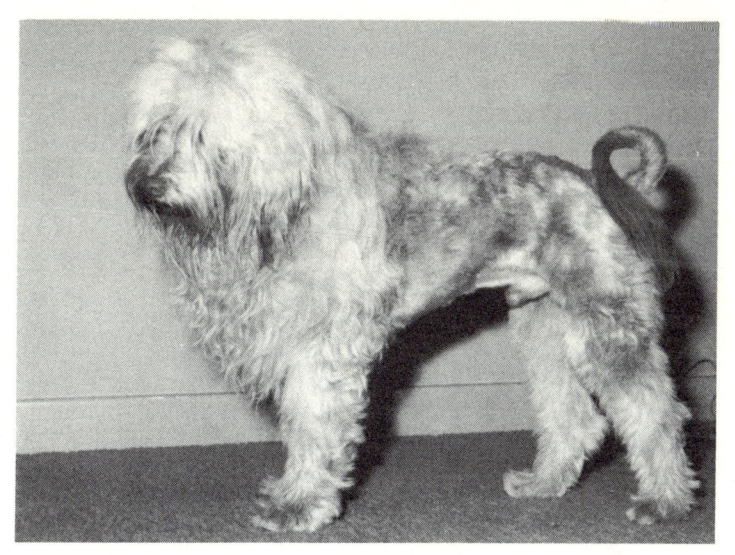

The little lion dog is reputed to be the rarest purebred dog in the world. There are only 30 in the U.S., 270 elsewhere. The breed originated in southern Europe several hundred years ago, and has been immortalized in tapestries, paintings and sculptures. Several were owned by the Duchess of Alba and appear in Goya's portraits of her.

This staunch, strong little fellow is well adjusted and easily trained; full of fun and joyous play with adults, children and other dogs. He is a fine pet in city apartments but hardy enough for country living. The coat is slightly harsh, medium in length, and may be clipped or unclipped. The lion mane is apparent even when not accented by clipping. The tail with plume is carried high over the back.

    HEIGHT: Male—10–15 inches   Female—9–13 inches
    WEIGHT: Male—9–12 pounds   Female—8–10 pounds
    COLOR: Any color but pure white
    COAT: See above

Maltese

Known as the ancient dog of Malta, the Maltese has been an aristocrat of the canine world for more than 28 centuries. At the time of the Apostle Paul, the Roman governor Publius of Malta owned a Maltese named Issa. The Greeks built tombs for their Maltese and often used them as subjects for paintings. So treasured were the dogs that in the Elizabethan period a Maltese was sold for today's equivalent of $10,000.

The noble toy dog is covered with a cloak of long, silky white hair which needs constant grooming. He is gentle-mannered and refined, but some can be snappish. He craves human companionship and needs a great deal of love and attention to make him feel secure. He seems fearless and full of energy, but is fragile and often has physical problems. He suffers occasionally from respiratory ailments, must be fed with care and exercised sufficiently to prevent skin eruptions.

HEIGHT: Male—5 inches Female—5 inches
WEIGHT: Male—2–7 pounds Female—2–3 pounds
COLOR: Pure white
COAT: Silky, long, straight
Registered with the AKC (toy group) and UKC

Manchester Terrier

The Manchester district of England was known for two "poor men's sports"—rat-killing and rabbit-coursing, so it was logical for the Manchester terrier to develop there. He is the result of a cross between the rat-killing black-and-tan terrier and the whippet.

The alert Manchester is a popular house dog but still possesses the characteristics of a fine ratter. His short coat is sleek and clean and hardly sheds. He does not require much outdoor activity. One bad habit is his barking. This should be controlled.

HEIGHT AND WEIGHT: Male standard—16 inches; 16–22 pounds
Female standard—14–15 inches; 12–16 pounds
Male toy—7 inches; 9–12 pounds
Female toy—6–7 inches; 5–9 pounds

COLOR: Black and tan

COAT: Glossy, smooth, dense

Registered with the AKC (terrier group)

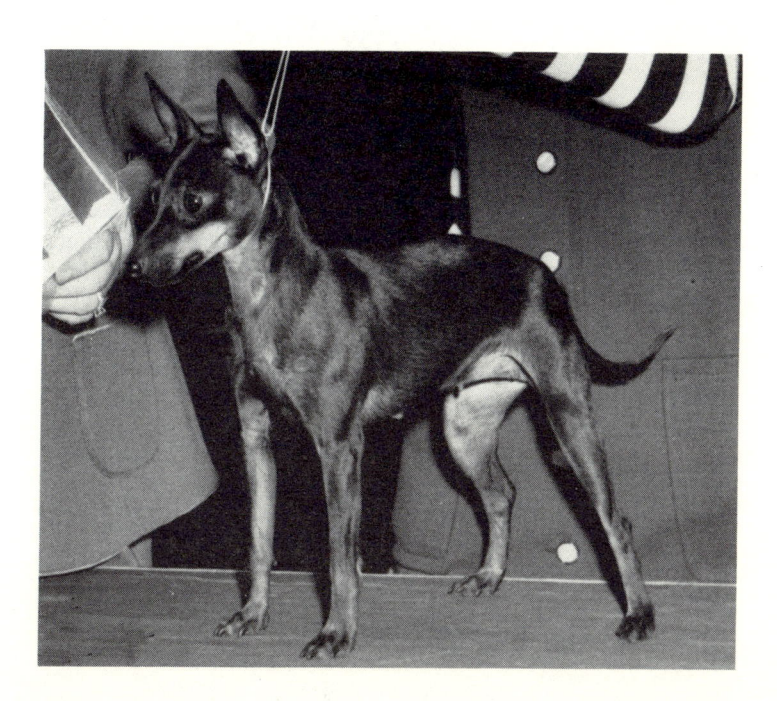

Mastiff

Little is known for sure about the mastiff previous to the past 100 years. Some believe he originated in Tibet and was taken to Persia, Egypt, Greece, and eventually to England, where he has been bred for over 2,000 years. (Caesar describes a dog like the mastiff in his records of the invasion of Britain in 55 B.C.) He was used in bull- and bear-baiting; followed his master to war; guarded against wolves and other predators; traveled in packs to hunt deer and lion.

The mastiff's personality does not fit his appearance. He is a terrifying-looking giant but is really gentle, affectionate, and friendly. Without any mean streak, he can be trusted completely with children; but because of his size he may hurt them just by leaning on them.

- HEIGHT: Male—30–33 inches   Female—27½–31 inches
- WEIGHT: Male—175–185 pounds   Female—165–175 pounds
- COLOR: Apricot, silver-fawn or dark fawn-brindle
- COAT: Short, coarse, close-lying

Registered with the AKC (working group)

Mexican Hairless

The Mexican hairless probably originated in China (not Mexico) and the breed goes back for centuries. Brought to this continent by the Aztecs, the dog has enjoyed considerable favor for generations. Loyal and devoted, he makes an interesting and playful pet especially for apartment dwellers, and is very trouble-free. His totally hairless body is easy to keep clean and free of parasites, yet is surprisingly sturdy. The dog generally enjoys a long life.

The hairless has several unusual characteristics: he loves to lie in the sun and gets a tan; when unhappy, he actually weeps tears. His skin is very warm to the touch (normal temperature runs from 102° to 104°).

HEIGHT: Male—10–12 inches Female—9–10 inches
WEIGHT: Male—5–15 pounds Female—5–10 pounds
COLOR: All colors from light pink to black

Miniature Bullterrier

This product of crosses among bulldogs, white English terriers and Spanish pointers has had many shapes, sizes and colorings, but is now stabilized. He's a vigorous small dog who can hold his own with just about anything. Tenacity, courage and fire are his immediately apparent attributes, but he is also good-tempered and amenable to discipline.

    HEIGHT: Male—11–14 inches   Female—10–13 inches
    WEIGHT: Male—12–17 pounds Female—10–15 pounds
    COLOR: Any color
    COAT: Shiny, crisp, short, smooth
    Accepted in AKC Miscellaneous Class

Miniature Pinscher

The miniature pinscher originated in Germany but has been bred almost as much in the Scandinavian countries. He was named the *Reh Pinscher* because he resembled a very small species of deer in German forests. After World War I his popularity soared, and importations to the U.S. increased.

The miniature pinscher is a sturdy, vigorous, alert little dog; very animated, and to some a born show dog. He is extremely confident—sure he will impress someone—but can be temperamental and does not always respond well to training. Sometimes he is snappish. His short coat requires little grooming. The owner of a miniature pinscher should know dogs and be willing to spend much time working with him.

HEIGHT: Male—11–11½ inches Female—10–10½ inches
WEIGHT: Male—9–10 pounds Female—8–9 pounds
COLOR: Red, rust-red, coal black, or brown with rust or yellow
COAT: Hard, smooth, short, lustrous

Registered with the AKC (toy group) and UKC

Miniature Schnauzer

The miniature schnauzer, derived from the standard schnauzer, was produced by crossings of small schnauzers and affenpinschers. He was recognized as a breed separate from the standard schnauzer in 1899.

The miniature is robust and active. Though still a fine ratter, he has gained popularity as a house dog and is very suitable to city apartments—for one reason: he's a good watchdog. He is healthy, active and good with children. Generally he enjoys a long life. His coat requires very little attention.

HEIGHT: Male—13–14 inches Female—12–14 inches
WEIGHT: Male—14–15 pounds Female—13–14 pounds
COLOR: Salt-and-pepper; black and silver; solid black
COAT: Hard and wiry

Registered with the AKC (terrier group)

Neapolitan Mastiff

Also called the Italian mastiff, this is a large, short-haired dog much like the more familiar mastiff bred in England but smaller. A good companion and watchdog, he can be aggressive if given the command; but generally he is quiet and easygoing and eager to please. He is easily trained.

HEIGHT: Male—25–29 inches   Female—23–27 inches
WEIGHT: Male—105–115 pounds   Female—95–105 pounds
COLOR: Black or gray, dappled or mottled
COAT: Short, coarse, tight to body

Newfoundland

The Newfoundland originated on the Island of Newfoundland and his ancestors probably were brought there by fishermen from Europe. Most authorities agree that he evolved around the seventeenth century as the result of crossings of the Great Pyrenees and native dogs, wolves or huskies. Dogs from these crossings were taken to England, where careful breeding took place to give us today's Newfoundland.

The Newfoundland is a true working dog who is totally at home in the water. His webbed feet are large and strong and enable him to travel through heavy marshes. His coat protects him in icy waters, and his lungs are strong enough to allow him to swim great distances. He possesses a natural lifesaving ability and has been known to save drowning men. He is a great friend and companion, even-tempered and trustworthy around children, and devoted to protecting his family. He needs a good deal of exercise every day.

HEIGHT: Male—27–28 inches Female—25–26 inches
WEIGHT: Male—140–150 pounds Female—110–120 pounds
COLOR: Dull coal black
COAT: Flat and dense, rather coarse and oily
Registered with the AKC (working group)

Norwegian Elkhound

The Norwegian elkhound is the same today as he was countless years ago, when his physical characteristics developed from his needs. His compactness and robustness were nature's requirements for a dog that could hunt daily in a rugged, cold country. His tremendous stamina enabled him to hunt elk, herd flocks and defend tribes against wolves and bears. He has such an acute sense of smell that he can detect an elk two or three miles away.

Norway's primary contribution to the dog world, the Norwegian elkhound is a trustworthy, fearless and dependable animal. He is very quick to learn and to adapt to new situations. He is also extremely aggressive and a real barker. Possessing a strong will, the dog requires an owner who knows much about training, for he requires much supervision.

HEIGHT: Male—19–20½ inches Female—18–19 inches
WEIGHT: Male—45–50 pounds Female—40–50 pounds
COLOR: Gray with black tips
COAT: Thick, hard, smooth-lying

Registered with the AKC (hound group)

Norwich Terrier

The Norwich is rather a newcomer to the terrier group. Developed in England in 1880, he soon gained popularity with Cambridge students. Some feel he should be known as the Cantab terrier in recognition of the collegiate environment that made him popular. His ancestors most probably are the Irish and English terriers and the old Border terrier.

Norwich terriers enjoy going out with the horses, and have been used in hunts in the U.S. They love to chase foxes, badgers and rabbits. Like all terriers, they are hard workers, full of spirit and strength. It is best that they live in the country and be kept busy, but I know many city and suburban families that swear by them, too. They are good watchdogs.

HEIGHT: Male—10–11 inches   Female—9–10 inches
WEIGHT: Male—10–14 pounds   Female—10–12 pounds
COLOR: Red and red-wheaten; black and tan; grizzle
COAT: Wiry, hard and very straight
Registered with the AKC (terrier group)

Old English Sheepdog

The old English sheepdog goes back about 150 years, but his exact origin is wrapped in mystery. He was first developed in the west of England. Some believe that the Scotch bearded collie was highly influential in his development, while others claim his ancestor was the Russian Owtchar.

The old English sheepdog is a fine worker. He naturally likes to tend cattle and sheep, but he is a good home dog—affectionate, smart and gentle. He loves children and plays well with them. But he should never be confined because he becomes bad-tempered. This is a clean dog that adapts to any weather since his coat serves as an insulator against both cold and heat, but he needs a good brushing daily. Because of his bangs, his eyes are weak; and puppies must be shielded from very bright light until the hair grows down over them.

HEIGHT: Male—23–25 inches   Female—21–24 inches
WEIGHT: Male—60–65 pounds   Female—55–60 pounds
COLOR: Gray, grizzle, blue, merle with or without white
COAT: Profuse and of hard texture, shaggy and free of curl

Registered with the AKC (working group)

Otter Hound

The otter hound was most popular in England at the end of the nineteenth century, where around twenty packs were regularly used for hunting the otters that preyed on fish in rivers and streams. There are varying opinions as to his origin. Some say he is a cross between the southern hound and Welsh terrier; others, that he is an almost exact duplicate of the Vendee hound of France. The earliest description of the otter hound, written in the early 1300's, tells of his hunting abilities.

The one purpose of the otter hound is the killing of otters. Bred mainly for his working qualities, he is a fearless fighter and an excellent swimmer aided by his webbed feet. He has a very sensitive nose and is diligent about investigating scents.

HEIGHT: Male—25–26 inches Female—24–25 inches
WEIGHT: Male—60–65 pounds Female—55–60 pounds
COLOR: Blue-gray and white; black and tan
COAT: Hard, crisp, coarse and oily

Registered with the AKC (hound group)

Papillon

Known in the sixteenth century as the dwarf spaniel, the papillon is yet another toy breed that noblewomen held in such esteem that they invariably held them in their laps when sitting for portraits. Madame de Pompadour and Marie Antoinette were among his admirers. As time passed, the dwarf spaniel—who started out with large, drooping ears—gradually developed erect, fringed ears that bore a resemblance to a butterfly. From these came the papillon name. (Droop ears still appear in litters, and both varieties are judged together.)

The papillon is an elegant dog with a fine bone structure. The only sporting toy breed, he serves as a very good ratter if necessary; but he's basically a house dog that likes to be loved and attended to. He has keen hearing and is able to give a quick alarm. His coat needs faithful grooming; but since he reacts to temperature extremes, he should not be bathed often for he is likely to catch cold.

HEIGHT: Male—11 inches Female—10 inches
WEIGHT: Male—9–10 pounds Female—5–8 pounds
COLOR: Either two-colored or tricolored—usually white and black; white and sable; white and some shade of red; or white and black with tan spots
COAT: Profuse, shiny, slightly wavy

Registered with the AKC (toy group)

Pekingese

The Pekingese comes from the Orient. Known as early as the eighth century, he was held on sacred ground. Theft of one of these valued dogs was punishable by death. As a result of the British looting of the Imperial Palace in Peking in 1860, the Pekingese entered the western world. He quickly became popular in America and was made a registered breed in 1909.

The Pekingese is a decorative lap dog. He keeps to himself, does not like to be scolded and does not make friends easily. Often noisy, he is not suited to a house full of children. He is best off living the city life in an apartment with older people. For them he makes a fine companion. He does not need a great deal of exercise, and should not be taken out on cold or damp days. If overfed, he can develop asthma. He should have a daily brushing.

HEIGHT: Male—8–9 inches   Female—6–8 inches
WEIGHT: Male—8–10 pounds   Female—6–8 pounds
COLOR: Fawn, red, black, black and tan, sable or brindle with black mask on face
COAT: Long, straight, flat, coarse

Registered with the AKC (toy group) and UKC

Pembroke Welsh Corgi

The Pembroke Welsh corgi is not as old as the Cardigan Welsh corgi; even so, his history traces as far back as 1107. His ancestors came across the Channel with Flemish weavers in response to the invitation of Henry I, and eventually took up residence in Wales. This dog comes from the same family as the Keeshond, Pomeranian, chow chow, Norwegian elkhound, Samoyed and Finnish spitz. He looked very much like the old Schipperkes. Despite his low-slung build, there is no trace of dachshund in him. During the nineteenth century, the Pembroke and Cardigan corgis were crossbred. But now all crossbreeding has stopped.

The Pembroke Welsh corgi is most at home on a farm. He is alert and energetic and is helpful with young, nervous colts. He is also a good ratter and weasel-killer. Generally calm and healthy, he may live up to eighteen years. He needs an opportunity to run several times a day, but if trained early, can adapt to an apartment that is not too confining.

HEIGHT: Male—11–12 inches   Female—10–11 inches
WEIGHT: Male—20–24 pounds   Female—18–22 pounds
COLOR: Red, sable, fawn or black and tan with white on legs, chest and neck
COAT: Medium-length, dense, straight but with some waviness allowed

Registered with the AKC (working group)

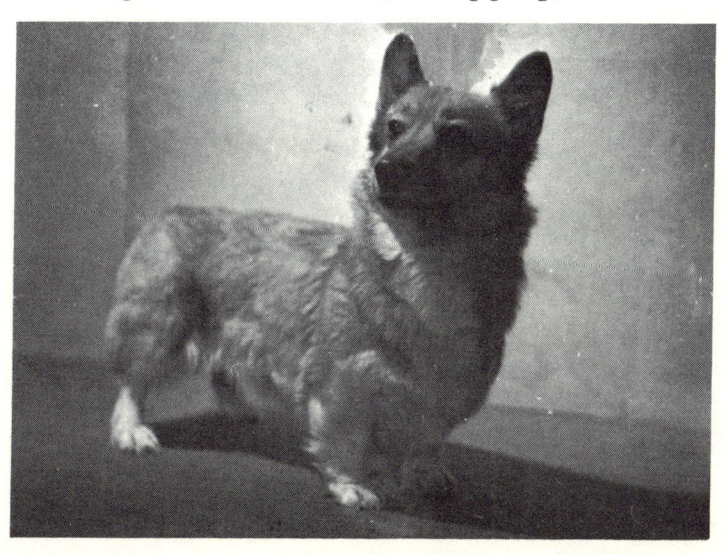

Pharaoh Hound

One of the oldest domesticated dogs, the Pharaoh hound is depicted on the walls of the earliest Egyptian tombs. Taken by the Phoenicians to Malta, the breed was preserved in its natural state and jealously guarded. Its popularity is growing in the U.S., for owners have found the dogs to be very keen, alert and affectionate. Their sharp sight and scent and graceful, free movement make them excellent for hunting. They are also good watchdogs and eager-to-please house dogs.

HEIGHT: Male—23–25 inches   Female—21–24 inches
WEIGHT: Male—55–65 pounds   Female—50–60 pounds
COLOR: Tan to rich chestnut
COAT: Short and glossy

Picardie Shepherd

Here's a family dog that doesn't waste any time in warning strangers that they had better be coming to his home on friendly business or else. Originating in northern France, he was used by the Gallic tribes before the Roman conquest to protect his owners against marauders and to herd sheep. He is still used in that country for home protection and police work. He's even said to be the guardian of France's missile silos.

There are only about 1,500 Picardies in the world. The bitch pictured is one of a tiny handful in the United States.

HEIGHT: Male—24–26 inches   Female—22–24 inches
WEIGHT: Male—60–70 pounds   Female—50–60 pounds
COLOR: Brindle to gray-black
COAT: Like goat hair—straight, dry, medium-long

Plott Hound

In Germany the ancestors of the Plott hound were valued for their ability and gameness in fighting wild boars. Brought to the Great Smoky Mountains of Tennessee and North Carolina by Jonathan Plott in 1750, they soon became highly efficient in fighting the black bears of the area. By keeping the breed pure and free of any outcrosses, Mr. Plott improved its quality and hunting prowess steadily; but his family didn't want to market the dogs and as a result they are not widely known. However, in 1946, the United Kennel Club recognized the Plott hound as a separate breed, and the number is slowly growing.

The Plott hound is a heavy-set, well-muscled dog with large ears that should spread 21 inches from tip to tip. Courageous and confident, he is used to hunt coyote, wolf, mountain lion, deer, wildcat and all small game. He is not terribly fast but has great endurance and superior treeing instinct.

HEIGHT: Male—22–25 inches Female—21–24 inches
WEIGHT: Male—50–65 pounds Female—40–55 pounds
COLOR: Brindle or brindle with black saddle
COAT: Smooth, fine, glossy
Registered with the UKC

Pointer

The development of the English pointer took place in Great Britain beginning around the eighteenth century, but the breed was known in Spain, Portugal, France and Belgium before this. He is a mixture of foxhound, greyhound, bloodhound and the setting spaniel, which played a key role in the development of most bird dogs. In 1650, the pointer was used to locate and point hares, and the greyhound was allowed to chase and kill them. In the eighteenth century, when wing shooting was fashionable, the pointer was known as a superior gun dog.

This is the perfect dog for a hunter. Developing quickly and acquiring hunting instinct at a very early age, he is agile, full of energy, courageous and able to put his total concentration on the hunt. He is recognized as the best bird-finding dog extant and so should not be sheltered from a country life with opportunity for lots of exercise. His short, neat coat takes care of itself. Because he can have a quick temper, he is really not very good with children.

HEIGHT: Male—24–25 inches   Female—23–24 inches
WEIGHT: Male—55–60 pounds   Female—50–55 pounds
COLOR: White with liver, lemon, orange or black markings
COAT: Smooth, shiny, short, dense

Registered with the AKC (sporting group)

Pomeranian

Descended from the sled dogs of Iceland and Lapland, the Pomeranian belongs to the spitz group. He derives his name from Pomerania, where most of his breeding took place. In the early nineteenth century, some Pomeranians weighed nearly 30 pounds. Slowly, after years of breeding smaller specimens, they became the dogs we know today.

The Pomeranian has a docile nature, and is easier to train than most dogs. He should be trained early in life, however; otherwise, he'll try to run the house. He is best suited to small homes and apartments, and preferably to families without children. He is active and sturdier than other toy breeds.

HEIGHT: Male—6–7 inches   Female—5½–6½ inches
WEIGHT: Male—5–7 pounds   Female—3–5 pounds
COLOR: Black, brown, red, orange, cream, wolf-sable, blue or white
COAT: Long, straight and glistening
Registered with the AKC (toy group) and UKC

Poodle

Known for years as the national dog of France, the poodle actually originated in Germany and was brought to France in the fifteenth century. The name comes from the German *pudel*, meaning "to splash in the water." Today we have three varieties of poodle: the standard, miniature and toy. It is believed that the standard is the oldest. Because he was used often as a water retriever, it seemed best to clip his coat to facilitate swimming. This started the custom of clipping to enhance the dog's appearance. Throughout time, the poodle has been referred to in literature and art—perhaps more so than any other breed. He has gained greatest popularity in the United States but is held in esteem all over the world.

The poodle has an air of distinction and dignity but is actually a great show-off. He is a quick learner and fine companion. His coat requires much care, and if you prefer to have it clipped, it becomes pretty costly since the hair grows very fast. His ears must also be watched, for the hair there sometimes blocks ventilation and drainage, and the ear passages can become blocked with wax. He is also subject to progressive retinal atrophy.

HEIGHT AND WEIGHT:	Male standard—15 inches and over; 45–55 pounds
	Female standard—15 inches and over; 40–50 pounds
	Male miniature—15 inches and under; 15–16 pounds
	Female miniature—15 inches and under; 14–15 pounds
	Male toy—Under 10 inches; 6–7 pounds
	Female toy—Under 10 inches; 5–6 pounds
COLOR:	Black, brown, white, blue, apricot, silver or café au lait
COAT:	Very profuse, harsh, dense

Registered AKC (non-sporting group) and UKC

Portuguese Water Dog

Known for hundreds of years, the Portuguese water dog is believed to have come from Russia. But his real worth was discovered in the Algarve section of Portugal, where he was the close companion of the fishermen. Possessing the rare talent of diving as deep as twelve feet to retrieve lost gear or even fish, he was a valued member of each fishing vessel's crew. He can swim five miles with ease using an unusual breaststroke.

The dogs are very hardy and adaptable, content to live in city or country. They are friendly, gentle with children, calm and sensible, eager to please. In their untrimmed state, they are gay and appealing; in their show clip, quite stylish. Their coats are curly and do not shed appreciably.

HEIGHT: Male—16–22 inches   Female—14–20 inches
WEIGHT: Male—35–55 pounds   Female—30–45 pounds
COLOR: Black or brown
COAT: Shaggy and curly

Pug

This small, sturdy dog has brought pleasure and pride to his owners for several centuries. Originating in China, he was brought to Holland by traders but remained in relative obscurity until imported into England. There he soon captivated influential noblewomen and, though the breed standard has been changed a good deal since the original was drawn up in 1883, the popularity of the pug continues unabated.

The pug is not a delicate toy. On the contrary, he is compact, well muscled and strong, with a massive, short-faced, round head. He gives great affection and demands a great deal in return; is a fine playmate for thoughtful youngsters, and a neat companion for adults. His coat is soft and easy to keep clean. But he despises hot weather, and because of breathing difficulties, should not be left in hot automobiles or stuffy apartments.

- HEIGHT: Male—11 inches   Female—10–11 inches
- WEIGHT: Male—14–18 pounds   Female—14–18 pounds
- COLOR: Apricot, fawn or black
- COAT: Short, smooth, soft

Registered with the AKC (toy group)

Puli

The puli, a Hungarian sheepdog, has been used by Magyar shepherds for over 1,000 years. He is similar to the Tibetan terrier, who may have been his ancestor. His coat is like no other. It is unkempt and tangled, so matted that it serves as protection against the weather and vicious animals. Because it is usually dull black, the dog was originally used to drive the sheep during the day since these animals respond more readily to dark dogs. And he was also more visible to the shepherds.

The puli is vigorous, active, tireless, nervous and very aggressive. To control wandering sheep, he will jump on their backs and return them to the fold. He is not fond of strangers, children or apartments but is primarily a worker. The plural of puli is pulik.

    HEIGHT: Male—17–19 inches   Female—16–18 inches
    WEIGHT: Male—30–35 pounds   Female—25–32 pounds
    COLOR: Black; also various shades of gray or white
    COAT: Dense and weather-resistant; straight, wavy or slightly curly

Registered with the AKC (working group)

REDBONE COONHOUND

Many dogs are called redbones but the true redbone coonhound has been bred pure for a long time. He was first named Saddleback because he had black saddle markings on his red coat; but these markings have since been eliminated. The foundation stock originated in Georgia and is supposed to contain blood of both the bloodhound and old Irish hound.

The redbone coonhound specializes in hunting raccoons but

is also used to trail and tree bear, cougar and wildcat. A good trailing dog, he is more heavyset than other coonhounds.

    HEIGHT: Male—22–26 inches   Female—21–25 inches
    WEIGHT: Male—50–70 pounds   Female—45–65 pounds
    COLOR: Solid red preferred; a little white allowed on feet and brisket
    COAT: Smooth, fine, dense

Registered with the UKC

REDTICK COONHOUND

The Redtick is a first cousin of the Bluetick coonhound. They share the same antecedents; have the same prowess in the hunt; and except for coloring are identical.

    HEIGHT: Male—22–27 inches   Female—20–25 inches
    WEIGHT: Male—55–80 pounds   Female—45–65 pounds
    COLOR: Reddish-tan, thickly mottled
    COAT: Medium-coarse and short, but appearing smooth and glossy

Rhodesian Ridgeback

Sometimes called the African lion hound, the Rhodesian ridgeback comes from South Africa. During the sixteenth and seventeenth centuries, the Dutch, Huguenots and Germans emigrated to that land bringing with them Danes, bloodhounds, terriers and other breeds. These dogs mated with the native hunting dog that was half wild and had an unusual ridge on his back. The eventual result was the Rhodesian ridgeback, a breed that served many needs of the Boer settlers. He was a watchdog, hunter and excellent companion.

The ridgeback is rarely quarrelsome or noisy. He is devoted to his master—a real one-man dog—but can be very stubborn and should be trained early in life. He can withstand great changes in weather, and can go without water for more than twenty-four hours.

HEIGHT: Male—25–27 inches   Female—24–26 inches
WEIGHT: Male—70–75 pounds   Female—65–70 pounds
COLOR: Light-wheaten to red-wheaten with a little white on chest and toes
COAT: Dense, short, glossy and sleek

Registered with the AKC (hound group)

Rottweiler

The Rottweiler originally served as a cattle-driver for the Roman legions when they conquered Rottweil in the south of Germany 1,900 years ago. When the Romans left, their dogs stayed behind. Aside from herding cattle, they also served as guards for their owners; and such was the fear they inspired that their masters often tied their purses around the dogs' necks.

The Rottweiler is a fine dog for farm life because he likes lots of freedom and is basically a worker. He is faithful and diligent, calm and obedient, and very easily trained for a job. But his innate stubbornness calls for a firm hand.

HEIGHT: Male—23¾–27 inches Female—21¾–25¾ inches
WEIGHT: Male—80–90 pounds Female—75–85 pounds
COLOR: Black with tan and dark brown markings on cheeks, muzzle, chest, legs and over both eyes
COAT: Short, coarse, flat

Registered with the AKC (working group)

Saint Bernard

Long cherished for his storied talent for finding lost travelers in the mountains, the huge, lovable Saint Bernard is not the tough, indomitable and often incredible lifesaver he used to be. Monks at the Monastery of the Order of St. Augustine, high in the Alps, still raise Saints, but sadly state that the basic instincts of the breed have been bred out to produce a more shapely dog who is supposed to be more gentle and patient but who has made news on several recent occasions for killing children. I find this as hard to accept as you; but must point out that such things happen when people inbreed dogs as indiscriminately as some have Saint Bernards.

Saints today are either long-haired (the more common) or short-haired; but both are still the imposing dogs with mammoth appetites known as far back as A.D. 980. They must be treated with respect and demand your affection; in return, the carefully bred dogs are loyal, placid, quiet companions for both adults and children. They are, of course, miserable in warm weather; and in winter they would rather be outdoors.

HEIGHT: Male—27–29 inches   Female—25–27 inches
WEIGHT: Male—155–170 pounds Female—140–160 pounds
COLOR: Various shades of red or brindle with white markings on chest and feet
COAT: Either short and dense or medium-length and slightly wavy without being shaggy

Registered with the AKC (working group) and UKC

SALUKI

The royal dog of Egypt, the saluki possesses a greyhound body with feathered ears, tail and legs. Depicted on tombs of around 2100 B.C., he was the only animal permitted to sleep in the sheikh's tent. The Moslems believed he was sent to them by Allah, and he was so highly regarded that his body was often mummified like the bodies of the Pharaohs. He was used to hunt gazelles, jackals, foxes and hares.

The saluki possesses keen sight and blazing speed. He is accustomed to living a hard life in any climate. He is aloof and undemonstrative; can be temperamental and is not suitable for youngsters.

HEIGHT: Male—23–28 inches   Female—18–24 inches
WEIGHT: Male—55–60 pounds   Female—45–55 pounds
COLOR: White, cream, fawn, gold, red, tan; white, black and tan; or black and tan
COAT: Smooth, soft, silky
Registered with the AKC (hound group)

Samoyed

The Samoyed is much like the primitive dog and has stayed pure for thousands of years. His name comes from the Samoyeds, a tribe that lived on the White Sea in Russia and depended on the dog for herding reindeer and driving sleds.

The Samoyed is strong, gentle and never looks for trouble. A faithful companion, he is good with children and an excellent watchdog. But you will have difficulty housebreaking him and teaching him to follow orders and not to chew on things. He is best suited to a cold climate.

HEIGHT: Male—21–23½ inches   Female—19–21 inches
WEIGHT: Male—50–65 pounds   Female—35–50 pounds
COLOR: Pure white; white and biscuit; cream
COAT: Dense and straight
Registered with the AKC (working group)

Schipperke

The Schipperke, or "little captain," as he was once called, is a small version of the Belgian sheepdog from which he's descended. He resembles no other breed. He has a heavy black coat with a handsome ruff, an almost foxy expression, and a thickset body. He is a reliable watchdog, good house dog and very amiable with children. If not overfed and if exercised often, he should have an unusually long life for a small dog.

HEIGHT: Male—12½–13 inches Female—12–12½ inches
WEIGHT: Male—16–18 pounds Female—14–16 pounds
COLOR: Black
COAT: Abundant and harsh
Registered with the AKC (non-sporting group)

Scottish Deerhound

Great value has always been attached to the deerhound, or Royal Dog of Scotland. Known as far back as the early sixteenth century and owned by no one of lower rank than an earl, this charming, courageous dog is best suited for pursuing and killing deer. He was such a favorite of Scottish chieftains that he was used as ransom for noblemen.

The deerhound's value is not solely based on his rarity but also on the great speed and strength that enable him to capture a Scottish deer weighing over 250 pounds. In addition, the dog is devoted to his master and family. He is quiet and dignified, keen and alert, and very easy to train. He is excellent around children.

HEIGHT: Male—30–32 inches Female—28–31 inches
WEIGHT: Male—85–110 pounds Female—75–95 pounds
COLOR: Dark blue-gray preferred; also gray, yellow, sandy-red
COAT: Harsh, wiry, up to 4 inches long
Registered with the AKC (hound group)

Scottish Terrier

The history of the Scottish terrier is full of controversy. None of the many theories and legends is conclusive because a good deal of crossbreeding undoubtedly occurred. There is no record of the dog prior to 1880, when the first standard was drawn up.

For such a little dog, the scottie possesses much power and confidence. Strong and alert, he rarely feels inferior to anyone. He is a one-man dog and his affection for that person rarely can be swayed. He's good with children only if he has been raised with them. He has a definite body odor and suffers from itching skin to such an extent that he spends a lot of time under beds scratching his back on the rails.

- HEIGHT: Male—10 inches   Female—9–10 inches
- WEIGHT: Male—19–22 pounds   Female—18–21 pounds
- COLOR: Steel gray; brindle or grizzled; black-wheaten
- COAT: Very hard and wiry, about 2 inches long

Registered with the AKC (terrier group)

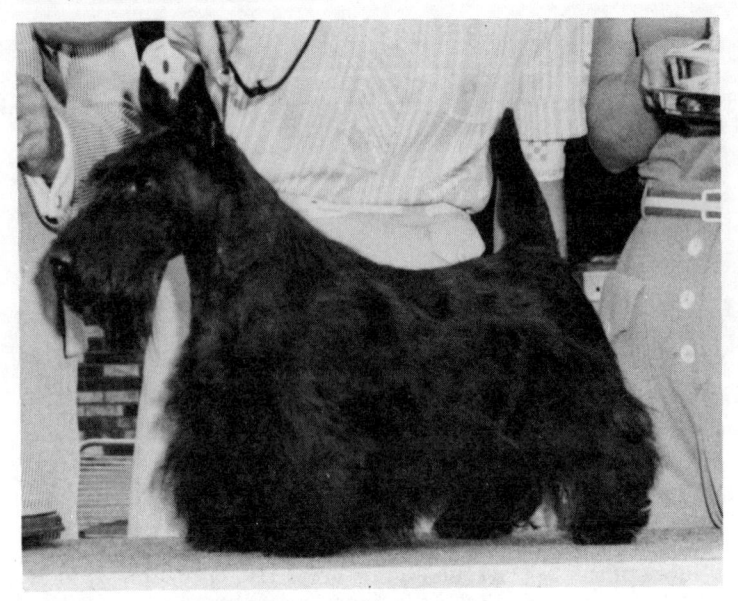

Sealyham Terrier

The Sealyham was named after the breeder's estate, Sealyham, located in Haverfordwest, Pembrokeshire, Wales. Since 1850 the dog has excelled as a hunter of foxes, badgers and otters. His ancestors are numerous: the Pembroke Welsh corgi, Dandie Dinmont, bullterrier and West Highland white terrier.

The Sealyham is naturally self-willed and needs early, firm training. Once trained, he is an excellent house dog and is happy to be around children. He is a loyal and alert companion, almost always full of energy. He makes a fine apartment dog and a good guard since he is acutely aware of any disturbance and barks readily. He is subject to occasional skin ailments.

HEIGHT: Male—10½ inches Female—10 inches
WEIGHT: Male—21 pounds Female—20 pounds
COLOR: All white or white with lemon; tan or badger markings on head and ears

Registered with the AKC (terrier group)

Shetland Sheepdog

The Shetland sheepdog is a small version of the collie. He came from the Shetland Islands, a rugged area known for contributing smaller breeds of domestic animals such as Shetland ponies, sheep and cattle. His ancestors are the King Charles spaniel and the old Scottish hill collie. He was given public recognition in 1840 in records telling of his guarding sheep in the highlands. But it was not until 1914 that the breed received a separate classification as Shetland sheepdog and not Shetland collie.

The Sheltie is a top-notch working dog. His innate instinct is to herd sheep, pigs and goats; and his size is an asset, for he is able to go into areas and jump over obstacles that stymie his larger friends. He is agile and strong yet docile and devoted, very sensitive to human feelings, and determined to please. He is happy to live in a small home because he doesn't take up much room or care to roam. He is an able watchdog. His coat requires much grooming. He is subject to the ailment "collie eye."

HEIGHT: Male—14–16 inches Female—13–15 inches
WEIGHT: Male—15–16 pounds Female—14–15 pounds
COLOR: Combination of black, merle and sable
COAT: Long, straight, harsh

Registered with the AKC (working group) and UKC

Shih Tzu

Depending on which account you believe, the Shih Tzu was introduced to China either from the Byzantine Empire or Tibet many hundreds of years ago. His name comes from the fact that, as depicted in the ancient *Imperial Dog Book,* he looks something like a lion; and *shih tzu* means lion. He was also called the "chrysanthemum-faced dog" because his face hairs grow in all directions. (Both ideas are pretty fanciful; to me he looks more like the typical Hollywood Chinese philosopher.) He was a pet of royalty and because of this was almost wiped out during a recent revolution.

The Shih Tzu carries himself with royal arrogance. He's alert and active; feisty and plucky. He's very adaptable and trustworthy with children; but very wary if they frighten him. He likes the outdoors; but don't let him wander into the underbrush or high grass because that will just compound your already difficult daily grooming chore. He enjoys good health but tends to have some difficulty breathing (this, however, can be corrected by minor surgery).

HEIGHT: Male—9–10½ inches   Female—8–9 inches
WEIGHT: Male—12–14 pounds   Female—10–12 pounds
COLOR: Any color
COAT: Luxurious, long, dense, straight or slightly wavy

Registered with the AKC (toy group)

Siberian Husky

Bred in Siberia as a sled dog, the Siberian husky, or Siberian Chukchi, was first seen in Alaska in 1909. Highly valued through the centuries for his endurance and racing ability, he soon began to win friends with his affectionate, gentle nature. He is happiest in cold climates but is becoming a very popular pet in all kinds of American homes. He is clean and easy to care for, happy, biddable, eager and so friendly that he may wander off in search of companionship if not well trained and loved by his owner. On the negative side, he is extremely strong-headed; quickly bored and destructive if left alone; and sheds several times a year.

The UKC name for this breed is Arctic husky.

HEIGHT: Male—21–23¼ inches Female—20–22 inches
WEIGHT: Male—45–60 pounds Female—35–50 pounds
COLOR: All shadings of gray, tan, black or white
COAT: Very thick, soft, medium-length

Registered with the AKC (working group) and UKC

Silky Terrier

A native of Australia, the silky terrier is most often found there as a pet in suburban homes. For many years, he was known as the Sydney Silky to honor the city of his origin. He comes from a cross between the Australian terrier and Yorkshire. We do not know if he came by chance or by careful planning.

The silky is loved by Australians. He is quite helpful on a farm since he goes after rats and snakes. He is friendly but aggressive and perhaps too energetic. A true terrier, he hardly sits down and therefore is not a dog for nervous people. But he is a good companion, devoted and smart. Housebreaking is difficult and grooming can become a chore.

HEIGHT: Male—10 inches   Female—9–10 inches
WEIGHT: Male—9–10 pounds   Female—8–9 pounds
COLOR: Black and tan
COAT: Glossy, flat, fine
Registered with the AKC (toy group)

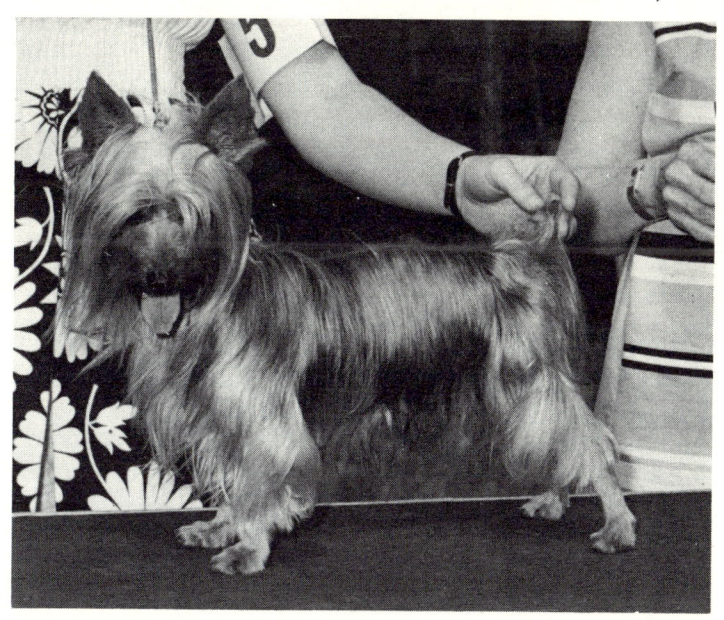

Skye Terrier

A resident of the Island of Skye of Scotland, from whence comes his name, the Skye terrier has attained his present appearance within the past 100 years. But we know from the old British book, *British Dogges,* that the long-coated fellow dates back to the 1600's. In those days he was used to fight off vicious animals and was a renowned burrower and swimmer. In the nineteenth century, he became known to nobility and was a particular favorite of Queen Victoria.

The Skye terrier is elegant and agile. He is twice as long as he is high, and his flowing coat serves as a protection against brush and encounters with other animals. He has a strong sense of smell and can follow a scent—especially that of a badger—accurately. He also has keen sight and hearing, and is a serious and fearless fighter when necessary. He never seems quite certain that he is loved, and demands a great deal of affection from his owner.

HEIGHT: Male—9 inches   Female—8½ inches
WEIGHT: Male—24–25 pounds   Female—23–24 pounds
COLOR: Black, dark or light blue, gray, fawn or cream
COAT: Hard and straight, 5½ inches long
Registered with the AKC (terrier group)

Soft-coated Wheaten Terrier

The soft-coated wheaten terrier, or Irish wheaten as he's sometimes called, is a relative of the Kerry blue and Irish terrier; a descendant of the old black-and-tan English terrier. On Irish farms he is a cattle dog, ratter and shooting companion. In the U.S., he's mainly just a pleasant fellow—good-tempered yet spirited, not as aggressive as some other terriers.

His coat is his pride. It starts out dark red or deep brown and takes as much as eighteen months to turn to a shade of ripe wheat—anywhere from silver to pale gold. The hair is moderately long, soft and silky and should not be trimmed.

HEIGHT: Male—18–19 inches　Female—16–18 inches
WEIGHT: Male—35–45 pounds　Female—30–40 pounds
COLOR: Ripe wheat
COAT: Abundant, medium-long, soft, silky, slightly wavy

Registered with the AKC (terrier group)

Spinone Italiano

Known as the Italian pointer, the spinone is more hound than pointer in appearance. And as a hunter, he belongs to the old slow-footed school prior to the era of wing-shooting. Nevertheless, he is preferred above all other gun dogs in northwest Italy.

The spinone is efficient, hard-working and sturdy. His yellow to pale brown eyes under bushy brows are endowed with a keen expression.

HEIGHT: Male—23–26 inches   Female—20–23 inches
WEIGHT: Male—50–56 pounds   Female—45–50 pounds
COLOR: White or white with yellow or fawn patches
COAT: Short, harsh, straight; undercoat very thick and flat

Accepted in AKC Miscellaneous Class

Staffordshire Bullterrier

The genealogy of the Staffordshire bullterrier has been figured out, but it's so complicated that I leave it to the fanciers to worry with. Enough to say that this is a dog with mixed bulldog and terrier ancestry, and as might be expected, he was originally bred for fighting and is a tough, courageous customer when he chooses to be. But like other dogs of fearsome appearance, he is generally quiet, stable and affectionate. He is particularly fond of children.

HEIGHT: Male—14–16 inches   Female—14–16 inches
WEIGHT: Male—28–38 pounds   Female—24–34 pounds
COLOR: Red, fawn, white, black, blue or any of these with white. Also brindle or brindle with white
COAT: Smooth, short, close

Registered with the AKC (terrier group)

Standard Schnauzer

The standard schnauzer is an old German breed. In Mecklenburg, there is a fourteenth-century statue of a hunter and his schnauzer, which looks very much like today's schnauzer. His portrait appears often in fifteenth- and sixteenth-century art. The breed originated in Württemberg and Bavaria. They were mainly cattle-drivers and rat catchers, and later they were involved in police work and war dispatch service.

The standard schnauzer is responsible and fearless. He seems to perceive approaching danger and so has always served as a good guard. He loves his master's family, including the children, but is not particularly friendly with those he doesn't know. Robust, high-spirited and affectionate, he likes to play, enjoys water and can be taught to retrieve. He needs trimming in spring and fall, and brushing every day. His only real fault is his stubbornness. (For information about the miniature schnauzer, see p. 346.)

HEIGHT: Male—19–20 inches   Female—17–19 inches
WEIGHT: Male—32–37 pounds   Female—27–35 pounds
COLOR: Black or pepper-and-salt
COAT: Close, hard, wiry
Registered with the AKC (working group)

Sussex Spaniel

The Sussex spaniel, taking his name from Sussex, England, dates to the middle of the nineteenth century. He was used for shooting in England where game was abundant and hunting on foot common. Because of the very different conditions in the United States, he has not been imported to a great extent.

Although the companionable Sussex spaniel lacks the speed of the springer and cocker, he has a sensitive nose and is a serious hunter; but since he's slow, he calls for a great deal of patience on the part of his handler. He is strong and steady, never fidgety. He has very little "doggy" odor.

HEIGHT: Male—15–16 inches Female—14–15 inches
WEIGHT: Male—40–45 pounds Female—35–40 pounds
COLOR: Rich golden liver
COAT: Dense, flat, slightly waved
Registered with the AKC (sporting group)

Telomian

The sturdy Telomian is still in the process of development. He is evidently a very old breed, but until 1963 he was known only to the aborigines of Malaysia as a sort of general-purpose dog used sometimes for hunting but kept mainly for companionship. Then a pair was brought to the United States for breeding. Thanks to their new diet and environment, their offspring and descendants are about half again as large; and other changes may be forthcoming. In the meantime, the dogs are being raised and studied by the members of the Telomian Dog Club of America, through which all puppies are sold.

The Telomian is commonly compared to the basenji, to whom he is thought to be linked. Like the basenji, he is difficult to train but is less wary of humans and more socially responsive. He makes the same yodeling or crowing sounds that distinguish the basenji and also barks much like a cocker spaniel. He's affectionate and good with children.

HEIGHT: Male—16–19 inches   Female—15–18 inches
WEIGHT: Male—25–30 pounds   Female—22–27 pounds
COLOR: Any shade of sable with white spots and ticking
COAT: Short and smooth

Tennessee Treeing Brindle

The Tennessee treeing brindle is a new breed developed by Earl C. Phillips and his sons in Illinois from the brindle mountain dogs used by the Cherokee Indians in the Appalachians and, about 1840, the Oklahoma territory. These differed—as does the present breed—from other coon dogs in that they preferred treeing game to trailing. In the sixteen years since the Phillips family started their project, the breed has been refined to a standard and has become popular from coast to coast.

The brindles are fast hunters with good scenting ability and sometimes climb well up into trees after their prey; yet despite their love of the hunt, they thrive on companionship with humans. As one owner writes, "I best describe my female as hunting brains and house brains. She handles herself well in whatever atmosphere she's in."

HEIGHT: Male—18–24 inches Female—16–22 inches
WEIGHT: Male—35–50 pounds Female—30–40 pounds
COLOR: Brindle or black with brindle trim
COAT: Smooth, short, crisp

Tibetan Mastiff

This aggressive sentinel and guard dog of long-ago Tibetan herdsmen has only recently been introduced to the U.S. Although the breed seems to have been the forerunner of all mastiff breeds as well as Saint Bernards and Great Pyrenees, the dogs are a good deal smaller but have many of the same characteristics. Biddable and with great dignity, they make excellent guardians for home and family.

HEIGHT: Male—24½–28½ inches Female—22–25 inches
WEIGHT: Male—80–90 pounds Female—75–85 pounds
COLOR: Black; black and brown; black and red; black and honey
COAT: Long, harsh and thick

Tibetan Spaniel

Originating in Tibet, these charming spaniels were revered and cherished long before the Christian era. They were shown and bred in England in 1905, but it wasn't until 1971 that they were seen in any number in the United States.

True to their long-ago heritage, Tibetans still love to lie on walls or steps and keep watch over their property, but they are unnecessarily yappy. They are cool to strangers, devoted to their family. The males make the better pets. They do not adjust happily to kennel life for they yearn for human companionship, but are quite independent. More alert, happy and active small dogs would be hard to find. Females generally come into heat only once a year. Males almost always outnumber females in litters.

    HEIGHT: Male—10 inches   Female—10 inches
    WEIGHT: Male—9–15 pounds Female—9–15 pounds
    COLOR: All colors and mixtures
    COAT: Silky, medium-long

Tibetan Terrier

From ancient Tibet the Tibetan terrier moved to India, then England, and finally to the United States. He was registered with the AKC in 1973.

Considered a holy or lucky dog in his native land, this is a bright, good-natured little fellow something like the old English sheepdog. Despite his heavy coat, which sheds little, he is adaptable to any climate. Though generally quiet, he is a good watchdog with a bark to give a prowler pause, because it starts on a deep note and rises like a siren.

HEIGHT: Male—14–16 inches Female—12–14 inches
WEIGHT: Male—18–30 pounds Female—16–25 pounds
COLOR: Any color or colors
COAT: Profuse, long, fine, straight or wavy outercoat over a fine, woolly undercoat

Registered with the AKC (non-sporting group)

Toy Fox Terrier

The toy fox terrier is a bred-down version of the smooth-coated variety of standard fox terrier. He was at one time occasionally called an American toy terrier. For the history and characteristics of the little breed, see Fox Terrier.

    HEIGHT: Male—10 inches   Female—10 inches
    WEIGHT: Male—3½–7 pounds   Female—3½–7 pounds
    COLOR: White and black with tan trim preferred; also white and tan or white and black
    COAT: Short, satiny, full-textured

Registered with the UKC

Treeing Walker Coonhound

The treeing Walker coonhound is the most popular foxhound in this country. True-bred examples are found wherever foxhunting is a popular sport.

For many years George Washington Maupin and John Walker, fellow Kentuckians and friends, bred and raised the hounds that had become almost native to Kentucky and Virginia. Through wise breeding and by using only the finest specimens, they came up with a hound that soon won wide popularity. But never totally satisfied with the strain, Maupin and Walker developed an outcross from which our modern Walker coonhound comes. Known as a treeing hound for the way he trees his quarry, the Walker is a splendid, tireless, plucky hunter with an excellent nose and good speed. He is graceful, energetic, ambitious and fearless.

HEIGHT: Male—22–27 inches Female—20–25 inches
WEIGHT: Male—50–75 pounds Female—40–65 pounds
COLOR: White predominating with black and tan spots
COAT: Smooth, fine, dense, glossy

Registered with the UKC

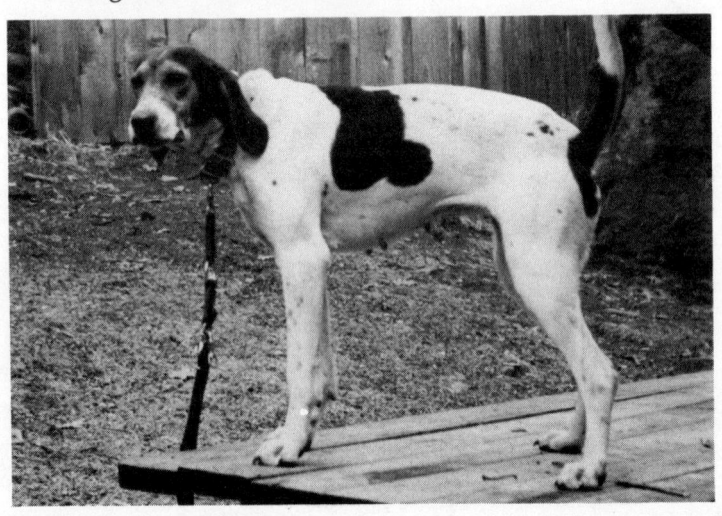

Trigg Hound

A fine foxhound developed in Kentucky under the supervision of Col. Hayden Trigg, this hunting dog is descended from Irish stock that was crossed with the Walker hound. He is notable for his rugged character, great speed and tireless spirit. A good-looking, sturdy dog, he is not thin but rangy.

HEIGHT: Male—23–24½ inches   Female—20–22 inches
WEIGHT: Male—45–55 pounds   Female—35–45 pounds
COLOR: All colors
COAT: Smooth, fine, dense

Vizsla

The Vizsla, or Hungarian pointer, is a favorite hunting dog of the Hungarians. His ancestors were the companions of the Magyars who invaded central Europe over 1,000 years ago. A fourteenth-century Hungarian manuscript tells of a dog resembling the Vizsla used in falconry. His innate hunting ability has been preserved through the ages.

Combining qualities of the pointer and retriever, the Vizsla is totally a one-man dog. He does well on upland game, especially rabbits, and waterfowl. He appears aristocratic and is almost snobbish with all except his immediate family. However, he is stubborn, often nervous, and without early training can become very destructive—especially if confined too much.

HEIGHT: Male—22–24 inches   Female—21–23 inches
WEIGHT: Male—45–60 pounds   Female—40–55 pounds
COLOR: Rust-gold or dark sandy yellow
COAT: Short, smooth and dense

Registered with the AKC (sporting group)

WEIMARANER

The weimaraner is a fairly new German dog dating to the early nineteenth century. One of his ancestors was the bloodhound. When wolves, wildcats, deer and lions were common in Germany, the weimaraner was used by sportsmen as an able, quick hunting dog. Then when big game became rare, he was trained into a retriever and bird dog. German sportsmen were proud to own a weimaraner and made it difficult for others to acquire one. Finally, in 1929, an American sportsman was made a member of the German Weimaraner Club and was allowed to bring back two dogs to the States.

If trained at an early age, the weimaraner makes a fine shooting dog. He has a good sense of smell, remarkable tracking ability and is basically fearless. He is a better watchdog than most hunting dogs. But although he is good with his family, he can be a misery because he chews on everything in sight and can be very stubborn and disobedient. If not given things to do, he dreams up activities on his own. He is also a show-off if permitted.

HEIGHT: Male—25–27 inches   Female—23–25 inches
WEIGHT: Male—70–85 pounds   Female—55–70 pounds
COLOR: Shades ranging from mouse-gray to silver-gray
COAT: Smooth, short and sleek

Registered with the AKC (sporting dog) and UKC

Welsh Springer Spaniel

By studying old prints and manuscripts, we can be rather certain that the Welsh springer spaniel goes back about 400 years. He is found mainly in Wales and the west of England, where he was bred and used purely for working purposes. More recently, the breed has made its way into other countries with varying climates.

The fervor and strength of the Welsh springer spaniel are hard to equal. He never tires and has such a keen nose that he sometimes wanders off looking for the source of enticing smells. If trained early, he becomes an obedient retriever. He is also an admirable family dog and is gentle with children. To keep him in good shape, he must be given adequate exercise.

HEIGHT: Male—16–17 inches Female—15½–16½ inches
WEIGHT: Male—35–40 pounds Female—32–37 pounds
COLOR: Rich dark red and white
COAT: Straight or flat, thick and silky
Registered with the AKC (sporting group)

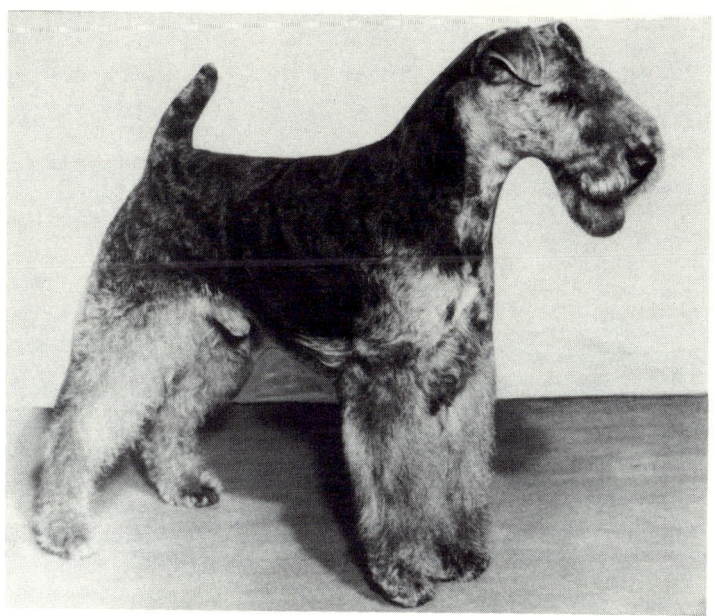

Welsh Terrier

The Welsh terrier has changed very little over the years. His black and tan coloring is the same. He was a sporting dog used to hunt otter, fox and badger and is still occasionally used for hunting. Old prints and paintings indicate that he dates back hundreds of years to the rough-haired black-and-tan terriers.

Though built to hunt, the Welsh terrier is more often seen as an apartment dog. He has much energy and is excellent for young people. He sheds little, is devoted to his family, easy to handle, and has a rather steady disposition with people; but he can be aggressive with other dogs. He is long-lived.

HEIGHT: Male—15 inches Female—14 inches
WEIGHT: Male—20 pounds Female—18–19 pounds
COLOR: Black and tan or black, grizzle and tan
COAT: Wiry, hard, abundant, close
Registered with the AKC (terrier group)

West Highland White Terrier

The West Highland white terrier shares the same ancestors as the scottie, Dandie Dinmont and cairn. He was at one time called the Roseneath terrier and also the Poltalloch terrier, because the breed as we know it originated on the estate of the Malcolms of Poltalloch in Argyllshire, Scotland.

This small white, hardy dog is quite Scotch. He is full of personality, determination and needs little pampering. He loves the outdoors and will romp in the snow on the coldest days; hunt, or run with great speed. He has no fear of animals, people or his environment. Within the home, he is affectionate. Being quite individualistic, he needs early training.

HEIGHT: Male—11 inches Female—10 inches
WEIGHT: Male—15–19 pounds Female—13–17 pounds
COLOR: Pure white
COAT: Hard, 2 inches long, free of curl
Registered with the AKC (terrier group)

Whippet

Sometimes referred to as the English greyhound, the whippet is the fastest dog of his weight—capable of speeds of up to 35 miles an hour. His forte is racing, and in Lancashire and Yorkshire he was called "the poor man's racehorse." His basic stock seems to have come from crosses between English greyhounds and various terriers. The English developed the whippet over 100 years ago for the so-called sport of chasing rabbits in a pen. In this country, he first appeared in Massachusetts, which for a time was the center of whippet racing.

The whippet is diminutively handsome and dignified. He has a pleasant disposition, is easy to housebreak, and doesn't shed. He likes living in a house but should be exercised often. As a watchdog, he earns a good rating but he's inclined to be skittish.

  HEIGHT: Male—19–22 inches   Female—18–21 inches
  WEIGHT: Male—18–28 pounds   Female—12–20 pounds
  COLOR: Gray, tan or white
  COAT: Close, smooth and firm

Registered with the AKC (hound group)

Wirehaired Pointing Griffon

The wirehaired pointing griffon originated in Holland in the last quarter of the nineteenth century, but he is mainly thought of as French since it was in France that major developments took place in his breeding. Despite a hazy ancestry, authorities feel he is a mixture of setter, spaniel, otter hound and German short-haired pointer. He is the only pointer with a harsh coat recognized by the AKC.

The wirehaired griffon is particularly adapted to swampy country because of this coat. In the field he is slow and deliberate, but has a keen sense of smell, points well and is also a good retriever. He is even-tempered, reserved and calm; good with a family, and attached to his master.

HEIGHT: Male—21½–23½ inches   Female—19½–21½ inches
WEIGHT: Male—50–60 pounds   Female—45–55 pounds
COLOR: Steel gray with chestnut splashes; gray-white with chestnut splashes; chestnut; or dirty white mixed with chestnut
COAT: Harsh, dry, stiff, never curly

Registered with the AKC (sporting group)

Xoloxcuintle

Known familiarly as the Xolo, this breed existed in Mexico at the time of the Aztecs, who valued the dogs highly as a food delicacy. Humorous effigies of the dog have been discovered in ancient tombs. Modern-day country folk in Mexico believe the dog has powers to ward off many ailments from asthma to malaria. Old people still take the dog to bed with them, because they are unusually warm (normally 104°).

The Xolo is somewhat like the Manchester terrier, graceful in movement with well-proportioned slender legs; but he is hairless except for a little fluff on the head and tip of the tail. The skin tans just as human skin does and must be rubbed with cream to prevent it from becoming too dry. Perhaps because his lack of coat gives him a slight inferiority complex, he is very aggressive toward large, hairy dogs; but he's gentle with children, small animals and even cats. He barks rarely and then in an impressive loud, low tone.

HEIGHT: Male—16–20 inches Female—15–18 inches
WEIGHT: Male—25–30 pounds Female—20–30 pounds
COLOR: Black to charcoal gray; dark bronze

Yorkshire Terrier

The Yorkshire terrier breed is not very old, and it is one that man developed so secretively that there are few definite records of his ancestors. Most probably he is descended from the Skye terrier and black-and-tan terrier; but the Maltese and Dandie Dinmont also may have had some influence on him. Within twenty years of the Yorkshire's beginning, the dogs were dwarfed so greatly that they are now among the smallest in the vast canine family. Though originally favorites of the working classes, they made their way into more fashionable circles in the late Victorian era.

This toy terrier is lovable, fearless and strong-bodied. He is friendly with people and other animals, loyal to his owner, and very healthy. He does demand attention, but this is not hard to give once you have survived a long housebreaking siege and as long as you forgive his lapses into stubbornness. His long, flowing coat requires nearly 30 minutes of attention daily. He is ideal for apartment living.

HEIGHT: Male—9 inches   Female—8–9 inches
WEIGHT: Male—7–8 pounds   Female—4–6 pounds
COLOR: Dark steel-blue and tan
COAT: Straight, long, glossy with silky texture
Registered with the AKC (toy group)

Credits

Page
- 18 Photo: Cherie Suhie.
- 43 Photo: Cherie Suhie.
- 64 Saint Bernards from Beau Cheval Kennels.
- 65 Lhasa Apsos litter bred by Barbara Wood and Brenda O'Donnell. Anbara Lhasa Apsos. Photo: Barbara Wood.
- 91 Photo: Margaret Noyes.
- 115 Photo: Arman G. Hatsian for *The Hartford Courant*.
- 174 Chinese fighting dog pups from Aitochi Kennel.
- 202 Photo: *The Greenwich Time*.
- 224 German wirehaired pointer from Wireland Kennels.
- 230 West Highland white terrier puppy from Eilmor Kennel.
- 237 Affenpinschers; Richard and Sharon Stremski, owners. Vroni Kleine Kennels. Photo: Evelyn Shafer.
- 239 Airedale terrier (Ch. Aristocrat of White House); White House Kennels.
- 240 Akita (Aitochis Fuji); Jean M. Fein, owner. Aitochi Kennel. Photo: Martin Booth.
- 241 Alaskan malamute (Beowulf's Danska); Beth J. Harris, owner. Beowulf's Hilltop.
- 243 American Eskimo (Morlock's King Snowball); F. K. Morlock, owner.
- 244 American foxhound (Hewly Striping); Stanley D. Petter, Jr., owner.
- 245 American Staffordshire terrier (Ch. Willynwood Ronin); William F. Peterson, owner. Willynwood Kennels.
- 246 American water spaniel (Katie of Swan Lake); John H. Barth, owner. Swan Lake Kennels.
- 247 Anatolian shepherd dogs (Peki, Topaz and Zorba); Lt. R. C. Ballard, U.S.N., owner.
- 248 Australian cattle dog (Fischer Jarmo Blue Anna); Cal and Bonnie Fischer, owners. Quarter Circle F Ranch.
- 249 Australian kelpie. Photo: American Kennel Club.
- 250 Australian shepherd (Lownes' Tuck of Coppertone); Richard W. Lownes, owner.
- 251 Australian terrier (Ch. Tinee Town Talkbac); Mrs. Milton Fox, owner. Pleasant Pasture Kennels.
- 252 Basenji (Ch. Betsy Ross' Kingola of Ber Vic); Betsy and Ross Newmann, owners. Betsy Ross Kennels.

404 / THE DOG LOVER'S ANSWER BOOK

254 Beagle puppies from Fulmont Beagles.
255 Bearded collie (Polaneid Yankee Doodle); Linda and Robert W. Fish, owners. Polaneid Kennels. Photo: Chase's Photography.
256 Bedlington terrier (Ch. Homer's Aphrodite); Frances N. Homer, owner and breeder. Photo: William P. Gilbert.
257 Belgian Malinois (Ch. Lagardaire de la Mascotte Royale); Dr. and Mrs. Dale M. Diamond, owner. Photo: American Kennel Club.
258 Belgian sheepdog (Ch. High-Mount's Charmin); Helena Tompkins, owner. High-Mount Kennel.
259 Belgian Tervuren (Fillette de Mont Chaussée); Mrs. Charles L. Pitman, owner. Photo: Evelyn M. Shafer.
260 Bernese mountain dog (Gordo); Susanne M. Gagnon, owner. Photo: William P. Gilbert.
261 Bichon Frise (Ch. Beau Monde the Actor); Marie and Marijane McAuliffe, owners.
262 Black-and-tan coonhound; Donald Iden, owner. Berghafen Kennels. Photo: Ritter.
263 Bloodhound (Ch. Trails Dandelion Charro); Lillian Sayre and Lonnie Sayre Lang, owners. Trails Bloodhounds.
264 Bluetick coonhound (Reefer); Russell Barbaresi, owner.
265 Border collie; Pat Kuchma, owner.
267 Borzoi (Ch. Blythe Spirit of Rising Star); Nadine Johnson, owner. Rising Star Kennels. Photo: Hodges and Associates.
269 Bouvier des Flandres (Ch. Odelette du Posty Arlequin); Mrs. Ray Hubbard, owner. Madrone Ledge Kennels. Photo: Brooks Photographers.
270 Boxer (Ch. Boxella's Rodger); Joseph Heine, owner. Boxella Kennels.
271 Boykin spaniel; W. B. Boykin, owner.
272 Briard (Ch. Man de Ville's O. J. Britt); Don Mandeville, owner. Briards de Beauxjolis. Photo: Missy Yuhl.
273 Brittany spaniel (Ch. Redgy of Little Egypt); Miz Temple, owner. Little Egypt Kennels.
274 Brussels griffon (Ch. Toto); Mrs. Thomas J. Coburn, owner. Photo: Alexander.
276 Bullmastiff; Nellie and Joseph Wisotzky, owners. Keytu Bullmastiffs.
277 Bullterrier (Rocky C. of Holcroft); Alfred T. Bibby, owner. Holcroft Kennels.
278 Cairn terrier (Ch. Woodstation Highland Rogue); Ken and Ruby Widicus, owners. Happy Day Kennels.
279 Canaan dog (Adam me Beth ha Emunah); Mrs. Judith K. Ardine, owner. Beth ha Emunah Canaan Dogs.
280 Cardigan Welsh corgi (Ch. Rollingwood's Blue); Priscilla Benkin, owner. Rollingwood Cardigans.
281 Catahoula leopard dog (Double Blue); Susan Gray, owner.
282 Cavalier King Charles spaniel (Can. Ch. Pargeter Fergus of Kilspindie); Miss Elizabeth Spalding, owner. Kilspindie Cavaliers.
283 Chesapeake Bay retriever (Ch. Crispin Roderick); John and

CREDITS / 405

Karen Ann Wood, owners. Bustrywood Kennel. Photo: Earl Graham.
284 Chihuahuas (Ch. Terrymont Maple Sugar Candy and Ch. Terrymont Trifle Bit of Candy); Mr. and Mrs. Herbert Terry, owners. Terrymont Kennels. Photo: *Cleveland Press.*
285 Chinese crested dog. Photo: Lucas Photography, Virginia Beach, Virginia.
286 Chinese fighting dog (Kung Fu); Mr. and Mrs. Victor Seas, owners. Walnut Lane Kennel.
287 Chinese Imperial Ch'in (Didi); Ruth Aston, owner. Photo: Bill Wade.
288 Chinese Temple dog (Aijya de Lau Shou Sying); Ruth Aston, owner.
289 Chow Chow. Photo: Evelyn Shafer.
290 Clumber spaniel (Ch. Oakhill Ambrose); Mr. & Mrs. C. W. Marion, owners. Oakhill Kennels.
291 Cocker spaniel (Chief Joseph Brandt); Mr. and Mrs. Philip W. Schwartz, owners.
292 Collie (Bellhaven Enchanting Lancer); Mrs. Inga Holm, owner. Holmhaven Collies.
293 Coton de Tulear (Pride of Beechwood); Mrs. John F. Casey, owner.
294 Curly-coated retriever (Ch. Siccawei Black Rod); N. Dale Detweiler, owner. Windpatch Kennels. Photo: William P. Gilbert.
295 Dachshunds (Ethel and Oscar); Mrs. John H. White, owner.
296 Dalmatian (Ch. Panore of Watseka); Carol Schubert, owner. Watseka Kennels.
297 Dandie Dinmont terrier (Ch. Ceolaire Checkmate); Carol M. Canora, owner. Ceolaire Kennels. Photo: Thelma Fracchia.
298 Doberman pinscher (Ch. Regulus of Marks-Tey); Everett and Norma Thompson, owners. Ki-Jan Dobes.
299 English cocker spaniel (Ch. Tolgate Tamara); Tolgate Kennels.
300 English coonhound (Plumlees Blue Dotty). Photo: UKC, Kalamazoo, Michigan.
301 English foxhounds. Photo: Evelyn Shafer.
303 English shepherd; Mr. and Mrs. John Blankenship, owners. Tennlea Farm.
305 English toy spaniel (Prince Charles variety). Photo: Evelyn Shafer.
306 Field spaniel (Ch. Squires Pilgrims Promise); Carl Steifel, Jr., owner. Five Sons Kennels. Photo: William P. Gilbert.
307 Finnish spitz (Cullabine Gadabout); Bette Isacoff, owner.
308 Flat-coated retriever (Ch. Mantayo Bronze Clipper); Sally J. Terroux, owner. Terroux Training Kennel.
310 French bulldog (Ch. Koch's Bobo); Miriam Koch, owner.
311 German shepherd (Irish and Indian Ch. Vagabond of Buttas); Mrs. J. M. Barrington, owner.
312 German short-haired pointer (Ch. Strauss's Happy Go Lucky); Mrs. Ann Serak, owner. Serakraut Kennels.
313 German wirehaired pointer (The King of Wireland); Bill and Janet Hesting, owners. Wireland Kennels.

314 Giant schnauzer (Gretta Von Alde); Ken and Ruby Widicus, owners. Happy Day Kennels.
315 Glen of Imaal terrier; Francis J. Kelly, owner.
317 Gordon setter (Ch. Sangerfield Smokey); Margaret Sanger, owner. Sangerfield Kennels. Photo: Evelyn M. Shafer.
318 Great Danes (Ch. Harpie von Meistersinger and Ch. C'est Si Bon von Meistersinger); owned and bred by Meistersinger Kennels.
319 Greater Swiss mountain dog (Carinthia's Cato); Mr. and Mrs. Merle Wilson, owners. J. Frederick Hoffman, breeder.
320 Great Pyrenees (Ch. Quibbletown Leo the Lion); Mrs. Walter R. Moore, owner. Zodiac Kennels.
321 Greyhound (Ch. Colonial Acres Lady Luck); Walter W. Schenck, owner. Colonial Acres Kennels. Photo: Rob Paris Studio.
323 Ibizan hound (Khafre); Susan Banner, owner.
324 Iceland dog (Loppi of Olafsvellir); Mrs. M. A. Beach, owner.
325 Irish setter (Misty Meadows Rusty); Linda and Matt Halprin, owners. Misty Meadows Farm.
326 Irish terrier (Ch. Kincora's Kerry-Ann Girl); J. M. O'Connor and S. G. Young, owners. Kincora Kennels.
327 Irish water spaniel (Ch. Mallyree Mr. Muldoon): Mallyree Kennels.
328 Irish wolfhound (Shea of Shannon); Mrs. Douglas Van Dyke, owner.
329 Italian greyhound (Ch. Colonial Acres Bittersweet); Walter W. Schenck, owner. Colonial Acres Kennels. Photo: Rob Paris Studio.
330 Jack Russell terriers; Mrs. Henry A. Rudkin, Jr., owner. Trelawney Kennel.
331 Japanese spaniel (Ai Jya de Gwei Dzu); Ruth Aston, owner.
332 Keeshond (Ch. Milmar's Key Flyer); Marilyn Miller, owner. Milmar Keeshonden.
334 Komondor (Ch. Pannonia's Jeges Medve); Candy and Jerry George, owners. Jeges Komondorok. Photo: Ward W.Wells.
335 Kuvasz (Ch. Von Elfins Kiraly-Joshua); Terrymont Kennels, owners. Von Elfin Kennels. Photo: Evelyn M. Shafer.
336 Labrador retriever (Jessfield Buckshot); Mrs. W. W. Wickersham, owner.
337 Lakeland terrier (Ch. Darbi's Checkmate); Donald and Barbara Riter, owners. Photo: Martin Booth.
338 Lhasa Apsos (Ch. Rgyal Kagtsa-Po); Barbara Wood, owner. Anbara Lhasa Apsos.
339 Little lion dog (The mouse d'Eayre); Mrs. Charles B. Cook, owner.
340 Maltese (Ch. Nika's Bonus); Mrs. Ruth B. Hager, owner. Nika Kennels. Photo: William P. Gilbert.
341 Manchester terrier (Ch. Lady Minuette Star of Essex); Alice A. Lovely, owner. Photo: Evelyn M. Shafer.
342 Mastiff (Ch. Harold of Shute); Griffith Ranch, owners.
343 Mexican hairless; Mrs. Howard L. Sherman, owner. Photo: Hess Photographers.

344 Miniature bullterrier (Albanian Moxie); David J. Stoia, owner. Ruth Gordon Kennels.
345 Miniature pinscher (Davina's Twinkle Toes); Mrs. Karlina Evans, owner. Davina Kennels.
347 Neapolitan mastiff (Arno Di Alaric); Alaric Neapolitan Mastiffs.
348 Newfoundland (Ch. Little Bear's James Thurber); V. A. Chern, owner. Little Bear Kennels. Photo: Jansken.
349 Norwegian elkhound (Ch. Dame Brittney Sands); Carl and Janice Bloomfield, owners. Jan-Car's Norwegian Elkhounds.
350 Norwich terrier (Pumpernickel); Mr. and Mrs. Duncan Sutphen, owners.
351 Old English sheepdog (Ch. Ragbear Bobmars Hillary Mist); L. A. Woody Nelson, owner. Moptop Kennels.
352 Otter hound (Ch. Specter's Alabaster); Martha C. Thorne and Susan P. King, owners. King Hill Kennel.
353 Papillon (Ch. Cadaga's Salute); Susan P. King, owner. King Hill Kennels. Photo: William P. Gilbert.
355 Pembroke Welsh corgi (Ch. Mackson's Princess-Belle); Frank F. Bell, owner. Bell-Fast Kennels.
356 Pharaoh hound (Divels Mina); Mrs. Rita Laventhall Sacks, owner. Beltara Kennels.
357 Picardie shepherd (Iaouen de Kerangat); Evans Hunt, owner.
358 Plott hound (Bluff Creek Sue); Steve Herd, owner. Bluff Creek Plott Hounds.
362 Portuguese water dog (Ch. Leão Algadbiorum); Mrs. Herbert H. Miller, Jr., owner. Farmion Kennels.
363 Pug (Ch. Koch's Happy Go Lucky); Miriam Koch, owner. Photo: William P. Gilbert.
364 Puli (Fritzi Scheff); Mrs. P. Kries, owner.
365 Redbone coonhound. Photo: National Redbone Coonhound Association.
367 Rhodesian ridgeback (Jungle Jolly Sunday's Child); Ruth M. Christopher, owner. King Hill Kennel.
368 Rottweiler (Ch. Dux von Hungerbuhl); Dr. Elizabeth Eken and P. G. Rademacher, owners. Rosden's Rottweilers.
369 Saint Bernard (Sir Mouser Von Bourban); Thad P. Lempicki, owner.
370 Saluki (Ch. Srinagar Jen Araby Krisna); Dr. Winifred B. Lucas, owner. Srinagar Kennels. Photo: Sudwig.
371 Samoyed (Ch. Winterway's Beowulf); Tom Quigley, owner. Taymyr Samoyeds.
373 Scottish deerhounds (Ch. Gwent's Hallelujah, Ch. Gwent's Magnificat and Jessica of Gwent); Mrs. Cecelia Arnold, owner. Deerhound Digs Farms. Photo: Mrs. C. Arnold.
374 Scottish terrier (Ch. Tambrae Tulla); Charlene Hallenbeck, owner. Lochnel Kennel. Photo: Hal Carrier.
375 Sealyham terrier (Pearson's Show Star); Mrs. Raymond Dunleavy, owner.
376 Shetland sheepdog (Ch. Astolat Galaxy); Constance B. Hubbard, owner. Astolat Kennels. Photo: Evelyn M. Shafer.
377 Shih Tzu (Ch. Witch's Wood Yum-Yum); Dr. and Mrs.

J. Wesley Edel, owners. The Emperor's Kennels.
379 Silky terrier (Ch. Gay Wolf of Iradell); Wilcroft Kennels, owner. Photo: William P. Gilbert.
380 Skye terrier (Ch. Tarskavaig Great Scot of Iradell); Robert Morsey, owner. Photo: Jansken.
381 Soft-coated wheaten terrier (Gramaehree's Roderick Dhu); Suzann Bobley and Barbara Miller, owners. Max-Well Kennels.
382 Spinone Italiano (Black Friar's Duck Soup); Annita Kuyfbeck Mann, owner.
383 Staffordshire bullterrier (Ch. Gamecock Another Brinsley Lad); Claude Williams, owner. Ashton Kennels. Photo: Chase Ltd.
384 Standard schnauzer (Max); Mrs. H. Vernon Scott, owner.
386 Telomian (Sam); A. M. Palumbo, owner.
387 Tennessee treeing brindle (Buck Creek Bucky); Ben Phillips, owner. Buck Creek Farm Kennel.
388 Tibetan mastiff (Ausable's Chang-Du); Joan Gilman and Linda Stone, owners. Ausable Kennels.
389 Tibetan spaniel (Rdo-Rje Rig-Zin of Amroth); Amroth Kennels.
390 Tibetan terrier (Ch. Zim Sha's Tasha Ti Song); Anne Keleman, owner.
391 Toy fox terrier (Ch. Hopkins Skippers Beryl); Phil and Eliza Hopkins, owners. Hopkins Toy Fox Terrier Kennel.
392 Treeing Walker coonhound (Swaney's Bawling Bonnie); Frank Swaney, owner.
393 Trigghound; Herbert O. Lamb, owner.
394 Vizsla (Ch. Glen Cottage Lake Barat); Mrs. Marion I. Coffman, owner. Cariad Kennels.
395 Weimaraner; Capt. and Mrs. Karl Zittel, owners.
396 Welsh springer spaniel (Sharon Brent); Jean Paskiewicz, owner. Walean Kennel.
397 Welsh terrier (Ch. Bengal Wiredot Welsh Prince); Nyle Layman and James Koss, owners. Janterrs Kennels.
398 Seven-week-old West Highland/white terrier; Mr. and Mrs. Fred Smith, owners. Photo: Barbara Wood.
399 Whippet (Ch. Colonial Acres King O' Clubs); Walter W. Schenck, owner. Colonial Acres Kennels. Photo: Rob Paris Studio.
400 Wirehaired pointing griffon (Waldschloss Rotebart); Anna May Metz, owner. Waldschloss. Photo: William P. Gilbert.
401 Xoloxcuintle. Photo: The American Hairless Dog Club, Norfolk, Virginia.

Index

Abdomen, swollen, 151
Affenpinscher, 237
Afghan hound, 238–39
African lion hound, 367
Age
    breeding and, 161, 163
    to buy dog, 52, 54–55
    placing puppies and, 199
Aging dogs, 228–33
Airedale terrier, 239–40
Akita, 240–41
Alaskan malamute, 241–42
Allergies, 45, 150
American Coonhound Association, 28
American Eskimo, 242–43
American Field Stud Book, 28
American foxhound, 243–44
American International Border Collie Registry, 28
American Kennel Club (AKC), 27–28
    breeds registered, 29–30
    registration with, 57–58, 187–188
    shows, 209–17
American (Pit) bullterrier, 244–45
American Staffordshire terrier, 244–45
American water spaniel, 246–47
Anatolian shepherd dog, 247

Anemia, 137
Antecedents, 15
Antifreeze, 155
Apartments, 36, 41–42, 73
Apron, 24
Arthritis, 145
Artificial insemination, 164
Attack dogs, 221–22
Australian cattle dog, 248
Australian kelpie, 249
Australian shepherd, 250
Australian terrier, 251
Automobiles, 114, 141–42
    chasing of, 115–16
    injuries by, 152–53, 206–7

Babblers, 225
Baby, new, resentment of, 23
Bandages, 153
Barking, 110, 112–13, 206, 207
Basenji, 252
Basset hound, 253
Bathing, 93–94, 199–200
Beagle, 254–55
Bearded collie, 255–56
Beauty spot, 24
Bedding, 74
Bedlington terrier, 256–57
Bee stings, 156
Begging, 112
Belgian Malinois, 257–58
Belgian sheepdog, 258–59

Belgian Tervuren, 259–60
Bench shows, 210, 212
Bernese mountain dog, 260–61
Bichon Frise, 261
Bicycles, 116
Bitch. *See* Females
Biting, 111–12, 129, 204–5
Black-and-tan coonhound, 262
Bladder stones, 145
Blaze, 24
Bleeding, 153
Blenheim spaniel, 305–6
Blindness, 146–47, 231
Blinkers, 225
Bloat, 141
Blooded dog, 29
Bloodhound, 263
Bloom, 92
Bluetick coonhound, 264
Boarding, 68–69
Boat, living on, 119
Bones, broken, 142
Bones (for food), 88
Border collie, 265
Border terrier, 266
Borzoi, 267
Boston terrier, 268
Bouvier des Flanders, 269
Boxer, 270
Boykin spaniel, 271
Brace Class, 215
Breath, foul, 149
Breeding, 158–73
  age of female, 161
  age of male, 35
  feeding and, 84–85, 167, 173
  hip dysplasia and, 133–34, 162
  unplanned, 38–39
  whelping and, 168–73
Breeds, 237–402
  list of, 29–33
  number of, 27
  popularity of, 33–34
  recognized, 29
  standards for, 34
Briard, 272

Brindle, Tennessee treeing, 387
Brisket, 27
Brittany spaniel, 273
Brush (tail), 27
Brushing, 90, 187
Brussels griffon, 274
Bulldog, 275
  French, 310
Bullmastiff, 276
Bullterrier, 277
  American (Pit), 244–45
  miniature, 344
  Staffordshire, 383
Bumps on head, 25
Burns, 155
Burrs, 93
Buying a dog, 41–59

Cairn terrier, 278
Calluses, 151
Canaan dog, 279
Candy, 88
Cardigan Welsh corgi, 280
Care and handling, 60–73
Carpeting, 65–66, 110
Carpus, 25
Carrion, rolling in, 22–23
Carsickness, 141–42
Castration, 36
Catahoula leopard dog, 281
Cataracts, 146–47
Cats, 24, 117
Cattle dog, Australian, 248
Cavalier King Charles spaniel, 282
C.D. and C.D.X., 122–24
Certificates, 49, 58, 187–90
Champion dogs, 216–17, 218
Chasing, 115–17, 118
Chesapeake Bay retriever, 283
Chewing, stopping, 110–11
Chicken killers, 206
Chien Berger de Brie, 272
Chihuahua, 284
Children, 23, 42–43, 53, 168, 186
Chills, 176

INDEX / 411

Chinese crested dog, 285
Chinese fighting dog, 286–87
Chinese Imperial Ch'in, 287–88
Chinese Temple dog, 288–89
Ch'ins, 287–88, 331
Chops, 25
Chow chow, 289–90
Circling moves, 22
City living, 36, 41–42, 73
Classes, competitive, 121–22, 213–14
Cleaning, 65
Cleft palate, 177
Clipping, 90
Clumber spaniel, 290–91
Coat of dog, 90–99, 200. *See also* Hair
  double, 24–25
Coats (apparel), 68
Cocker spaniel, 21–92
  English, 299–300
Collars, 66–67, 177
  flea, 96–97, 177
Collie, 292–93
  Bearded, 255–56
  Border, 265
Colors of dogs, 23–24
Colostrum, 179
Come, teaching dog to, 106
Communicating by dogs, 21
Companion Dog, 122–23
Companion Dog Excellent, 123–124
Constipation, 140–41, 229
Convulsions, 144
Coonhounds
  black-and-tan, 262
  bluetick, 264
  English, 300–301
  redbone, 365–66
  redtick, 366
  treeing Walker, 392
Corgis, 280, 355
Coton de Tulear, 293–94
Cough, kennel, 143
Cowhocked, 26
Crackers, 88

Crossbreed, 29
Croup, 27
Crying by puppies, 102–3
Cryptorchid, 35
Culling a litter, 176
Curly-coated retriever, 294–95
Cuts, 151–52

Dachshund, 295–96
Dalmatian, 296–97
Dam. *See* Females; Mother dogs
Dandie Dinmont, 297–98
Dandruff, 150–51
Deafness, 135, 231
Death, 233
Deer, 206
Deerhound, Scottish, 373
Defecation, 22, 65, 193
Destructive dogs, 111
Dewclaws, 26, 184–85
Diabetes, 144
Diarrhea, 140
Diet. *See* Feeding
Dips, tick, 97
Distemper, 129–30, 195
Doberman pinscher, 298–99
Docking of tails, 182–84
Dognapping, 207
Dragging rear, 136
Dribbling, 40, 229
Drowning, 156
Dysplasia, 131–34, 162

Ears, 147–48, 184
  cropping of, 197
Eclampsia, 173
Eczema, 150
Eggs, 87
Electrical shocks, 156
Elevators, 62
Elkhound, Norwegian, 349
Enemas, 128
English bulldog, 275
English cocker spaniel, 299–300
English coonhound, 300–301
English foxhound, 301
English greyhound, 399

412 / INDEX

English setter, 302
English sheepdog, 351
English shepherd, 303
English springer spaniel, 304
English toy spaniel, 305–6
Entropion, 145
Eskimo, American, 242–43
Estrum, 37
Excrement, 22, 65, 193
Exercises, obedience trials and, 122–25
Expression, 25
Eyes, 15, 16, 25, 95, 184
    diseases of, 145–47

Falls, 155
False pregnancy, 39
Family pets, 41–48
Fat, supplementary, 88, 94
Fears, 117–18
Feathering, 24
Feeding, 80–89, 127
    of aging dogs, 228
    breeding and, 84–85, 167, 173
    of puppies, 179–80, 191–94, 200
    Females, 36–37, 40, 48
        boarding at home, 38
        breeding and, 160–61, 164, 166–73
        fighting of, 61
        as guard dogs, 37
        heat of, 37–38, 40, 203
        as hunters, 37
        vs. males as pets, 45–46
        mongrel litters, 38
        spaying of, 39, 133
        staining by, 38
Fencing, 64, 78–79
Field spaniel, 306
Field trials, 226
Fighting, 61
Fighting dog, Chinese, 286–87
Finding a dog to buy, 48–49
Finnish spitz, 307
First aid, 151–54

First dog, 15
Flank, 27
Flat-coated retriever, 308
Fleas, 95–96, 177
Flews, 25
Food. See Feeding
Foreign countries, 59, 72
Forelegs, parts of, 25–26
Formulas, 179, 191
Foxhounds, 243–44, 301
Fox terrier, 309
    toy, 391
French bulldog, 310
Fruit, 86
Full Cry Kennel Club, 26
Fur. See Coat; Hair

Gait, faults in, 26–27
Gardens, 63
Garlic, 84
Gas, 89, 141
German shepherd, 311
German shorthaired pointer, 312
German wirehaired pointer, 313
Gestation period, 167
Gestures, understanding and, 21
Giant schnauzer, 314
Gift dogs, 54–55, 59
Glen of Imaal terrier, 314–15
Glove, hound, 92
Golden retriever, 315–16
Goose-rump, 27
Gordon setter, 317
Grass, 88, 99
Great Dane, 318–19
Greater Swiss mountain dog, 319–20
Great Pyrenees, 320–21
Greyhounds, 321–22, 329, 399
Griffons, 274, 400
Grilles for autos, 70
Grooming, 90–99, 187
Guard dogs, 54, 114, 219–23
    females as, 37
    Turkish, 247
Guide dogs, 226–27
Gun dogs, 223–26

Habits, bad, 109, 111
Hair, 65, 137. *See also* Coat
    care of, 90–99
Handicapped person, 45, 121
Handlers, professional, 216
Handling of dogs, 60–61
    puppies, 185–86
Hard pad, 130
Harness, 67
Harrier, 322
Haw, 145
Head bumps, 25
Health care, 126–57
Hearing, 15–16, 184
Heart disease, 142–43
Heartworm, 137–40, 195
Heat, sexual, 37–38, 40, 203
Heat loss, panting and, 19
Heel, teaching to, 108
Height, measurement of, 26
Hematomas, 147
Hemorrhaging, 153
Hepatitis, 130–31, 195
Hindlegs, parts of, 25–26
Hip dysplasia, 131–34, 162
Hock, 26
Hookworms, 135–36
Hormones, heat and, 40
Horses, 118
Hotels, 70
Hounds, 30. *See also* Coon-
    hounds; Foxhounds; Grey-
    hounds; Wolfhounds
    Afghan, 238–39
    African lion, 367
    basset, 253
    Ibizan, 323
    otter, 352
    Pharaoh, 356
    Plott, 358
    Trigg, 393
Housebreaking, 103–5
Housing, 74–79
Howling, 16, 17
Humming by mother dog, 17
Hungarian pointer, 394
Hunting dogs, 37, 223–26
Husky, Siberian, 378

Ibizan hound, 323
Iceland dog, 324
Illness, 126–57
Imperial Ch'in, Chinese, 287–88
Inbreeding, 158–59
Inherited ailments, 131, 134–35
Injuries, 151–54, 206–7
Insecticides, 97
Insurance, 205, 228
Intelligence of dogs, 20
International Fox Hunters' Stud
    Book, 26
Irish setter, 325
Irish terrier, 326
Irish water spaniel, 327
Irish wheaten, 381
Irish wolfhound, 328
Italian greyhound, 329
Italian mastiff, 347
Italian pointer, 382

Jack Russell terrier, 330
Japanese Ch'in, 331
Japanese spaniel, 331
Judges, 122–23, 216, 217
Jumping on people, 113

Keeshond, 332
Kelpie, Australian, 249
Kennel cough, 143
Kennel run, 77
Kennels, 68–69, 201–3
    buying from, 51, 53, 54
Kerry blue terrier, 333
Kidney disease, 229
Killer dogs, 205–6
King Charles spaniel, 305–6
Kiss marks, 24
Knuckling, 27
Komondor, 334
Kuvasz, 335

Labor, 169–70
Labrador retriever, 336
Lakeland terrier, 337
Learning, 20. *See also* Training
Leashes, 67, 107–8, 203
Legal problems, 201–7

Legs, 25–27
  ailments of, 142
  lifting of, 35
Leopard dog, Catahoula, 281
Leptospirosis, 131, 195
Lhasa Apsos, 338
Liability, 204–5
Lice, 99
Licenses, 203–4
Licking, 60
Life-span of dogs, 228
Lifting a dog, 60, 185
Linebreeding, 158–59
Lion dog, 339
Lion hound, African, 367
Liquid medicines, 128
Litter
  raising of, 174–200
  registration of, 187–90
  selling of, 197–98
  size of, average, 161
Little lion dog, 339
Livestock killed by dog, 205–6
Lost dogs, 62

Malamute, Alaskan, 241–42
Males, 35–37
  breeding and, 162–64, 166
  vs. females as pets, 45–46
  fighting of, 61
Malinois, Belgian, 257–58
Maltese, 340
Manchester terrier, 341
Mane, 24
Mange, 149
Mantle, 24
Manure, rolling in, 22–23
Mask, 24
Mastiff, 342
  bullmastiff, 276
  Neapolitan, 347
  Tibetan, 388
Mastitis, 178–79
Mating. See Breeding
Maturity, 35
Meat, 81, 86
Medical care, 126–57

Memory of dog, 20–21
Metatarsus, 25–26
Mexican hairless, 343
Minerals, 88
Miniature bullterrier, 344
Miniature pinscher, 345
Miniature schnauzer, 346
Miscellaneous class, 31, 32, 215
Mites, ear, 147, 148
Moneymaking in puppies, 198–199
Mongrels, 29, 38–39, 46–47
Monkey dogs, 237
Monorchidism, 35–36
Motels, 70
Mother dogs, 20–21, 168–73, 177, 180–81, 185, 186, 193
Mountain dogs, 260–61, 319–20
Mounting, 40, 114
Moving, 59, 72–73, 231
Musical note, howling and, 16
Mutt, 29
Muzzle, 25, 148

Nails, 94–95, 185
Naming, 56–57, 190
National Coursing Association, 26
National Stock Dog Registry, 26
Neapolitan mastiff, 347
Neighbors, 22, 89
Nephritis, 229
Newfoundland, 348
Night hunts, 226
Nipping habit, 111–12
Nipples, 167–68
"No" in training, 109
Noises, 118
Non-sporting dogs, 31
North American Sheepdog Society, 28
Norwegian elkhound, 349
Norwich terrier, 350
Nose, sickness and, 127
Number of dogs, 15, 27, 33
Nursing, 173, 191

INDEX / 415

Obedience schools, 100–101, 120
Obedience trials, 120–25, 208
Odor, 92
Oil in diet, 94
Old dogs, 228–33
Old English sheepdog, 351
Old people, 44
Operations, 127
Organizations, 28
Orphaned pups, 181
Otter hound, 352
Outbreeding, 159
Outdoor living, 74–79
Outdoors, taking puppies, 196
Overweight, 82, 83

Packs, dog, 117
Paddling, 27
Pan-feeding, 191–92, 193
Panting, heat loss and, 19
Papers, 49, 58, 187–90
Paper-training, 103
Papillon, 353
Paralysis, 144
Parks, 70
Pastern, 25
Patches, circular, 137
Paw, injuries of, 151, 155
Pawing at people, 113
Pedigree, 29, 46–47, 122
Pekingese, 354
Pembroke Welsh corgi, 355
Pens, 77–78, 196–97
Pet shops, 51, 202
Pharaoh hound, 356
Picardie shepherd, 357
Picking up dog, 60, 185
Picture-taking, 64
Pills, 128, 155
Pinscher
  Doberman, 298–99
  miniature, 345
Pit bullterrier, 244–45
Placentas, 170, 171
Plants, 63
Plott hound, 358

Plucking, 91
Plume, 27
Pneumonia, 143
Point, coming to, 223
Pointer, 359
  German, 312, 313
  Hungarian, 394
  Italian, 382
Pointing griffon, wirehaired, 400
Poisons, 154–55
Pomeranian, 360
Pompon, 27
Poodle, 361–62
Popularity of breeds, 33–34
Porcupines, 157
Portuguese water dog, 362–63
Potatoes, 87
Pound, 56
Pregnancy, 167, 173
  false, 40
Premium list, 212
Prescription diets, 85–86
Prince Charles spaniel, 305–6
Pug, 363–64
Puli, 364
Punishment, 101–2, 105
Puppies
  buying, 41–59
  raising, 174–200
Purebred, 29, 46–47
Purring, 17
Putting down, 176–77, 231

Rabies, 128–29
Raising puppies, 174–200
Rare breeds, 32
Redbone coonhound, 365–66
Redtick coonhound, 366
Referral services, 49
Registration, 49–51, 56–57
  organizations for, 28
  procedure for, 58, 187–90
Retinal atrophy, 146
Retrievers, 225–26
  Chesapeake Bay, 283
  curly-coated, 294–95
  flat-coated, 308

Retrievers, *continued*
  golden, 315–16
  Labrador, 336
Rewarding, 102
Rhodesian ridgeback, 367
Riding on dogs, 63
Ringworm, 137
Rottweiler, 368
Roughhousing, 60–61
Roundworms, 136
Ruby spaniel, 305–6
Ruff, 24
Rugs, 65–66, 110
Running
  away, prevention of, 72–73
  speed, 19, 114–17
  with pack, 117
Runs, 75–77
Runt of litter, 46
Russian wolfhound, 267

Saint Bernard, 369–70
Saluki, 370–71
Samoyed, 371
Schipperke, 372
Schnauzers, 314, 346, 384
Schools, obedience, 100–1, 120
Scottish deerhound, 373
Scottish terrier, 374
Scraps, 85, 89
Scratching, 60
  of door, 112
Sealyham terrier, 375
Seeing Eye dogs, 226, 227
Selling of litter, 197–98
Setters, 302, 317, 325
Sexual activity, 35–40. *See also*
  Breeding
Shar-Pei, 286
Shedding, 17–18
Sheepdogs, 258–59, 351, 376
Shelters, 59
Sheltie, 376
Shepherds
  Anatolian, 247
  Australian, 250
  English, 303

Shepherds, *continued*
  German, 311
  Picardie, 357
Shetland sheepdog, 376
Shih Tzu, 377
Shock, 152
  electrical, 156
Shock collars, 67
Shows, 120–25, 208–18
Siberian husky, 378
Sickness, 126–57
Sight of dogs, 15, 16
Silky terrier, 379
Singing dogs, 17
Sires, 35, 162–64. *See also*
  Males
Sitting, training for, 106, 109
Skin ailments, 150–51
Skunks, 157
Skye terrier, 380
Sleeping, 18
Sleeve dog, 287–88
Slobbering, 113
Smell
  sense of, 16
  dog odor, 92
Smooth fox terrier, 309
Snakebites, 156
Sneezing, 22
Sniffing, 22, 113
Soft-coated wheaten terrier, 381
Spaniels
  Boykin, 271
  Brittany, 273
  Cavalier King Charles, 282
  Clumber, 290–91
  cocker, 291–92, 299–300
  field, 306
  hunting and, 225
  Japanese, 331
  springer, 304–5, 396
  Sussex, 385
  Tibetan, 389
  toy, English, 305–6
  water, 246–47, 327
Spaying, 39, 133
Speed of dogs, 19

INDEX / 417

Spinone Italiano, 382
Spitz, 242, 307
Splay feet, 26
Sporting dogs, 29
Spots on dogs, 24
Sprays, flea and tick, 96, 97
Springer spaniels, 304–5, 396
Staffordshire bullterrier, 383
Staffordshire terrier, 244–45
Staining by female, 38
Stand, teaching to, 108
Standard Foxhound Stud Book, 28
Standard schnauzer, 384
Standards for breeds, 34
Stay, teaching to, 109
Stifle, 26
Stings, 156
Stirrup cup dog, 287–88
Stitches, 154
Stodghill ARF Registry, 28
Stools. See also Defecation, loose, 193
Stop, 25
Strange dogs, 62
Stripping, 91
Stud book, 162
Sussex spaniel, 385
Swallowing foreign objects, 154
Sweaters, 68
Sweating by dog, 19
Swelling, abdominal, 151
Swimming, 19–20, 98

Tags, 71
Tails, 27, 142
    American- vs. English-bred, 34
    docking of, 182–84
Talking to dog, 21
Tapeworms, 136
Tar, 92
Taste, sense of, 16
Tattooing, 68
Team of dogs, 215–16
Teeth, 95, 148–49, 184
Television, 16

Telomian, 386
Temperament, 36–37
Temperature, 128
Tennessee treeing brindle, 387
Terriers, 30–31
    Airedale, 239–40
    American (pit) bull, 244–45
    Australian, 251
    Bedlington, 256–57
    Border, 266
    Boston, 268
    bull, 244–45, 277, 344, 388
    Cairn, 278
    Dandie Dinmont, 297–98
    fox, 309, 391
    Glen of Imaal, 314–15
    Irish, 326
    Jack Russell, 330
    Kerry blue, 333
    Lakeland, 337
    Manchester, 341
    Norwich, 350
    Scottish, 374
    Sealyham, 375
    silky, 379
    Skye, 380
    soft-coated wheaten, 381
    Staffordshire, 244–45
    Tibetan, 390
    Welsh, 397
    West Highland white, 398
    Yorkshire, 402
Tervuren, Belgian, 250–51
Testicles, 35–36
Thigh, 26
Thirst, 229
Thorns, 155
Throat, objects in, 154
Thunderstorms, 117–18
Tibetan mastiff, 388
Tibetan spaniel, 389
Tibetan terrier, 390
Ticks, 97–99
Toenails, 94–95
Toy dogs, 30–31
Toy fox terrier, 391
Toy spaniel, English, 305–6

418 / INDEX

Toys for puppies, 196
Trails, beating, 63
Training, 100–19
   advanced, 120–25
   guard dog, 219–23
   housebreaking, 103–5
   hunting dogs, 223–25
Tranquilizers, 155
Traveling with dogs, 68–72
Treeing brindle, Tennessee, 387
Treeing Walker coonhound, 392
Tricks, teaching, 119
Trigg hound, 393
Trolley, 77–78
Tumors, 144
Turkish guard dogs, 247
Two dogs, 47–48
Tying up dog, 77–78

U.D. and U.D.T., 124–25
Understanding by dogs, 21
United Kennel Club, 28, 31–32
   breeds registered, 31
   registering with, 188–90
   shows, 218
United States
   breeds in, 29–33
   number of dogs in, 15
Upholstery, 65, 111
Urination, 22, 35, 145
   cleaning after, 65
   dribbling, 40, 229
   training and, 103–5
Utility class, 124–25

Vacations, 70
Vaccination, 195
Vegetables, 86
Veterinarian, 126
Vicious dogs, 36. *See also* Biting

Vision of dogs, 15, 16
Vitamins, 85, 87–88
Vizsla, 394
Vomiting, 65, 141, 193
   induction of, 154

Walker coonhound, treeing, 392
Walking the dog, 107–8
Wandering, 36, 117
Watchdogs, 114. *See also* Guard dogs
Water dog, Portuguese, 362–63
Water spaniel, 246–47, 327
Weaning, 191–92
Weimaraner, 395
Welsh corgis, 280, 355
Welsh springer spaniel, 396
Welsh terrier, 397
West Highland white terrier, 398
Westminster Dog Show, 212–13
Wheaten terrier, soft-coated, 381
Whelping, 168–73
Whipworms, 136
Whistles, 106, 223
Wirehaired fox terrier, 309
Wirehaired pointing griffon, 400
Withers, 25
Wolfhounds, 267, 328
Words, understanding of, 21
Working dogs, list of, 30
Worms, 135–40
   worming, 194–95
Wounds, 151–54

Xoloxcuintle, 401

Yorkshire terrier, 402

Zoning laws, 202–3